Published by Louisiana State University Press
lsupress.org

Manufactured in the United States of America

Designer: Andrew Shurtz
Typefaces: Kings Caslon, Adobe Caslon Pro

Portions of this book were previously published as "Respectability Politics and
Early African American Literature," in *African American Literature in Transition,
1750–1800,* ed. Rhondda Robinson Thomas (Cambridge: Cambridge University
Press, 2022), copyright © 2022 by Cambridge University Press.

Cataloging-in-Publication Data are available
from the Library of Congress.

ISBN 978-0-8071-7979-6 (cloth: alk. paper)
ISBN 978-0-8071-8072-3 (pdf)
ISBN 978-0-8071-8071-6 (epub)

RACE

AND

RESPECTABILITY

IN AN

EARLY

BLACK

ATLANTIC

CASSANDER L. SMITH

LOUISIANA STATE
UNIVERSITY PRESS
BATON ROUGE

RACE AND
RESPECTABILITY
IN AN
EARLY BLACK
ATLANTIC

CONTENTS

RESPECTABILITY POLITICS, a term popularized by Evelyn Brooks Higginbotham in the early 1990s, is the self-policing that occurs when members of an oppressed group seek to model (and condemn those in the group who do not model) the cultural and social mores of a dominant group with the belief that doing so will eliminate the oppression and promote equality. I first conceived of *Race and Respectability in an Early Black Atlantic* in 2012 after the shooting death of the Florida teen Trayvon Martin. The heartbreak his family suffered, and continues to suffer, joined a collective, cultural grief, a trauma, for Black America. The more conservative element among us dealt with that grief by clinging to a narrative of respectability politics. We, for example, homed in on Martin's dress and debated whether the hoodie he wore that evening portended some nefarious intent.[1] Mainstream media inundated us with stories about Martin's supposed past criminal proclivities, like possession of marijuana that reportedly led to a school suspension. There was an impulse to dismiss him as a thug, his premature death a *natural* and fitting conclusion to a misspent youth. This assessment found credence in the fact that he did not submit to George Zimmerman's interrogation. In fact, Martin spoke back—and apparently fought back. As I listened to people try to explain, if not outright justify, the killing, I was confronted by the sheer power of respectability politics to deem Black lives, especially young ones, as worthy of death if those lives do not adhere to arbitrary standards of conduct. I also saw respectability politics as an operation of self-control, a deep, abiding need by Black folk to believe that we can exert some measure of power to mitigate the effects of white supremacy. If we walk right and talk right and bow right, we tell ourselves, our bodies will not become vulnerable to the kind of violence that has historically claimed the lives and souls of too many Black people. This is, of course, a false sense of security.

Black America was forced to confront the myth of respectability like never before on May 25, 2020, when police officers in Minneapolis killed George Floyd, one cop pressing a knee into his neck and holding it there for some nine minutes. The cop did this on a busy street, in broad daylight with his black-gloved hand resting casually at his side and a pair of shades sitting atop his head. He did this even as bystanders protested—one an off-duty firefighter who recognized Floyd's physical distress and pleaded with the cops to check his pulse. Floyd's crime? He paid for items in a convenience store with a counterfeit twenty-dollar bill that he may or may not have known was counterfeit. Besides the coldness registered on the face of the cop pressing the life out of Floyd, the most disorienting aspect of the moment—at least for Black America—had to be the release of video footage that showed what happened leading up to the moment of the killing. In that video, a police officer walks up to the driver side of Floyd's car, gun drawn. Floyd gets out of the car; police promptly handcuff him, then lead him over to the sidewalk. He sits down on the pavement against a building. From what we can see, Floyd does not resist. He does not reach for an officer's gun or taser. He does not try to run away or fight. He does what Black people have been taught to do for generations—comply. That compliance does not save his life. Instead, events escalate to the point of his death. All those excuses that people—both white and Black—propagated to explain Trayvon Martin's death do not, cannot apply with Floyd.[2] Respectability politics failed Floyd; it failed Breonna Taylor, who was sleeping in the comfort of her own home in Louisville, Kentucky, on the night of March 13, 2020, when police officers barged into her home and killed her while raiding her apartment in search of drugs that did not exist.[3] Respectability politics failed Ahmaud Arbery, who was hunted down and killed in the street on February 23, 2020.

To be clear, respectability politics failed Trayvon Martin.

Even in the wake of these murders of Black lives, we continue to retreat behind that rhetoric of respectability. When people took to the streets in protest after Floyd's death, Black leaders and news commentators filled the airwaves with pleas for people to protest "peacefully," propping up the idea that there is a right and wrong way to protest.[4] News coverage even homed in on peaceful protestors and castigated those caught looting and starting fires.[5] But is there really a *right* way to protest?[6] Football quarterback Colin Kaepernick began a silent, nonviolent protest in 2016 by first sitting and then kneeling during the playing of the National Anthem before games. Other athletes of various races and across other sports joined in, including soccer all-star Megan Rapinoe. The protest did not involve looting, burning, or physical bodily harm. Still the protest sparked national outrage. Former president Donald Trump took umbrage—on behalf of America—and called Kaepernick a "son of a bitch."[7] Similarly critical, retired football player, Olympiad, and former Georgia senatorial candidate Herschel Walker condemned US Olympic athletes who would use the global platform in Tokyo in 2021 to stage nonviolent protests by, for example, taking a knee or turning their back during the playing of the National Anthem. "This is the United States of America," he insisted in an interview with Fox News in July 2021. "If people don't like the rules here, . . . why are you here?"[8]

Respectability politics compels us to attach a moral judgment to forms of protest. Today, for example, we shun the militancy of activist leaders like Malcolm X. We praise the nonviolent strategies of the Rev. Dr. Martin Luther King Jr. He gets a national holiday; elementary schools and streets in every major city bear his name. The irony, of course, is that King, in at least one instance, leveraged Black militancy and white violence to advance the civil rights movement. In his "Letter from a Birmingham Jail," he explains to his white, liberal, ministerial readers that he stands between two "opposing forces in the Negro community." One is the force of apathy, populated by Black Americans who have accepted the status quo mostly out of a sense of hopelessness and exhaustion. The other force he describes as "one of bitterness and hatred" consisting of Black Americans who come "perilously close to advocating violence." That force, according to King, fuels the rise of Black Nationalist groups, like the Nation of Islam. These groups, according to King, are "nourished by the Negro's frustration over the continued existence of racial discrimination." He warns his ministerial colleagues:

> I am grateful to God that, through the influence of the Negro church, the way of nonviolence became an integral part of our struggle. If this philosophy had not emerged, by now many streets of the South would, I am convinced, be flowing with blood. And I am further

convinced that if our white brothers dismiss as "rabble rousers" and "outside agitators" those of us who employ nonviolent direct action, and if they refuse to support our nonviolent efforts, millions of Negroes will, out of frustration and despair, seek solace and security in black nationalist ideologies—a development that would inevitably lead to a frightening racial nightmare.[9]

King understood full well that the peaceful marches would evoke white rage, a violent response that could be leveraged to elicit sympathy for the cause. Violence was an essential element of the civil rights movement. However, we describe the history of that movement in terms of its nonviolent aspects.[10] We are driven by a need to do this, in part, because of respectability politics.

We want to protest but to do so in ways that are acceptable; the goal is oxymoronic. Social protests by design transgress; they disrupt the status quo, which makes protest an inherently violent act. Rather than acknowledge this, however, we hold onto the myth that there are right and wrong ways to protest racism and white supremacy—and maybe there are. My point is not to exonerate those who commit crimes like burglary, arson, assault, and so forth during riots and protests. My point is that the dichotomy that characterizes our discussions of riots and protests is a false one, and it is embedded in a deeper impulse to police the behavior of Black Americans, to describe the ways we act in terms of right and wrong—respectable versus disrespectable. That dichotomy has long circumscribed Black America. This book is an effort to address the Black community's centuries-long obsession with respectability politics by analyzing its (dys-)function in an early Black Atlantic world.

This book was many years in the making. I want to thank the following people who read drafts of chapters, listened to me drone on about the book, and/or provided the scholarly community that kept me energized through the process of writing: Philathia Bolton, Kristina Bross, Tara Bynum, Lauren Cardon, Katy Chiles, Brigitte Fielder, Casarae Abdul-Ghani, Miles P. Grier, Trudier Harris, Nicholas Jones, Yolanda Manora, Joycelyn Moody, Désha Osborne, Albert Pionke, Kerry Sinanan, Deborah Weiss, and Kelly Wisecup. Thanks, as well, to the communities of the Mahindra Humanities Center (Harvard), the Graduate Center (CUNY), the English Department at Northwestern University, and the University of Alabama's Honors College for carving out spaces where I could try out many of the book's ideas before committing them to print.

I owe a debt of gratitude, as well, to the Huntington Library, UA's College of Arts & Sciences Leadership Board, and UA's Research Grants Committee. These entities provided funding that allowed me to conduct research for the book. Thanks, as well, to Cambridge University Press for permission to incorporate into the book portions of my essay "Respectability Politics and Early African American Literature," which appeared in *African American Literature in Transition: 1750–1800,* edited by Rhondda Robinson Thomas (Cambridge: Cambridge University Press, 2022).

I very much appreciate the efforts of the editors and staff at Louisiana State University Press, especially James Long, who remained enthusiastic and supportive from the beginning. I appreciate his patience, diligence, and professionalism. Thank you to the outside readers, whose feedback challenged me to be more precise. Thanks, as well, to my research assistant, Isabelle Stephens, whose meticulous eye saved me from making more than a few errors in this work. In case it doesn't go without saying, any remaining errors are owed solely to my own fallibility.

I end my acknowledgments with a final thank-you to my parents, Mary and Thomas Davis, who taught me how to question respectability politics at an early age, and to Alberto Pérez-Huerta, who ultimately has made respectability politics a moot point in my life.

*RACE AND
RESPECTABILITY
IN AN
EARLY BLACK
ATLANTIC*

INTRODUCTION

Race and Respectability in an Early Black Atlantic reexamines the origins of African American literature by locating its earliest iterations within an ideology of respectability politics and by situating the literature within a larger Atlantic context. Since the election of this country's first Black president in 2008, respectability politics has assumed a newfound significance as political analysts and cultural critics alike attribute former president Barack Obama's popularity among Black voters to this idea of respectability. Obama, himself, peddled such narratives, especially during his presidential campaign and in the early days of his administration, when he delivered speeches to majority-Black audiences that chided them for bragging about an eighth-grade education and feeding their children "cold Popeyes" for breakfast.[1] "Obama," as Nia-Malika Henderson argues, "gave black respectability politics a social and political currency not seen before, legitimizing the kind of fault-finding critiques of African-American behavior that has been more common among conservatives."[2] Notions of respectability remain ever present in how people police the behavior of Black Americans, like tennis superstar Serena Williams, or in how we justify the shooting deaths of Black people by police and community vigilantes. In Black communities, even beyond the borders of what is now the United States, respectability politics is a double-edged sword; it *promises* upward mobility but also permits the oppressive violence done to Black bodies.

In general, respectability politics refers to the way members of a minoritized population—people of color, white women, immigrants, LGBTQIA+ communities, among others—adopt the customs and manners of a dominant culture in order to combat negative stereotypes about their subject group and gain cultural visibility and safety. One must walk, talk, dress appropriately, live in the right neighborhoods, value education, choose a career wisely,

1

attend church every Sunday, eschew criminal behavior, and assume a host of other proper attitudes and behaviors that illustrate their self-worth. Those who display virtue, presumably, enjoy the benefits of full membership within a culture; they expect that virtue to inoculate them against the detrimental effects of racism, sexism, homophobia, xenophobia, and so forth. Respectability politics demands the constant surveillance of oneself and others. As Tiffany M. Nyachae and Esther O. Ohito note, "the politics of respectability" is "fundamentally the politics of power."[3]

From the perspective of Black communities, which is the focus of this book, scholars typically locate the origins of respectability politics in the mid- to late nineteenth century. In her foundational study *Righteous Discontent: The Women's Movement in the Black Baptist Church, 1880–1920*, Evelyn Brooks Higginbotham examines Black respectability politics as a discourse emerging specifically out of communities of Black women's church and club movements at the end of the nineteenth century. She argues that Black women in these church contexts understood respectability as a tool of resistance to combat negative stereotypes about Black women specifically and the race in general. "The politics of respectability," she maintains, "emphasized reform of individual behavior and attitudes both as a goal in itself and as a strategy for reform of the entire structural system of American race relations."[4] She also argues that this "politics of respectability" helped to create a Black middle class that stood in opposition to and in judgment of both the perceived "idleness and vice" of a lower-class Black community and the "hedonism and materialism" associated with a Black "high society."[5] In this way, Higginbotham's work engages with Willard Gatewood's 1990 study of the rise of a Black aristocracy in America between 1880 and 1920. That aristocracy, according to Gatewood, centered on specific ideas about respectability, signaled in large part by one's genealogy: "Members of the aristocracy of color . . . had great pride in family background, education, and what was called 'respectability,' a term that included good breeding, manners, and proper conduct."[6]

Other scholars have built on Higginbotham's and Gatewood's work to emphasize the gendered and class politics implicated in Black respectability discourses. In his 2014 essay "The Rise of Respectability Politics," Frederick C. Harris argues that respectability politics is the product of an elite "black middle-class ideology" that emerged in the late 1800s.[7] It speaks to a "yearning for economic uplift in black communities," Harris maintains. He goes on to say that the "virtues of self-care and self-correction" at the center of respectability politics "are framed as strategies to lift the black poor out of their condition by preparing them for the market economy."[8] Victoria Wolcott, also, interrogates the mechanics of a Black bourgeois respectability, which she argues shaped urban communities in Detroit in the early twentieth century. Like Higginbotham, she notes that "respectability . . . was a gendered language usually deployed and defended by women."[9] More recently, Brittney C. Cooper has complicated the study of late nineteenth- and early twentieth-century Black women and their investment in respectability politics. While noting that "respectability discourse . . . constituted one of the earliest theorizations of gender within newly emancipated Black communities," Cooper argues that Black women intellectuals, such as Anna Julia Cooper, looked beyond respectability strategies to advocate on behalf of Black Americans.[10]

Situating Black respectability politics within a wider historical context, while also acknowledging its distinct features, Wolcott points out the deployment of respectability rhetoric in nineteenth-century American and British labor traditions. She notes two interrelated discourses of respectability that shaped United States and British societies, one embracing "the values of hard work, thrift, piety, and sexual restraint—values that were, theoretically, accessible to all classes and races and therefore routes of social mobility" and another that "emerged with the rise of the bourgeoisie in the nineteenth century and denoted class status and privilege through dress, deportment, and organizational affiliation."[11] These discourses, I would add, existed alongside rhetoric about racial uplift that abounded in Black American communities in the early and mid-nineteenth century, emphasizing self-reliance and personal responsibility as fundamental strategies in the fight for Black emancipation and equality.[12] That rhetoric was a precursor to the respectability strategies Higginbotham argues defined the Black church at the end of the nineteenth century.

All of this is to say that current studies privilege the late nineteenth and early twentieth centuries as formative in the development of Black respectability politics. What is more, these studies overwhelmingly address the subject as a phenomenon specific to the United States. In *Race and Respectability,* I posit that concerns about the manners and customs of people of African descent emerge even earlier and in spaces beyond the borders of what would become the United States. From the very beginning of the transatlantic slave trade and the rise of racial hierarchies, Black Africans advocated for particular forms of conduct and assimilation as a means to alleviate their oppression. If anything, I argue, a politics of respectability arose at the turn of the twentieth century out of a centuries-long process, the core elements of which begin to appear in the efforts of early Black Africans to navigate race, racism, and enslavement; they employ strategies of respect and respectability. Through various means, which I discuss in the pages that follow, early Black Africans strive for visibility, esteem, safety, uplift—and freedom. Their efforts, disparate and contingent upon time and place, anticipate the more formalized politics about which Higginbotham and others have elucidated. The process, not necessarily linear, reminds us that respect is a coping strategy that has long defined the Black experience in America and beyond.

As an early African American literary scholar, I am interested especially in how that coping strategy shaped early Black African expressions of identity. The strategies circumscribed literary aesthetics, particularly forms of life writing, poetry, and letters, a genre that has received little critical attention in early Black studies. In the pages that follow, *Race and Respectability* stages three interventions. First, it recontextualizes respectability politics as a process that Black Africans have employed to combat racial oppression and degradation. Second, it expands a "Black Atlantic" narrative by including West Africa as a key site for the expression of Black diasporic culture; it is itself a recipient of the diasporic production of new cultural forms as Black Americans repatriated to West Africa beginning at the end of the eighteenth century, taking with them concerns for respectability. Third, the book expands our understanding of early Black literary aesthetics. Blacks in America sought respect and respectability; their efforts circumscribed the aesthetic choices of Black writers, particularly in the epistolary form in the eighteenth century. Ultimately, this book expands discussions about Black respectability, illustrating its malleability over centuries and its central importance in the development of Black Atlantic cultures and what we would come to know of as a politics of respectability.

THE EARLY AMERICAN ROOTS OF
BLACK RESPECTABILITY POLITICS

In 1600, a free, mixed-race, unmarried woman living in Querétaro, a province in north-central Mexico, petitioned a local magistrate to verify her legal status. The woman, named Isabel de Olvera, planned to travel to Santa Fe, New Mexico, along with her employer, as part of the Juan Guerra de Resa expedition. She worried that those she encountered along the journey might not acknowledge her free and unattached status. She requested from her local magistrate a signed affidavit attesting to her free status. She explains to the town official her plans to travel on an expedition to New Mexico. She says she has "reason to fear" that she "may be annoyed by some individual" given the fact that she is "a mulatta." She understands that it is "proper to protect my rights in such an eventuality by an affidavit showing that I am a free woman, unmarried and the legitimate daughter of Hernando, a Negro, and an Indian named Magdalena." She needs an affidavit, then, to prove she is "free and not bound by marriage or slavery." Depending upon the legality of such a document, she insists, "I request that a properly certified and signed copy be given to me in order to protect my rights, and that it carry full legal authority. I demand justice."[13]

For historians like Dedra McDonald and Quintard Taylor, de Olvera's petition is significant because of what it tells us about the earliest presences of people of African descent in what would become the United States. The most popular story of origin for the arrival of Black Africans on American shores centers on 1619 Jamestown. For McDonald and Taylor, however, the western frontier is equally, if not more so, crucial in the story about Black African origins in America. What is more, McDonald argues specifically, de Olvera presents an opportunity for us to learn more about how women of color fared on a Spanish and western frontier.

As a literary scholar, I find the passage striking for its representation of respectability. In this case, respectability assumes the form of legal legitimacy. De Olvera makes it clear that she was born a "legitimate" child and justifies her actions as "proper." She insists that the letter is a matter of justice and seeks the protection of documentation to enforce a level of respect she seems to have enjoyed in Mexico. She eschews the model of respectability most common to women in colonial New Spain, that of marriage.[14] As a kind of protofeminist gesture, she equates marriage with slavery, celebrating her freedom from both. This is not to say that her unmarried status disrupts the power structure of a patriarchal system, which infantilizes and confines women through matrimony. De Olvera very much participates in that system—even though she claims a different model of respectability—as she appeals to its power in seeking legal protection. Her rhetorical and political moves evoke what Steve Stern calls "pluralizing the patriarchs."[15] Focusing specifically on gendered power dynamics in colonial Mexico, Stern argues that early American women mobilized patriarchal systems on their behalf by setting in opposition patriarchal figures in a kind of checks-and-balances strategy. By petitioning, appealing—or threatening to complain—a woman like de Olvera could curb the power of one patriarchal figure by deploying the authority of another, more superior, figure, such as a regional magistrate. De Olvera employs this strategy in anticipation of the trouble to come—for a single, freeborn woman of color traveling the frontier roads of New Spain. Her understanding of respectability is informed by imperial expansion and settler colonialism; she pursues the affidavit, after all, upon deciding to leave conquered territory to occupy more (newly) conquered territory. The mechanics of gender complicate her efforts.

In some ways, she anticipates the tragic mulatta trope prevalent in nineteenth- and twentieth-century African American literature. In novels like William Wells Brown's *Clotel* (1853), Harriet Wilson's *Our Nig* (1859), Charles Chesnutt's *The House behind the Cedars* (1900), and even Harriet Jacobs's slave narrative *Incidents in the Life of a Slave Girl* (1861), mixed-race women mobilize various patriarchal structures in an often fatal attempt to protect their perceived virtue against the lewd desires of white men. De Olvera, then, is an early representation of how mixed-race women embody modes of respectability to negotiate their precarious status. As McDonald notes, "To be black and female in the Spanish and Mexican northern frontier required racial and gender consciousness, wariness, and willingness to indulge in a wide variety of cross-cultural strategies, both formal and informal, for survival."[16] I would add to this that de Olvera employs respectability as a survival strategy. Her actions do not rise to the level of respectability politics as de Olvera does not engage in acts of self-policing or monitoring the behaviors of other Black women, which are major tenets of what we understand as respectability politics today. Importantly, however, aspects of her behavior—the effort to protect herself, to be seen as respectable—provide an early indication of how and why respectability mattered for people of color, why they would be invested in a strategy predicated on respect. Indeed, respect and respectability appear as prevalent tropes in the texts of Black people endeavoring to negotiate their freedom and humanity. De Olvera's white counterparts would have been vulnerable, too, by virtue of being women in this frontier space, but let us not forget the specific stakes attached to de Olvera's racialized otherness. Her legal status as a free woman can be called into question if others do not respect her lineage. So there is something singular about her efforts to secure a petition from the town magistrate using a strategy of respectability.

Conversations about respectability politics and people of African descent have not considered the example of de Olvera primarily because we have understood respectability politics as a phenomenon of the nineteenth and twentieth centuries. It might be tempting to deem de Olvera, then, an outlier in the seventeenth century. However, as I have argued elsewhere, her example joins that of several others to suggest that people of African descent were concerned with respectability even in the seventeenth and eighteenth centuries.[17] And not just on a Spanish American frontier. Consider the following example of a Black woman, enslaved and living in Massachusetts in 1638, who was raped by an enslaved Black man at the behest of an enslaver. The enslaver ordered the violent act to ensure the woman's impregnation. Distraught and traumatized, the woman tearfully complained about the incident to a passerby. Her grief so moved that passerby, an Englishman named John Josselyn, that he related her story in the travel journal he published in 1674.[18] He narrates his encounter with the woman as follows:

> The second of October about Nine of the clock in the morning, Mr. Mavericks Negro woman came to my chamber window, and in her own Countrey language and tune sang very loud and shrill, going out to her, she used a great deal of respect towards me, and willingly would have expressed her grief in *English;* but I apprehended it by her countenance and deportment, whereupon I repaired to my host, to learn of him the cause, and resolved to intreat him on her behalf, for that I understood before, that she had been a Queen of her own Countrey and observed a very humble and dutiful garb used towards

her by another Negro who was her maid. Mr. Maverick was desirous to have a breed of Negroes and therefore seeing she would not
yield by perswasions to company with a Negro young man he had
in his house; he commanded him will'd she nill'd she to go to bed
to her, which was no sooner done but she kickt him out again, this
she took in high disdain beyond her slavery, and this was the cause
of her grief.[19]

In the past, I wrote about this textual moment as an illustration of the mediating influence of Black Africans on early American literature.[20] In the
present context, I discuss the moment as an example of the insidious nature
of respectability. Josselyn traveled twice to New England, in 1638 and 1663.
He kept a detailed journal from both trips, which he edited and published
as a single travel narrative in 1674. The text is organized as a series of dated,
episodic entries designed to inform English readers about the colonial New
England landscape. His encounter with this enslaved woman occurs during
his stay with a Massachusetts colonist named Samuel Maverick. Based on
archival work, historian Wendy Anne Warren surmises that the woman was
among the first group of enslaved Africans to arrive in the Massachusetts Bay
Colony by way of the Caribbean Providence Island in 1638.[21]

In terms of its literary significance, the passage tracks the woman's movement from visibility to invisibility that makes this, I would argue, a counter-
respectability narrative. I say counter-respectability because the woman
seems to reject the aspect of respectability that requires assimilation and
compliance. The rejection is registered, for example, in the fact that she
approaches Josselyn "in her own *Countrey* language and tune." Although
she apparently could speak English, Josselyn says, she chooses to initiate an
encounter with him on her terms. Also, she seems to have retained something of her preenslavement social stature as evident by the fact that another
enslaved woman serves her as maid, addressing her in a very "humble and
dutiful" manner, acknowledging the woman's royal status. It seems that
she endeavors to transfer to this new environment her old customs and status rather than accept the new station in life prescribed for her. She does
not comply with expectations, rejecting one of the primary forms of labor
demanded of enslaved Black women, procreation. As Jennifer Morgan has
argued in her influential study *Laboring Women: Reproduction and Gender*

in New World Slavery, the value of enslaved Black women resided in their ability to "produce both crops and other laborers" through reproduction.[22] This process, Morgan notes, simultaneously replenished the enslaved labor force and perpetuated ideologies of racial difference that naturalized the link between Black Africans and enslavement.

The woman exhibits a lack of respectability through her refusal to comply with Maverick's orders and assimilate to her new surroundings. At the same time, it seems she clings to her dignity, which is not the same thing as respectability. As Brittney Cooper points out, dignity is inherent, grounded in the acceptance of one's own humanity. Respectability is extrinsic and, in Cooper's words, "socially contingent."[23] Respectability, Cooper notes, assumes "that unassailable social propriety will prove one's dignity."[24] That is to say, one adopts *respectable* behavior to make one's dignity visible to others. Ironically, the woman in Josselyn's narrative makes herself visible to him precisely because she rejects social propriety (by refusing to comply with Maverick's orders and complaining publicly). Perhaps it is more accurate to say that she succeeds in translating into this colonial American landscape a form of respectability she enjoyed in her "own Countrey," social propriety implied by her deferential relationship with another enslaved woman in the household about whom we know even less.[25] It seems that Josselyn does register the woman's dignity, her humanity, if for only a moment, when he identifies with her grief. When he resolves to entreat Maverick on her behalf, he transforms from a mere observer of the scene into a participant. Josselyn makes clear this woman has actively resisted her enslavement, evident in how and why Maverick orders the rape in the first place: "she would not yield by perswasions."

One must wonder what compels Maverick to attempt persuasion first. Is it a general strategy applied to all enslaved women, or does he note, too, the exceptional status of this particular woman, a queen in her former country? Or is it an effort simply to avoid violent handling of human property, preserving value as much as possible? For whatever reason, he attempts to coax compliance from her. Failing that, he turns to violent coercion. Whatever forms of respectability the woman imagines herself embodying, despite all the ways her manners and comportment garner respect and sympathy, from others enslaved, from Josselyn—maybe even from Maverick, too—it does not shield her from the mechanics of a slavery system that deemed her more commodity than human. The woman's effect on Josselyn, alas, is short-lived. He abandons sympathy after talking with Maverick and discovering the "cause of her grief." The sympathetic mode gives way to a business mode. The woman's story, the bodily violation, the grief and trauma remind us of the stakes of respectability politics—as a strategy to emphasize one's humanity and create an immunity from oppressive, discriminatory systems. The enslaved woman living in Maverick's household enjoyed no such immunity. At first glance, a moment like this might seem to be wholly beyond a respectability paradigm as framed by Higginbotham. With this example, though, I wish to point out the ways in which this Black woman, like de Olvera before her, negotiates issues of respectability to assert her very personhood, which unites her in struggle with her Black counterparts of the late nineteenth and twentieth centuries. Her suffering challenges the efficacy of respectability as a coping mechanism.

Despite its failings, respectability has become a pervasive strategy among Black Africans. That strategy and the way it manifested in the textual record evolved over time and was shaped by sociopolitical phenomena such as European expansion into the Americas and invasive colonization, the Enlightenment movement, the Revolutionary War, the Great Awakening, and developing racial ideologies that spread through the early Atlantic. What is more, a preoccupation with respectability among Black Africans led to transformations in the Black life writing and poetry that first emerged in the eighteenth century, from figures such as Phillis Wheatley and Olaudah Equiano. Drawing inspiration from the examples of de Olvera and the woman in Josselyn's narrative, in this book, I home in on that first generation of Black Africans who wrote about and embodied tenets of respectability. I am interested especially in how that first generation of Black writers living in an eighteenth-century Atlantic world represented respectability—in terms of religious conformity, language acquisition, gender expression, and physical comportment/demeanor. I also am interested in the tensions between respectability and racial discourses that were just starting to be understood as fixed/immutable by the end of the eighteenth century. What was the transformative potential or limitation of respectability for Black subjects? And why did they believe respectability was the answer to equality? How might respectability have been a response by Black Africans to notions of race and gender, a way to circumvent the rigidity of identity categories? In

Race and Respectability, I make a case that early Black writing was a key avenue through which Black Africans self-constructed as civilized, assimilated—respectable—subjects in the early Atlantic world.

In general, writing assumed a unique significance for Black Africans, as did the function of authorship. Early Black literature pronounced Black humanity. Often, Black writers articulated that humanity in terms of social mores, economic accomplishments, and religious attitudes, all in an effort to address their oppression and promote equality. What is more, this writing strategy was not confined within the borders of what would become the United States. For example, when Black Americans who had fought on the side of the British during the Revolutionary War emigrated from the United States, they took with them to their new homes (in England, Nova Scotia, the Caribbean, and Sierra Leone) ideas about respectability. The rhetoric, then, was a phenomenon of a larger Atlantic world.

Over the next five chapters, I examine respect and respectability as tropes shaping the literature of an early Black Atlantic. As early Black writers navigate racism and enslavement, they display certain elements of what would become respectability politics by the turn of the twentieth century. They try out, as it were, notions of virtue, diligence, accommodation and assimilation, self-surveillance. In a couple of examples, they challenge these notions. Although the coping strategies of individuals in this earlier period do not map fully onto the paradigm Higginbotham first articulates in 1993, it is crucial to note that the idea of respectability as a means to navigate racial oppression did not first occur to Black people in the late nineteenth century. In short, a politics of respectability develops over time. I point to certain texts as examples to illustrate how and why it developed over some three centuries. These examples are flashpoints in early Black Atlantic culture, moments of heightened racial tension during which Black figures grapple with notions of respect and respectability.

The first chapter, "'No Rogue, No Rascal, No Thief': Respectability and 'Adam Negro's Tryal,'" centers on the legal and literary documents comprising the early eighteenth-century freedom suit of a Black man named Adam living in colonial Massachusetts. In 1700, Adam sued his enslaver, John Saffin, to enforce the terms of an indenture contract that Saffin sought to revoke on the grounds that Adam did not comport himself properly during the term of his indenture. Partly in response to Adam's suit, Saffin wrote a proslavery pamphlet that represents Adam as violent and surly. Through court documents, Adam constructs a counterimage, one that renders him compliant with the legal and social status quo. Scholars of African American literature consider Adam's court narrative the first in a long line of African American autobiography, a proto–slave narrative that has been dubbed "Adam Negro's Tryal." I recontextualize the court narrative, examining it as a debate about respectability, articulated in terms of obedience, depravity, and religious conformity. Saffin deploys respectability rhetoric as a tool to perpetuate myths of racial difference; for him, respectability and Blackness are contradictory terms. In pressing his claims to freedom, Adam rejects such notions. He demands respect, understood as visibility and a recognition of his humanity, by seeking a legal remedy for his enslavement. "Adam Negro's Tryal" functions as a prologue of sorts that illustrates a narrative tension between a white colonial imagination and that of an enslaved/indentured Black African over this idea of respectability. Because he did not pick up the pen himself, Adam must rely on the mediating mechanics of attorneys and courts to confirm his humanity.

Through "Adam Negro's Tryal," we see how respectability works as a racializing project in the early eighteenth century. Adam challenges that racial project. In subsequent chapters, I show how early Black writers, in a sense, advance Adam's challenge by refuting racializing discourses like that espoused by Saffin. They embody tenets of respectability to collapse racial difference or call out white supremacy. In chapter 2, "'Those Who Seem'd to Respect Me': Phillis Wheatley at the Border of Respectability," I discuss the poetry and letters of Phillis Wheatley. Other scholars have examined the way Black women at the turn of the twentieth century embodied respectability politics or rejected it to establish a particular kind of Black womanhood. In this chapter, I argue that Wheatley does neither. Refuting mainstream stereotypes through proper comportment and virtue, she advocates a respectability that does not prescribe specific roles to Black women and men. Through her poetry and letters, she assumes a universal Black voice, speaking from what Hortense Spillers refers to as the ungendered borders of early America. The example of Wheatley complicates the presumption of a constitutive relationship between Black respectability and gender; gender has overdetermined how we have come to understand the mechanics of respectability politics in Black communities. Adopting a gender-neutral literary persona, Wheatley offers herself up as a model of virtuous Blackness and in doing so, modifies racial and gendered codes of appropriate behavior.

Like Wheatley, the writer, merchant, and abolitionist Olaudah Equiano imagines himself as a model of Black virtue; Wheatley and Equiano directly refute cultural stereotypes of Black degradation that are sanctified and systematized by the Enlightenment movement at the end of the eighteenth century. In chapter 3, "(Some) Black Lives Matter: Olaudah Equiano and the Social Racial Contract," I examine Equiano's deployment of respectability rhetoric to critique the British slave trade in his 1789 autobiography, *The Interesting Narrative.* He does this by challenging the Enlightenment ideal of a social contract that bonds individuals together in a consensual form of civil government, the primary purpose of which, according to one of the theory's most prominent thinkers, John Locke, is to protect the life, liberty, and property of individuals. As an ideal, the social contract espouses equality and prioritizes the preservation of individual rights, understood to be natural, God-given. In practice, however, the social contract excludes Black Africans—both those enslaved and free. Despite Equiano's social and economic rise from enslavement to freedom, respectability does not translate into social visibility, inclusion. He adopts tenets of respectability, then, to exhibit Black humanity and critique the exclusion of Black Africans from the social contract. Respectability rhetoric enables him, through opposition, to magnify the inhumanity of the slave trade and the barbaric treatment to which he and other Black Africans are subjected, particularly in the West Indies. Equiano points out the racist underpinnings of the social contract, rendering it what Charles W. Mills has termed instead a "racial contract." In this chapter, I argue that Equiano manipulates respectability to undermine the tenets of that contract.

In the next two chapters, I examine the 1787 British colonization of Sierra Leone on the west coast of Africa. After the American Revolutionary War, England experienced an influx of indigent Black Loyalists. Abolitionists, led by the fervor of Granville Sharp, proposed creating a settlement in Sierra Leone for their relief. In the early years of that settlement, Province of Freedom, its residents emphasized respectability, extending many of the conversations that were unfolding in the United States and England around questions of emancipation and Black virtue, conversations made visible by figures like Equiano and Wheatley. Equiano, in fact, very briefly participated in the Sierra Leone repatriation plan, and Wheatley declined an offer to participate in a Black-led missionary expedition to Africa. In chapters 4 and 5, I track the ways in which concerns for respectability informed the literary/cultural landscape of Sierra Leone as it transformed into a refuge for Black Americans. Specifically, in chapter 4, "'My Poor Little Ill-Thriven Swarthy Daughter': Granville Sharp and the Respectability of Deportation to Province of Freedom," I discuss Sharp's rhetoric about the establishment of Province of Freedom. Through a close reading of those letters, reports, pamphlets, and treatises Sharp wrote in defense of the settlement idea, we can see how notions of respectability fit into his larger utopic vision of a space populated and governed by Black Africans on the African west coast. Importantly Sharp's ideas for Province of Freedom existed alongside—indeed, were complicated by—the material reality or lived experiences of those mostly Black African settlers tasked with the responsibility of realizing Sharp's vision. Mainly through letters exchanged with Sharp, they apprised Sharp of the settlement's progress, petitioned for more resources from Britain, and attempted to secure positions of power for themselves in the newly formed town, all while convincing Sharp of their respectability, a necessary rhetorical move as onlookers—those mostly white enslavers living at nearby trading forts—represented them as the antithesis of respectable. Like Equiano, settlers laid claim to the social contract. Letters were a primary vehicle through which they demanded inclusion by engaging in conversations about respectability.

In chapter 5, "'Send Me Over One Worthy': Reimagining Respectability in Sierra Leone," I extend the discussion by examining more closely the literary landscape that starts to emerge specifically in and about what became Freetown. The letter writing discussed in the previous chapter joins a wider body of texts written on behalf of Black settlers in the 1790s to control the narrative about Black settlement and respectability in the British colonial spaces of eighteenth-century Sierra Leone. Through narratives and letters, those early settlers maintained familial contacts, intervened in political and religious discourses, and contested the colony's power structure. As examples, I offer close readings of the texts of several Black Africans who were actively involved in the sociopolitical life of Freetown between 1792 and 1800. The texts in various ways embody and subvert notions of respectability that were intimately tied to ideas about liberty, justice, and upward mobility and illustrate how respectability rhetoric circulated through the Atlantic, shaping Black lives in the United States and West Africa alike. Together, these chapters make a point that for centuries respectability has been one of the most prevalent coping strategies that Black Americans have used to combat racial oppression and degradation. The book expands our understanding about emancipation and the struggles of Black Africans to negotiate enslavement and its dehumanizing rhetoric and consequences by illustrating Black Africans as agentive forces manipulating the sociopolitical landscapes in an early Atlantic world.

A BLACK LITERARY AESTHETICS
AND THE EPISTOLARY FORM

Race and Respectability illuminates the ways in which concerns for respectability circumscribed early Black writing, expanding our understanding of early Black literary aesthetics. To some extent, my approach dialogues with Rafia Zafar's *We Wear the Mask: African Americans Write American Literature* (1997); Vincent Carretta and Philip Gould's *Genius in Bondage: The Literature of the Early Black Atlantic* (2001); Joanna Brooks and John Saillant's *"Face Zion Forward": First Writers of the Black Atlantic, 1785–1798* (2002); and Nicole N. Aljoe's *Creole Testimonies: Slave Narratives from the British West Indies, 1709–1838* (2011).[26] These studies emphasize Black literary production in the eighteenth and nineteenth centuries and examine texts written or as-told-to by Black voices. *Race and Respectability* emphasizes the same kinds of texts, but it does so with a different historical and cultural framework, understanding early Black literary production as a moral endeavor, bound up with political and racial aims. Respectability shows up in this early Black literature through a preoccupation with good behavior, education and intellectual capacities, spiritual conversion, virtue, social propriety, even financial restraint and resourcefulness. Through texts, Black Africans communicated ideas about proper comportment, salvation, virtue, obedience, and education.

Respectability guided not only what eighteenth-century Black Africans wrote—or narrated to others—but also the genres or forms those texts assumed. Letter writing, in particular, was an important mode of expression. In epistolary studies, there is little engagement with the topic of early Black

African letters, this even though letter writing, relatively speaking, was a ubiquitous act in Black communities throughout the early Atlantic world.[27] Wheatley and Equiano penned letters, as did many of the Black settlers in Sierra Leone.[28] Letters offer valuable insight about literacy and literary practices among early Black Africans and speak to their efforts to construct social and political identities. They also employ letters to establish and maintain bonds with friends, family, and influential figures.

Letter writing in this period had a certain kind of democratizing potential in that anybody could write a letter to anybody so long as one could procure access to the most basic writing technologies. Generally speaking, by the end of the eighteenth century, as Mary A. Favret points out, "The letter had . . . become a phenomenally useful political tool, available to anyone with a pen."[29] Letters and their democratic power were central, in fact, in the forming and maintenance of British Empire in the long eighteenth century, as Eve Tavor Bannet argues. In *Empire of Letters,* Bannet examines letter-writing manuals, and their evolution over the century, and the ways in which those manuals taught epistolary practices to letter writers in Britain and its American colonies. She argues that letters became a key method for uniting the "far-flung" regions of the British Empire—the "three kingdoms and the American mainland and island colonies."[30] By the end of the eighteenth century, we could add Sierra Leone to this imperial map. As Bannet notes, "Letters were the only available technology for distance communication."[31] So, it was essential that people be taught proper epistolary form, Bannet maintains. "One of the functions of letter manuals," she argues, "during the long eighteenth century was to unite dispersed localities by facilitating the 'mutual communication' of persons with different local and regional dialects, pronunciations, mores, memories, levels of education and ranks."[32] That Black Africans should employ letter writing as a communicative strategy perhaps did not appear extraordinary to readers in England. As Bannet notes, "the eighteenth century naturalized the idea that anyone can (or should be able to) read and write a letter."[33]

Of course, the democratizing potential of letters must be qualified by the unique obstacles Black Africans encountered in gaining access to those writing technologies. The challenges were particular not only to race, gender, and class but also to time and place. In the United States, for example, Black slave codes increasingly criminalized Black education.[34] Black codes would not have been an issue for the settlers and West African kings in Sierra Leone, where they had some access to missionary schools. Instead, access to writing materials might have been their greatest barrier. Despite the obstacles, some Black Africans learned how to read and write in English, or they gained access to those who could, like the Temne King Niambanna II did by employing the services of a literate Sierra Leone colonist named Abram Elliot Griffith.[35] Frequently, they composed letters not for aesthetic reasons but to communicate needs and ambitions; their letter-writing skills, in many cases, reflected what Konstantin Dierks calls a "rudimentary," or baseline, level of mastery. In his study arguing for the centrality of letter writing in the rise of a (white) middle class in eighteenth-century America, Dierks outlines three modes of letter-writing instruction in a British Atlantic. In addition to a rudimentary level, most often reflected in the "lower sorts," according to Dierks, there also was a midlevel instruction focused on grammar and mechanics. The highest level emphasized "stylishly literary writing" and was practiced by an "affluent elite" class, those concerned with aesthetics.[36]

Black letters were a primary vehicle through which Black Africans articulated and enacted understandings about respectability. Usually people wrote letters to maintain relationships over (great) geographical distances. Transatlantic epistolary studies, like those by Sarah Pearsall and Susan Imbarrato, emphasize the circulation of letters through the Atlantic.[37] They have pointed out the ways in which letters helped to create early Atlantic cultures by maintaining familial bonds among family members and close associates separated by an ocean. Some Black Africans composed letters in this way, as an intimate, social practice. I discuss the letters of Wheatley (in chapter 2) and Mary Perth (in chapter 5) as examples. Those very same letters, though, and others penned by settlers in Sierra Leone (which I discuss in chapters 4 and 5) are designed to procure political power and illustrate Black humanity. Sierra Leone settlers especially employ letters as a form of "writing upwards," which Martyn Lyons describes as a genre of letter writing whereby there exists "social or political inequality between the correspondents."[38] Often, according to Lyons, this power differential necessitates that a less powerful letter writer employ sincere or subversive displays of deference, humility, supplication, and flattery with the ultimate goal of influencing the letter's more powerful addressee. In this way, letters bridged political distance, allowing those Black Africans I discuss in this book to enter public spheres. The public sphere perhaps held a particular allure for Black Africans because of what Jürgen Habermas describes as the space's tendency toward "parity."[39] The public sphere, he argues, "preserved a kind of social intercourse that, far from presupposing the equality of status, disregarded status altogether. The tendency replaced the celebration of rank with a tact befitting equals."[40] Even if one must genuflect in a letter to a person of higher rank, as Lyons explains, the letter nonetheless closes social and intellectual gaps through the interaction inherent in a letter exchange. Through letters, according to Habermas, "the individual unfold[s] himself in his subjectivity."[41] Letter writing, then, was a form of self-construction that some early Black Africans employed to make themselves more visible in public contexts. We can usefully broaden the epistolary conversation to interrogate how Black Africans participated in the imperial energies of Britain, endeavored to create and maintain familial bonds with family members in other regions, and affected politics. Black letters meditate on freedom, race, worship, voting rights, and Black humanity. Through this lyrical mode, the letters offer valuable information about the lives of Black Africans who utilize the letter form to self-construct as respectable citizens of a body politic.

EARLY BLACK STUDIES AND RESPECTABILITY

By focusing on how early Black emigrant communities (and a king) in West Africa subscribed to tenets of respectability, this book expands the ever-popular construct of "the Black Atlantic," a term Paul Gilroy theorized in 1993. In *The Black Atlantic,* Gilroy characterizes the culture created by Black Africans in the Western world as a transnational phenomenon that links Black Africans in all those regions (beyond Africa) that border the Atlantic Ocean. His work shifted the focus from Africa (as the central unifying feature of Black diasporic communities) to the waters of the Atlantic. He understood, for example, African American literature as a hybrid form created by the movement of Black African bodies and ideas through the Atlantic's watery routes. His is still a dominant model for discussing the diasporic experiences of Black Africans. However, a number of studies have since updated his perspective.[42] *Race and Respectability* further updates Gilroy's formulation of a "Black Atlantic" by shifting the focus back toward Africa as a site of Black diasporic cultural expression. If the Atlantic Ocean is a site of cultural origin, as Gilroy maintains, that culture not only manifests itself in Europe, the Caribbean, and the Americas but also in Africa, as illustrated by those settlers and Indigenous people living in Sierra Leone who, I argue in chapters 4 and 5, espouse tenets of respectability as a response to Enlightenment racism and slavery. Respectability was a preoccupation for Black diasporic populations, which consequently affected the literary (and sociopolitical) landscape of the Atlantic world.

Although Gilroy's model of a Black Atlantic has been prominent in the field of Black studies, seldom does Black studies feature the texts I examine in this book, focusing instead on content of our more modern times. Manning Marable says of Black studies scholarship that it is descriptive, corrective and prescriptive.[43] The work is descriptive in that it examines subject matter from the perspective of Black lives; corrective in terms of how it challenges negative stereotypes about Black people and culture; and prescriptive in its activist urgency, which is to say that the scholarship is rooted in public engagement. Marable argues, "The purpose of black scholarship is more than the restoration of identity and self-esteem; it is to use history and culture as tools through which people interpret their collective experience, but for the purpose of transforming their actual conditions and the totality of the society all around them."[44] *Race and Respectability* offers a perspective on early Black Atlantic lives that is descriptive, corrective, and prescriptive, speaking to the struggles of Black people today by calling on us to reckon with respectability politics as a centuries-long strategy that has proved an ineffective response to racism and white supremacy.

Building on Higginbotham's treatment of the subject, *Race and Respectability* provides a prologue of sorts by turning to the eighteenth century to illuminate a long-enduring preoccupation with respectability among early Black Africans, many of them situated in church contexts, both within and beyond the borders of the United States. What is more, this approach to respectability in the eighteenth century illuminates the murkiness of gendered difference within Black communities. As I illustrate through close readings of the poetics of Phillis Wheatley and the Methodist evangelism of Mary Perth in Sierra Leone, Black women sometimes conducted themselves in ways that were coded masculine at the time. For example, while Perth served as housekeeper for Freetown's governor and managed a boardinghouse for children, she also owned a goods store and voted in local elections. Her business acumen added to her social stature. She straddled the line between public and domestic (or private) spheres. If respectability politics was an essential strategy enabling earlier generations of Black Americans to theorize gender, as Brittney Cooper notes, part of that theoretical work was testing gender boundaries. In fact, respectability politics demanded it. As Higginbotham argues, respectability politics was a form of activism that compelled Black church women to move beyond the domestic sphere to advocate for racial equality in the public realm. Black women seeking respectability in the eighteenth century moved similarly.

Respectability has been so engrained in Black cultures over the centuries because of its concomitant discourse about self-improvement and racial uplift. It resulted in the rise of a Black middle class, an elite element within the race, and has been a reminder for Black Americans of their agency, challenging narratives of victimhood and abject powerlessness. It encourages Black Americans to seek out college, to pursue high-earning careers, to run for political office and build nonprofit organizations, to be a better self and achieve elements of the American dream. Speaking specifically from a hip-hop feminist perspective, Cooper, Aisha Durham, and Susana M. Morris articulate the gains of respectability politics as a "platform from which . . . progressive black women could indict the de jure and de facto racist and misogynist practices they experienced daily. Respectability politics has been a somewhat useful strategy for improving conditions for blacks."[45] The gains often associated with this politics, however, weigh against its detrimental effects. One effect, as E. Frances White points out, is that the strategy has reified a "good woman/bad woman dichotomy" that encourages Black women to strive for "good woman" status instead of exposing "the bankruptcy of the entire system."[46] Respectability politics, Durham, Cooper, and Morris acknowledge, "employs tactics such as surveillance, control, and repression" that actually reassert "dominant systems of power, namely white capitalist heteropatriarchy."[47] Importantly, it upholds the neoliberal fallacy that if Black folks would only take personal responsibility, then racism would cease to be a problem; this way of thinking ignores systems and structures of oppression that actually maintain racism.

Instead of taking responsibility, Black folks who subscribe to notions of respectability often end up taking the blame. In doing so, they suffer health consequences. According to Hedwig Lee and Margaret Takako Hicken, respectability politics is akin to "vigilance behavior," which they define as a hyperfocus on "care about appearance and language to get good service, avoid being harassed, receiving the same level of respect as White people, the avoidance of social situations and places, and preparing for potential prejudice and discrimination." This vigilance behavior leads one constantly to anticipate potentially "stressful situations," which "activates the body's primary stress response system." This, in turn, leads to issues such as poor sleep quality, hypertension, and depression.[48] Nevertheless, as Ta-Nehisi Coates points out, Black Americans cling to this survival strategy because the alternative is too difficult to grasp. "Respectability politics is, at its root, the inability to look into the cold dark void of history," Coates argues. "For if black people are . . . no part of the problem, if the problem truly is 100 percent explained by white supremacy, then we are presented with a set of unfortunate facts about our home."[49]

Discussions about respectability politics in Black communities, increasingly, acknowledge the problematic aspects of the discourse. Brando Simeo Starkey, for example, bemoans the tendency in Black communities to label as respectability politics, and subsequently dismiss, any commentary about racial uplift and progress.[50] Especially with the rise of the Black Lives Matter movement, there has been an impulse to claim triumphant narratives of Black resistance to respectability.[51] For some, Beyoncé has become an emblem for this kind of resistance.[52] The release of her song "Black Parade" in 2020 to commemorate Juneteenth led one cultural critic for National Public Radio to declare that the singer was "defenestrating respectability politics" as she sang in the song about embracing kinky hair and dreads.[53] Another columnist for the *New York Times* declared in the wake of Beyoncé's 2018 performance at the Coachella festival in California that she "rewrote the book on black respectability politics" because she headlined the show by spotlighting elements of Black culture; she sang the Negro national anthem, "Lift Every Voice and Sing," began the performance with a Nefertiti-inspired outfit, and evoked the sounds, choreography, and intellectual traditions of Black colleges and universities. All of this matters, according to *New York Times* opinion writer Myles E. Johnson, because "Black people often feel the need to edit parts of our culture and upbringing for the sake of appearing respectable. . . . Beyoncé's Coachella performance suggests that, as black people's power grows, we should intentionally amplify the culture that nurtured us. This anti-respectability politics that Beyoncé brought to the stage is what transformed her performance into a political statement."[54] The headline for Johnson's *New York Times* column anticipates an "end to respectability politics." This optimistic perspective belies the fact that many Black institutions remain mired in respectability politics, like those HBCUs celebrated in Beyoncé's performance.

For sure, Black colleges and universities, as Steve Mobley and Jennifer Johnson note, consistently "cultivate and encourage social change and racial uplift, and . . . are among the few places where Black culture is placed at the forefront, celebrated, and sustained." It is also the case, which Mobley and Johnson go on to say, that "many HBCUs have also produced a hidden curriculum that permeates their campus culture."[55] That hidden curriculum is one designed to police and modify "particular types of Blackness, thus making them palatable to White communities."[56] That is illustrated, for example, in the controversial decision by Morehouse in 2010 to implement a dress code, emphasizing *appropriate* forms of masculine attire, that was particularly hostile to nonbinary, non-gender-conforming students. HBCUs were founded beginning in the nineteenth century to promote upward mobility for Blacks—social and economic. The point here is not to denigrate HBCUs, of which I am a proud product. These spaces remain central cultural institutions in Black communities. The point rather is to point out the all-encompassing aspect of respectability politics; it shapes even spaces designed to disrupt the status quo. It has shaped the cultural history of Black people in the United States and beyond. Respectability politics is a specific kind of moralizing discourse coming out of marginalized communities. It is about conformity and assimilation, a way to gain status, to claim civil and human rights by adhering to hegemonic standards of social, religious, and political conduct. It also is a process that is coconstitutive with the development of early Black Atlantic cultures. *Race and Respectability* calls attention to Black people's long-enduring dependence on respectability, a coping strategy that takes as much as it gives.

A NOTE ON TERMINOLOGY

I apply to early Black African figures the terms "respect," "respectable," and "respectability." I do so at the risk of my analysis appearing anachronistic and presentist to some. Nonetheless, I insist on a reading of these figures within the context of respectability and respectability politics to emphasize threads that bind the experiences of Black peoples then and now. Throughout the book, I understand respect to mean esteem or regard for the humanity of Blackness. Although archaic, the *OED* formulation of respect is particularly useful. The *OED* defines respect as "Regard, gaze; visual attention. Esp. to have respect to: to direct one's gaze towards, to regard, look at; to face."[57] This definition speaks to the stakes inherent in achieving respect as it translates into visibility as opposed to invisibility. To be invisible is to be enslaved, to exist beyond the social contract. The idea for figures like Adam, Wheatley, Equiano, and those settlers in Sierra Leone is that their actions would alter other people's perceptions of them. Respect, then, is a quest to be seen, to have one's personhood acknowledged. Extending the *OED* construction, to be respectable is to be worthy of being seen/visible, to be worthy of consideration, of freedom and equality. Respectability in this same vein is the quality of being respectable, of having features that mark one as respectable and therefore worthy of visibility, of consideration, of freedom.

I use respectability politics specifically in reference to the paradigm Higginbotham identified in 1993. The paradigm is defined by key features, including assimilation, self-policing, safety, rhetorics of uplift, and gender reification that make it cohere as a politics. It would be imprecise to refer to as respectability politics the efforts of the figures discussed in this book's chapters as none of them reflects the paradigm fully. When taken together, however, their strategies speak to the ways in which a politics of respectability formed out of earlier Black Africans' engagement with tenets of respect and respectability. Note that I use the terms "politics of respectability" and "respectability politics" interchangeably, although I take to heart Lori Latrice Martin's larger point that the way we talk about "respectability politics" today has lost a good deal of the meaning that Higginbotham invested in the term "politics of respectability" in 1993.[58] Martin suggests that respectability politics is a corrupted, mutated present-day form of a concept that was highly nuanced as a lens for explicating the Black experience at the turn of the twentieth century. I do not mimic Martin's parsing out of terms. I wish to emphasize that our current discourse about respectability politics comes out of that earlier moment in the late nineteenth century, and that earlier moment comes out of still earlier moments. Rather than emphasizing the discontinuities, throughout this project I focus on threads pulling us from the moment in 1600 when a mixed-race woman secured a letter of protection enforcing her respectable status to the present-day, when people of African descent continue gravitating toward strategies to recommend them favorably in society.

"NO ROGUE,

NO RASCAL, NO THIEF"

RESPECTABILITY

AND

"ADAM NEGRO'S TRYAL"

IN 1694, A BLACK MAN living in Boston, Massachusetts, entered into a labor contract with a white Massachusetts judge and merchant; the contract would transform his legal status from slave to indentured servant to free man within seven years, provided he went on "cheerfully, quietly and industriously." Near the completion of that seven-year term, the enslaver revoked the contract, claiming that the man, named Adam, failed to remain productive and obedient in his service. In 1700, Adam sued that enslaver for his freedom. Historians and literary scholars alike read Adam's legal battle as a moment of slave resistance. Typically, we deem the body of documents resulting from the court case a prototypical slave narrative, an early example of textual self-fashioning that preceded the slave narrative proper. His efforts tell us something, too, about how a concern for respect manifested itself in some of the earliest textual records of Black lives in the Americas. Adam demanded respect; he deployed court apparatuses to earn that respect and with it his freedom. What we see in Adam's case is that respectability was a dividing line between civility (most often embodied by white, colonial Americans) and depravity (portrayed frequently through depictions of Black African behavior).[1]

The same year that Adam initiated his lawsuit, the Massachusetts jurist Samuel Sewall published the colony's first known antislavery tract, *The Selling of Joseph: A Memorial,* in which he argued that slavery was wrong because Black Africans, like whites, were the offspring of God. Therefore, to sell a man into slavery, according to Sewall, was akin to Joseph's brothers selling him to the Ishmaelites. Several months later, in 1701, the man enslaving Adam, named John Saffin, wrote a pamphlet in defense of slavery titled *A Brief and Candid Answer to a Late Printed Sheet Entitled, The Selling of Joseph.* In the text, Saffin points out that slavery is an institution grounded in biblical scripture. Citing examples of slavery in the books of Genesis, Exodus, Leviticus, and others, he argues "any lawful captives of other heathen nations may be made bond men as hath been proved."[2]

Sewall and Saffin's exchange constitutes one of the earliest slavery debates in British colonial America. Studies of Saffin's pamphlet, then, emphasize his rhetorical maneuvers in response to Sewall. The text, though, is equally remarkable for its engagement with Adam, as evident by a narrative Saffin appends to the pamphlet and references on the title page.[3] In that narrative, Saffin includes depositions from neighbors testifying to Adam's violent and surly disposition; he represents, or mediates, Adam's behavior and character through a lens of respectability. He includes a timeline of events that explains how and why he revoked the indenture contract and various means by which he and Adam sought arbitration. The arbitration began not in a courtroom but in the front parlor of the home of Sewall, who summoned Saffin at Adam's request. Whereas most studies concentrate on the main body of Saffin's pamphlet and his philosophical entanglements with Sewall, my discussion in this chapter shifts focus to the appendix, which is anything but an appendage. The very pamphlet might not have materialized if Adam had not been aggressive and effective in pressing his legal claims. In the purest sense of the term "respect," Adam compels Saffin to see him, to acknowledge him in the very text designed to negate Adam's personhood.

In this chapter, I examine Adam's and Saffin's deployment of respectability as a tool to define Blackness. For Adam, respect manifests in his willingness to abide by the laws of the colony and to seek persistently legal remediation for his grievances. He demands justice. Saffin presents Adam as the antithesis of respectable. Adam is not worthy of respect, according to Saffin, because he comports himself with violence and insolence. What is more, he normalizes the character portrayal, so that the presumed poor behavior of Adam correlates with a general depravity in Black Africans. In one regard, Adam succeeds as the courts ultimately side with him, granting him his freedom in 1703. Saffin's rhetoric in his narrative, however, is particularly consequential as his negative descriptions of Black character gained credence with the arrival of the Enlightenment movement to the Americas later in the century.

I begin the discussion of "Adam Negro's Tryal" with an overview and context for the conflict between Adam and Saffin. I then discuss the slavery debate between Saffin and Sewall, which centered on the issue of social order and the extent to which a Black presence in the colony disrupted that order. Both Sewall and Saffin ground their arguments in racial ideologies about Black degeneracy that challenge notions of Black humanity and respect. Finally, I examine Saffin's construction of Adam as unruly and disrespectful in the appended narrative. My reading of Saffin's pamphlet illuminates a tension between a white, colonial imagination and Black subjectivity, centered on respect.

For sure, "Adam Negro's Tryal" does not demonstrate many of the key elements of respectability politics based on the paradigm that Higginbotham sets forth in 1993. He, for instance, does not endeavor to self-police. Self-policing is a concern for comportment, demeanor; it is a form of assimilation designed to put a mainstream majority at ease and ensure one's safety. Adam is not critical or censorious of his own actions but, rather, of Saffin's. What is more, he claims that his comportment is a nonissue. Through his attorneys he insists that the manner in which he carried out his duties during the term of his indenture is not a condition for his freedom. In one key aspect, though, Adam's actions speak to respectability politics in that he is motivated by the same fundamental need for visibility, to be regarded as human in the face of racialized rhetoric. His demand for respect is a liberatory gesture and an issue of safety. If we understand respectability politics as a process that evolves over centuries, then, "Adam Negro's Tryal" illustrates the stakes inherent for Black Africans striving for respect. His example anticipates the motivations of later Black Africans, like Phillis Wheatley and Olaudah Equiano, who render themselves as respectable in response to racial discourses. Through respectability, early Black Africans stake a claim to freedom.

THE CHARACTER OF INDENTURE

The point of contention between Adam and Saffin was a conduct clause included in the indenture contract, which stated:

> Be it known unto all men by these presents, that I John Saffin . . . do by these presents, of my own free and voluntary will and pleasure, from and after the full end and expiration of seven years . . . make free my said Negro man named Adam . . . Always provided that the said Adam my servant do in the mean time go on cheerfully, quietly and industriously in the lawful business that either myself or my assigns shall from time to time reasonably set him about or imploy him in, and do behave and abare himself as an honest, true and faithful servant ought to do, during the term of seven years. (8–9)

Initially, in September 1701, the colony's high court, of which Saffin was a member, ruled in Saffin's favor, prompting Adam to appeal. A year later the court reversed the ruling and affirmed Adam's freedom, which led to more appeals and reversals. Over the course of three years, Saffin and Adam battled through the courts.[4] Adam sought his freedom; Saffin sought the return of his "property," whom he considered a fugitive slave. He argued that Adam violated the contract because he did not, in fact, carry out his duties "cheerfully, quietly and industriously." David Kazanjian offers a useful articulation of Saffin's aims as simultaneously an act of dispossession and possession. He notes that Saffin not only sought to dispossess Adam of his labor but also sought to "possess Adam with a certain being: the desire for, or love of, quiet industry on behalf of his master."[5] Kazanjian continues, "Saffin aims to function as master of Adam's work and his *being,* as both boss and conjurer."[6] For his part, Adam rejects, or mocks, in Kazanjian's words, this act of (dis)possession, insisting that he complied with the primary—indeed, the only—condition of the contract, that he serve for seven years.[7] In one appeal filed by his attorney, Adam argues that the clause referencing his demeanor and attitude is a consideration, not a condition for his freedom. Importantly, Adam's appeal points out that "there is no penalty in the said instrument if [Adam] did not serve [Saffin] faithfully during the abovesaid term of seven years. . . . [T]he enfranchisement is positive and not conditionall and liberty being a privilege, the greatest that can be given to any man save his life, it ought not to be forfeited upon trivial and frivolous matters."[8] Here, Adam eschews the very notion that comportment is linked to freedom, rejecting what we have come to understand as a core tenet of respectability politics.

That Saffin would use an indenture contract to control Adam's behavior was not unusual. Indenture contracts were formulaic legal documents that represented a mutual agreement of limited-term bondage. The contracts often included conditions or incentives that were specific to the individual being indentured. The incentives might consist of an allotment of land upon completion of the service, farming provisions, clothing, or money. Indenture contracts also could be used to monitor the conduct and control the morality of servants, which was the case for Adam. As Elisabeth Ceppi points out, "The stipulation of working cheerfully codifies the traditional discourse of humiliation, of the patient and cheerful acceptance of a servant's place."[9] That is to say, conduct clauses were part of a larger Puritan ideology of good masters and servants, the "ideal of covenant labor."[10] Focusing specifically on colonial Virginia, Warren Billings notes of the nature of indentured servitude contracts that "they were . . . instruments of social control designed to regulate, as strictly as law and community attitudes allowed, the lives of unruly and potentially quite dangerous" social elements, like immigrants, and I would add those enslaved.[11] The same could be said of indentures in colonial Massachusetts. Consider the following excerpt from a contract dated February 22, 1664, between Joseph Pike, a weaver, and a boy named Samuell Hadley, both of Essex County, Massachusetts:

> Samuell Hadley of Rowley . . . with the consent of his father George Hadley of Rowley bound himself to serve said Pike as an apprentice five years, and he was not to haunt ale houses, taverns or any tippling houses, not to keep bad company, nor to reveal his master's secrets, nor to be out of master's house at unlawful time of night without his master's leave; said Pike was to teach him to read and write well, teach him the trade of a weaver . . . and at the end of his time to have a good loom with the tackling and a good shuttle fit to set to work with.[12]

The terms of Hadley's indenture resonate with Adam's in that his conduct is under scrutiny. Clearly, this contract is designed not only as an appren-

ticeship but also as a moral compass. Adam's contract is particularly significant, though, because Saffin employs the conduct clause to racialize Adam.
Conduct, as Ceppi argues, became "a legal basis upon which white masters
like Saffin might claim authority to convert their black servants into slaves."[13]

Respectability rhetoric, then, enables Saffin to portray Adam as worthy
of enslavement; what is more, Adam signifies Black African depravity. In
his study of John Saffin's life and the rise of racial rhetoric in colonial Massachusetts, Albert J. Von Frank points out Saffin's general tendency to "catalog
the various peoples of the earth."[14] Saffin, Von Frank argues, is guided by
a puritanical notion of "chosenness," or exceptionalism as God's people,
which resulted in a general sense of cultural superiority. At one point in his
notebook, Saffin rehearses Mercator's derogatory classification of European
ethnic groups:

It would be to [sic] much to Reckon up the vertues of several Nations
in Europe: but as their vices (as who is without some) they are noted
in some short Sayings Viz.

The people of Franconia are foolish, rude & vehement
The Bavarians are Prodigall glutons & Railery.

. . . .

The Saxons Dissemblers, crafty, Self willed

. . . .

The Italians proud, Desirous of Reveng & witty.
The Spaniard's haughty, wise, Covetous.
The French Eloquent, intemperate, and rash.

. . . .

The Sarmatians are great Eaters, proud, & Theives.
The Greeks miserable.[15]

Within this context, then, one might understand the poem, titled "The Negro's Character," that Saffin includes in his 1701 pamphlet.[16] He describes
Black Africans:

Cowardly and cruel are those *Blacks* innate,
Prone to Revenge, Imp of inveterate hate.
He that exasperates them, soon espies
Mischief and Murder in their very eyes.
Libidinous, Deceitful, False, and Rude,
The Spume Issue of Ingratitude. (5)

One could argue here that Saffin denigrates Black Africans in this poem not as a racial project but as a reflection of the same cultural supremacy and xenophobia that infuse Mercator's catalogue of humanity. The moment could be read, which Von Frank does, as an illustration of the Puritan mind intent on thinking in typological terms, whereby the particular stands in for "the larger group or class to which it is seen as belonging."[17] I would argue that the racial work of the poem and of Saffin's representation of Adam in the pamphlet comes through in the very move to create an entire category of humanity based solely on the one identifying somatic feature of Blackness. What is more, the stakes attached to Saffin's poem and pamphlet are markedly different from those attached to Mercator's catalogue; Saffin aims to justify the enslavement of a category of people he has deemed inhuman.

For Saffin, respectability and Blackness were contradictory terms. However, it was not at all a consensus among white Massachusetts colonists that Blackness—and the negative traits associated with it—was immutable. This is suggested in the diary Samuel Sewall kept from 1674 to 1724. In his diary, Sewall writes on June 19, 1700, "Having been long and much dissatisfied with the trade of fetching of Negros from Guinea, at last I had a strong inclination to write something about it; but it wore off."[18] In 1700, something changes for Sewall. Sewall's diary is vague about the particulars of his defining moment, but in that same June 19, 1700, entry he mentions his visit with a "Brother Belknap," who shared with Sewall his plans to petition the courts to help an enslaved married couple gain their freedom. After that visit, Sewall resolved to voice his criticism, which, he notes in the diary, "makes me hope that I was call'd of God to write [*The Selling of Joseph*] . . .; lest his blessing accompany the same."[19] With this newfound zeal, Sewall played an active role in mediating the grievances between Adam and Saffin. Several months after publication of his pamphlet, Sewall summoned his fellow jurist Saffin to his house and attempted to appeal to Saffin's sense of justice to grant Adam his freedom.

In his diary, Sewall mentions that other influential Massachusetts men also had been galvanized into action, sparking a kind of proto–antislavery movement in Massachusetts. Besides Belknap, he previews Cotton Mather's plan to publish an essay advocating for the conversion of enslaved Black people. The ever-prolific Puritan minister published his *The Negro Christianized* in 1706.[20] In addition to the essay, Mather helped Massachusetts's Black residents form the Society of Negroes in 1693. This community centered on an agreed-upon set of nine rules that outlined what they perceived as proper conduct. Importantly, their perceptions were informed by Mather and a very orthodox Puritan sensibility. Among the rules, they agreed to meet and worship every Sunday evening, but not so long that it would interfere with their work obligations. They committed to learning and reciting a catechism and only admitting people into the society who had undergone proper instruction and examination by a "[white] Minister of God" like Mather.[21] They agreed to refrain from fornication, swearing, cursing, lying, and stealing. The members of this Negro society were called upon to behave in a manner similar to their white counterparts. In fact, codes of conduct, like the conduct clause included in Adam's indenture contract, were a common feature of colonial town governances, not unique to this society.

However, there is a singular quality with regard to what the Society of Negroes, its members enslaved, is called upon to do as they vow not to engage in "notorious disobedience or unfaithfulness unto their masters."[22] The rules required members to do good "to the other negro-servants" and included an anti–fugitive slave clause that promised they would "afford [runaway slaves] no shelter" but instead help to "do what in us lies, that [runaways] may be discovered and punished."[23] They also agreed to monitor each other's comings and goings and not stay out late, which anticipates laws established at the beginning of the eighteenth century directed specifically at Black Africans in the colony.[24] These rules suggest that the aim here is not simply to create another community of saints in colonial Massachusetts who only incidentally are Black. Beyond piety, the rules framing this society are concerned with the economic interests of the colony, with protecting the status quo, and with surveilling its Black enslaved population. Members agree to a strict code of self-policing with the idea that doing so will alter their status as cultural, social, and civic outsiders; ironically, the rules ensure their marginalized, dehumanized status as chattel.

Historian Wendy Anne Warren, noting Mather's guiding hand in draft-ing the rules, argues that those rules suggest that Mather saw "New En-gland's African inhabitants as potential makers of trouble."[25] In this way, Warren argues, Mather endeavored to build a society of Blacks that "might teach others about Christianity" and proper behavior.[26] Given the ubiqui-tous nature of such conduct codes in Puritan culture, even among white colonists, perhaps Mather did not see Black Africans in particular as "makers of trouble" but as collaborators in maintaining a Godly society.

Beyond what Mather *might* have intended when sponsoring this organi-zation, it is notable that a group of Black Massachusetts residents *agreed* to this form of self-policing. For its members, the society allowed them to live with a sense of self-control and determination. The rules illustrate the sheer power of respectability as an ideology that makes Black Africans complicit in their own oppression. This form of self-policing will become a cornerstone of respectability politics at the turn of the twentieth century. As an opera-tion of self-control, respectability allowed Black Africans then—as it allows them now—to live with an illusion of security, believing that if they comport themselves properly, their bodies will not become vulnerable to the physical violence and oppression that defined slavery and its cultural offspring in the United States. The Society of Negroes vowed to police themselves by a set of moral standards they understood would translate into some measure of freedom even as that set of standards formalized a system of surveillance that ensured their continued oppression.

Although Adam's actions suggest he does not subscribe to these notions of self-policing, he does comply with a status quo to a certain extent by seek-ing a legal remedy for his enslavement. It is not exactly clear, though, how or why he turned to Sewall to begin the arbitration of his case.[27] Perhaps he had read *The Selling of Joseph,* circulated just months before. Perhaps an advocate referred him to Sewall. For whatever reason, Adam requests an audience with Sewall, which leads to Sewall summoning Saffin to his house, where other magistrates were also present. Like Adam, Sewall deemed the condi-tional clause invalid, telling Saffin that liberty was "a thing of great value, even next to life."[28] A second magistrate, perhaps conceding the validity of the conduct clause in the terms of indenture, chastised Saffin for applying the clause too strictly to an enslaved Black man. He told Saffin that there was "much to be allowed for the behaviour of Negroes, who are so ignorant, rude

and bruitish, and therefore to be considered as Negroes."[29] After two days
of discussion with no resolution, those magistrates present at Sewall's house
agreed to entertain Saffin's and Adam's grievances in court. Adam finally
found resolution in November 1703, when the Superior Court of Judicature
ruled that "the said Adam and his heirs be at peace and quiet and free with
all their chattels from the said John Saffin Esquire and his heirs forever."[30]

In at least once instance, Saffin, himself, advocated for manumission of an
enslaved Black man, following King Philip's War in 1676. On July 1 of that
year, Wampanoag-allied forces attacked a community just outside of Boston.
They raided the home of Hezekiah Willet. After shooting and beheading
Willet, the Wampanoag took as captive the man Willet had enslaved, Jethro.
Jethro remained a prisoner of war among the Wampanoag for five days,
and because he could speak a little of their language, he was able to gather
important details about military strategy, including their plan to attack another English settlement. Out of a sense of loyalty to his English neighbors or
self-preservation or maybe even moral prudence, Jethro escaped and related
to English colonial forces all he had learned. His intel helped the English
stage a counterattack and turn the war in their favor. For his efforts, later
that year, Jethro was manumitted by court decree. The court acted on the
recommendation of Saffin, who had been named administrator of Willet's
estate.[31] The decree reads:

> In reference unto a negro named Jethro, taken prisoner by the Indi-
> ans, and retaken againe by our army, which said negro appertained
> to the estate of the successors of Capt Willett, deceased, our Gen-
> erall Court haue agreed with Mr. John Saffin, adminnestrator of the
> said estate, mutually, that the said negro doe forthwith betake him-
> self to his former service, and to remaine a servant vnto the succes-
> sors of the said Captaine Willett, vntill two yeers be expired from
> the date hereof, and then to be freed and sett att libertie from his
> said service.[32]

Rather than provoking racist poetry, Jethro's conduct compels Saffin to advocate on his behalf. It would seem that Jethro exhibits the good behavior,
or respectability, that Saffin claims Adam lacked. This 1676 moment complicates our understanding of Saffin's legal and rhetorical moves in Adam's

case, as it suggests at the very least a shift in Saffin's thinking about American slavery and the character of Black Africans between 1676 and 1701. Did Saffin have Jethro in mind when insisting in 1701, in "The Negro's Character," that Blacks were a degenerate people? Was Jethro the exception that proved the rule? At what point did Saffin decide the *bad* behavior of Adam rather than the *good* behavior of Jethro typified Black character? A simple answer for the difference in Saffin's treatment of Jethro and Adam is that Saffin did not claim Jethro as his property. So he had nothing to lose by advocating for the man's freedom.[33]

BLACK (DIS-)RESPECTABILITY
AND THE SOCIAL ORDER

The slavery debate between Sewall and Saffin centered on the issue of civil and spiritual order and the extent to which a Black presence threatened the colony.[34] Sewall suggests that the white, Christian community invites chaos upon itself through the institution of slavery. He makes a moral appeal, insisting, as Mason Lowance notes, that slavery is a "violation of God's ordinances."[35] What is at stake for Sewall is nothing less than the spiritual salvation of Massachusetts. He argues, "How horrible is the uncleanness, mortality, if not murder, that the ships are guilty of that bring great crowds of these miserable men and women."[36] For Sewall, the practice of slavery threatens the spiritual order of things, an order that determines Black Africans and their white colonial counterparts are bound together as "Sons of Adam," and "coheirs" of God's kingdom with "equal Right unto Liberty, and all other outward Comforts of Life."[37] From a spiritual perspective, according to Sewall, racial difference is a moot point. From a civil perspective, however, Sewall argues that racial slavery deteriorates living conditions for whites and Blacks alike because it forces an artificial, unnatural intimacy between races: "It is . . . most lamentable to think, how in taking Negros out of Africa, and Selling of them here, That which God ha's joyned together men do boldly rend asunder; Men from their Country, Husbands from their Wives, Parents from their Children."[38] He argues that slavery forces Black Africans into "our Body Politick as a kind of *extravasat* Blood."[39] He determines that "there is such a disparity in their Conditions, Color & Hair, that they can never embody with us, and grow up into orderly Families, to the Peopling of the

Land."[40] In this way, Sewall laments the creation of a system of servitude that forces "the Africans to become Slaves amongst our selves."[41] Not only does slavery force an artificial intimacy between Black and white, but it also disrupts the economic development of Massachusetts as, according to Sewall, "it would conduce more to the welfare of the Province to have White Servants for a Term of Year, than to have Slaves for Life."[42] What is more, the disrespectful and lawless behavior that Saffin ascribes to Black Africans' inherent nature, Sewall argues is a pernicious result of slavery. "Indeed they can seldom use their freedom well," Sewall concedes, "yet their continual aspiring after their forbidden Liberty, renders them Unwilling Servants," and, as a result, they engage in "Thefts, and other Immoralities" for which their "Masters" must answer.[43] Sewall, then, advocates for the abolishment of slavery on the grounds that it disrupts spiritual and civil order. As War-ren notes, Sewall "had trouble imagining a commingling of Africans with English; like so many white nineteenth-century abolitionists, his antislavery sentiment did not imply an inclusionary worldview."[44] He implicitly sup-ports the idea of racial difference and a public perception of Black Africans as unruly and morally corrupt.[45]

Saffin arrives at the same conclusion about Black African character but to make the opposite argument—that slavery is the best means for maintaining spiritual and civil order in the colony. Like Sewall, Saffin argues that Black Africans fit within a spiritual order. He writes, "We grant it for a certain and undeniable verity" that all men are "the creatures of God" (4). This, however, does not mean that "we ought to tender Pagan Negroes with all love, kindness, and equal respect as to the best of men," he insists (5). Racial difference, then, implied here through religious difference, matters for Saffin because it ensures a civil order that is hierarchical and that permits slavery. "It would be a violation of common prudence," he argues, "and a breach of good manners, to treat a Prince like a Peasant" and vice versa (5). For Saffin, slavery does not upset the spiritual order but protects it as Christians assume their rule over non-Christians (5).[46] Abolishing slavery, then, denies white Christians their God-given right to possess "bondmen." He argues, "all the sacred Rules, Precepts and Commands of the Almighty which he hath given the Sons of Men to observe and keep in their respective Places, Orders and Degrees, would be to no purpose" (2). Stoking public fears, Saffin further speculates that abolishing slavery would set loose a savage, heathen population to do as they please among the white community. "If there be not some strict course taken with them by Authority," he warns, "they will be a plague to this Country" (2).

Saffin's rebuttal to Sewall constitutes only part of his defense of slavery. In the appendix to his pamphlet, he makes the claim more explicitly that Black Africans exist as a disorderly element in the colony.[47] In that appendix, Saffin offers a chronological narrative of his conflict with Adam, including certain depositions from the trial records that characterize Adam as disobedient, lazy, violent, and unruly. What becomes apparent through a close reading of the appendix is the extent to which Saffin's argument is not about slavery solely as an economic system—or even a religious matter. Saffin is concerned with the maintenance of a social order and Adam's alleged transgression of that order.

THE TEXTUAL CASE

Saffin's *A Brief and Candid Answer* serves several purposes: to defend the practice of slavery, to defend Saffin's conduct as a judge and enslaver, and to secure his personal property; at the time of the pamphlet's publication, the courts were still debating the issue of Adam's freedom. He ends the main body of the pamphlet with the poem referenced earlier, "The Negro's Character," recasting his argument in verse form. Most reprintings of Saffin's pamphlet end the document with the poem, discarding the appendix. The practice of excluding the appendix from reprints began in 1866, when historian George H. Moore recovered the text and reprinted it, minus the appended narrative, in his *Notes on the History of Slavery in Massachusetts.*[48] As Abner Goodell speculates, Moore might have done this because the only surviving manuscript of the appendix ends in midsentence. Lines, or maybe even entire pages, appear to be missing.[49] Subsequent studies mostly have followed Moore's lead, focusing on the main text.[50] This trend of not attending to the appendix renders the dialogue between Sewall and Saffin as solely theoretical. It undermines Saffin's motivations, which were material, practical, and urgent. More important, failure to consider the appendix undermines the agentive moves of Adam.[51] Even as Saffin writes his pamphlet, Adam presses his claim in court and casts doubt on Saffin's own behavior as a judge and enslaver. At a hearing in September 1701, the first time Saffin and Adam appear in court, at a session of the Superior Court of Judicature held in Bristol, a jury ruled in favor of Saffin, determining that Adam was his enslaved property.[52] Magistrates, however, were apparently uneasy about the verdict because Saffin, who had been promoted to the Superior Court just a few weeks earlier, refused to recuse himself from the case. Some magistrates—like Sewall—suspected Saffin tampered with the jury.[53] Deciding to honor the jury's decision, the Superior Court remanded Adam back into Saffin's custody, but the court also decided to revisit the case in one year, while they investigated Saffin's conduct. By the end of 1701, when Saffin published his pamphlet, he had recovered his "property," but the case was by no means resolved. According to Dominik Nagl, Adam was able to sue for his freedom because slavery in colonial New England assumed a "curious legal form" that deemed Black Africans "property *and* persons at the same time—property in the sense that they could be traded and treated as commodities, and persons because they still were entitled to certain rights under the law."[54] That contradiction, Nagl notes, is based on Puritanical notions about civil and spiritual order, what he refers to as the "governmentality of slavery."[55] Despite his best arguments, then, Saffin could not deny Adam a legal stage. Consequently, he turned to print. Alongside Sewall's critique of slavery, Adam's actions motivate Saffin's pamphlet. The pamphlet is not, as one historian articulates it, "a dispute with Sewall *over* Adam [emphasis mine]."[56] Attending to the appendix illuminates Adam's role as a vital third party in the dispute.

Even though the appendix has survived only in part, one can glean well enough Saffin's rhetorical strategies in defending his choice to enslave Adam.[57] The tract is an assault on Adam's character, designed to justify slavery as an institution that can control the dangerous impulses of enslaved Blacks. The assault begins early in the text as Saffin relates when and how the conflict between himself and Adam started. Saffin explains that to begin Adam's indenture he hired him out, along with his farm Boundfield in Bristol, to a local farmer named Thomas Shepard. After several years, Shepard, fed up with Adam's work performance and attitude, insisted that Saffin remove Adam from Boundfield. Saffin then hired him out for brief periods to several other neighbors, before finally bringing Adam back to Boston sometime in the year 1700. In March 1701 Adam realized Saffin's intention to revoke his indenture when Saffin ordered him back to Bristol to begin yet another work contract. This time Adam "absolutely refused, and would not go" (7). One evening while Saffin was away on business, Adam, Saffin writes, "took his clothes out of the house by stealth, and went about the town at his pleasure; which said actions of his at Boston, had there been no other, was enough to forfeit his freedom" (7). Saffin's use of "stealth" connotes wrongdoing, conveying the idea that Adam stole away from the house in the dark of night the way a criminal might. He amplifies the criminality with the description of Adam walking around town "at his pleasure." From Saffin's perspective, this is audacious, brazen behavior because Adam clearly flaunts his disobedience. However, if Adam left Saffin's house by "stealth" and crept around, he did so in plain sight. He traveled through Boston openly; he did not leave the city or run away; presumably, he could have done so while Saffin was traveling. His departure from the house was not an escape attempt or a matter of disobedience. From Adam's perspective, it appears a matter of principle. Reading the moment against the grain suggests that Adam had no designs of stealing away from his enslaver but rather was enforcing the terms of the contract to which he and Saffin had agreed.

Further casting Adam's behavior as disrespectful, Saffin explains that soon after he returned home, Adam informed him in a "sawcy and surly" manner that he had been summoned to Sewall's house (7). Though resentful and enraged, Saffin "obey'd this Negromantick summons, and went to know what Captain Sewall had to say" (7). The use of the term "obey'd" in reference to Saffin's own actions contrasts the disobedience he assigns Adam. His use of the term "Negromantick" to describe the summons is of even greater significance—for several reasons. First, Saffin deploys the language of sorcery or black magic, this in the wake of the Salem witch trials, which had occurred less than a decade earlier in the colony. This could have been Saffin's attempt to stoke the same fears that fueled the witch trials in 1692, during which nineteen people were convicted of witchcraft and hanged. One man was pressed to death for refusing to enter a plea. Dozens more languished in jail for months—several died while awaiting trial—before a new governor put an end to the witch hunts in October of that year.

Second, Saffin's careful attention to diction here allows him to indulge in a character denigration of both Adam and Sewall. Saffin dehumanizes Adam by suggesting a link between the enslaved man and black magic. Adam is cast into a supernatural realm of sorcery, of evil and sin. The rhetoric of necromancy here echoes that of the Salem witch trials in that accusers and witnesses often attested to seeing a *black man* inflict harm on residents of Salem. According to those confessed witches and those claiming to be afflicted by witchcraft, this black man seduced residents, coaxed them to sign away their souls in his little book, and bid they serve him by performing acts of torture and other mischief upon their neighbors. He is often seen in the trial transcripts whispering into the ears of accused witches. According to some, he wore a black coat and hat and walked with a cloven foot. According to others, he assumed the form of accused witches. Whereas the "black man" in the witch trials is a kind of spectral presence, a ghost looming over the community, here Adam embodies that evil presence. He is a tangible, fleshly creature walking among the citizens of Boston, ready to infect minds. Indeed, he has already infected at least one, according to Saffin—Sewall's.

Saffin's character assault of Sewall is even more scathing than that of Adam. Back in 1692, Sewall had served as a judge on the Court of Oyer and Terminer, convened to oversee the trials. Once the trials ended and the court disbanded, the frenzy subsided. In the subsequent years, many in Salem understood that a grave mistake had been made. In 1697, the Massachusetts General Court declared a day of fasting and prayer. Many of the accused received pardons and financial restitution. Some of the accusers issued formal apologies, saying their testimony was a result, not of malice, but of poor judgment; they themselves had been victims of Satan's evils. Only one magistrate who had served on the Court of Oyer and Terminer issued a public apology—Sewall. On that day of fasting and prayer in 1697, Sewall handed a written statement to his minister, which the minister then read aloud to the congregation. In that letter, Sewall referred to his own guilt and assumed "the Blame and shame" of the events at Salem. He begged "pardon of men, and especially desiring prayers that God, who has an unlimited authority, would pardon that sin and all other his sins; personal and relative."[58] The witch crisis in 1692 was a moment of chaos in the colony. Based on the tenor of Sewall's apology, his supplication to God for pardon of both public and personal sins, Sewall was attempting to restore order and meaning to both his personal life and the community.

In calling the summons from Sewall "Negromantick," Saffin suggests that Sewall has intervened on Adam's behalf because he has been bewitched, influenced by evil forces just as he had been influenced back in Salem. Perhaps Saffin wants to evoke skepticism of Sewall's judgment in the present case. It is also possible that the moment is a bit tongue-in-cheek for Saffin, a subtle dig at a jurist who has allowed himself to be manipulated by "dark" forces for a second time. The moment may even function as a cautionary tale, a reminder to those same magistrates who at the very time of the pamphlet's writing and then publication were deciding Adam's fate. Saffin warns them not to succumb to the same witchery that has consumed Sewall. Perhaps Sewall, himself, is the sorcerer influencing the court to do his bidding. This is an especially striking moment in Saffin's text because it sharpens the image of himself as a guardian, a protector of communal order. He stands in opposition to Adam and Sewall. Unlike his fellow jurist, Saffin apparently is impervious to necromancy, equipped with a keen sight to see through it. As a result, he can protect the colony from evil presences, like Adam, in a way that other jurists failed to preserve the community nine years before in Salem and in a way that the contemporary courts were threatening to fail in their present deliberations. For those in the legal community and the reading public, Saffin presents a host of negative implications associated with the court proceedings initiated by Adam and supported by Sewall.[59]

ADAM AND THE SOCIAL THREAT

To emphasize Adam's disrespectful nature and further render him a threat to social order, Saffin includes in the appendix a series of depositions taken from his neighbors, including Thomas Shepard (or Shepherd), in whose household Adam lived for the first few years of his indenture contract. Unlike slavery in the southern colonies, in New England enslaved Blacks lived in closer proximity to their enslavers. They often slept in the same house, ate at the same table, and worked alongside each other.[60] The Shepard family's testimony bears out this spatial relation. At one point, Saffin even criticizes Shepard for setting "[Adam] at his table to eat with himself, his wife and children, (for which indeed I have blam'd him)" (6). This social structure, according to Dominik Nagl, enabled enslavers to manage enslaved Blacks in colonial Massachusetts through "close social surveillance."[61] Shepard seems to have adapted that strategy of surveillance.[62]

As a member of the Shepard household, Adam disrupted family life, according to Shepard. He habitually disobeyed Shepard, who maintains, "the said Negro man, having been a very disobedient, turbulent, outrageous

41

and unruly servant in all respects these many years . . . I dare no longer keep him in my house" (9). Oddly enough, Shepard does not mention any specific incidents to illustrate Adam's behavior. The specifics come from the deposition of a neighbor who witnessed an episode at the village mill when Shepard complained about the speed with which Adam performed a particular task. In response, the neighbor testifies, Adam "came up with his hand to Shepards face as if he would have struck him and jabbar'd, but I could not tell what he said, but it seem'd to me as if he challenged said Shepard or threatned him" (9). There are two points to note here: first, the deponent's testimony renders Adam as hyperaggressive; his rage is almost animalistic, amplified by his indecipherable speech, jabber. The second point to note is the potential for physical violence. Adam does not actually strike Shepard. The threat of violence seems to be the primary transgression. The moment reminds readers of what is possible if Adam and Black Africans in general are granted freedom.

Shepard's wife, Hannah, also testifies in a joint deposition with Shepard; she claims that on separate occasions Adam wielded an ax and a knife against her husband to "cut off his head" (10). Her testimony focuses almost exclusively on Adam's threatening behavior, which becomes more outrageous. There is no mention of the incidents leading up to his violent outbursts or "mad fits (which were many)" (10). Her testimony serves one purpose, to intensify the representation of Adam as violent. This intensification is necessary for Saffin to prove that Adam's behavior surpasses what one judge deemed the general tendency of "Negroes, who are so ignorant, rude and bruitish, and therefore to be considered as Negroes" (7). Shepard's daughter Sarah also testifies, claiming that "Adam did give me ill words, and strike me in the time of his service with my father" (10). Although we now have a specific act of physical violence, the deposition treats it as a minor episode. Sarah does not elaborate on how or why the incident occurred. She does not express outrage, judgment, or fear in the deposition. In fact, she quickly turns toward Adam's impertinent actions within the home and the disrespect he exhibited toward her parents. She testifies that Adam "was very disobedient to my mother when she spake to him for to do anything, as the laying on a logg on the fire or any such thing, and mock and deride at her when she did speak to him" (10). His insolent behavior, Sarah says, "was much to my fathers damage" (10).

In each deposition, the particulars of the deponents' complaints differ but not the general idea—that Adam was a disobedient slave always on the verge of violence. The final deposition included in the appendix continues the character assault. The deposition involves a Captain Timothy Clarke, employed to oversee fortification of Castle Island, just south of Boston. After a court initially rules that Adam legally is enslaved to Saffin, Saffin hires him out to Clarke in October 1701. The incident at Castle Island begins as a battle of wills. Clarke orders Adam to dig a trench. According to Clarke, Adam performs the task improperly and ignores Clarke's efforts to correct him. In response to Adam's recalcitrance, Clarke asks, "You rascal, why don't you do it as I ordered you" (12). Adam responds that he is "no rogue, no rascal, no thief" (12). Perhaps shocked by Adam's daring display of insolence or feeling the need to make a public example of him, Clarke swings a stick at Adam. Then he tells Adam, "You shall do as I bid you" and pushes him (12). Adam pushes back and tells Clarke that "if [Clarke] struck him he would strike [Clarke] again" (12). Not to be outdone, Clarke hits Adam again with the stick. Adam snatches it and breaks it. A full-fledged fight ensues, or, as the deponent represents it, an attack from which Clarke is "rescued" (12). Several workers rush over to separate the two men. Adam purportedly is so full of rage that he "got one of the labourers hands in his mouth, and had like to have bit it off" (12). The fight illustrates what had only been suggested before—that Adam is violent and unruly; once again there is the animalistic rage, this time indiscriminate as he fails to differentiate between the source of his rage—Clarke—and those attempting to restore the order and peace. His display of superhuman strength requires the efforts of several workers and garrison soldiers or else he "had like to have spoilt [Clarke]" (12). At first glance, this scene performs the necessary work for Saffin.

A Counternarrative

The representation of Adam's actions produces a subtext even as it appears to solidify Saffin's argument. By telling Clarke that he is "no rogue, no rascal, no thief," Adam rejects the dehumanizing labels. Of note in particular is the last of the three characteristics he disavows—theft. Adam's legal battle centers on the issue of ownership and who has the right to possess his body and the labor that body produces. By declaring himself "no thief," Adam asserts himself to

Saffin, to Clarke, even to the court that has remanded him back into Saffin's custody, and to anybody else who would claim that he has stolen something from Saffin by exercising his freedom. This point perhaps might have resounded especially for those who had read Sewall's tract and his argument that enslaved Blacks were indeed humans who had the right to basic liberties.

Saffin might intend the moment as one in which Adam is dehumanized as a thuggish brute. If we read the moment from Adam's perspective, the scene reflects a legitimate frustration. The incident occurs in early October 1701, after what had been a year so far of legal battles in which Adam's situation deteriorated. Since 1694 he had been working with the expectation of the freedom to come. In 1701, he was once again enslaved, Saffin having chosen to trifle with something as sacred as his freedom. One can imagine the regret Adam must have felt in not running away when he had the opportunity. He also might have felt that the social order and legal order of the day—even Sewall—had failed him. He had acted within socially acceptable boundaries, and it had not worked. Now, in October 1701, he was facing an intolerable future of perpetual servitude.

By the time Clarke strikes Adam on Castle Island, perhaps he believes he has nothing to lose in striking back. Instead, he finds a target for all his frustration. It should be noted that although Clarke and Saffin deem the moment an attack, a display of uncontrollable violence, Adam does exercise a measure of restraint leading up to the fight. He first warns Clarke; Clarke initiates the physical contact. As a supervisor, he does not deescalate tensions but enflames them. After the shoving match, Adam again *warns* Clarke to stay back. Only after Clarke strikes him a second time does Adam succumb to his frustration. This might have been a life-changing moment for Adam, like the confrontation Frederick Douglass describes a century and a half later between himself and the notorious "slave-breaker" Mr. Covey in his 1845 *Narrative of the Life*.[63] Douglass says of the encounter: "This battle with Mr. Covey was the turning point in my career as a slave. It rekindled the few expiring embers of freedom, and revived within me a sense of my own manhood. It recalled the departed self-confidence, and inspired me again with a determination to be free."[64] Perhaps the fight between Adam and Clarke sparked a renewed effort in Adam to attain his freedom.

In response to a 1702 ruling that reversed Adam's enslavement, Saffin petitioned the court, "the said vile Negro is at this day set at large to go at his pleasure, in open defiance of me his master in danger of my life, he having threatened to be revenged of me and all them that have cross't his turbulent humor to the great scandal and evil example of all Negros both in town and country whose eyes are upon this wretched Negro to see the issue of these his exorbitant practices."[65] Saffin suggested that Adam's impertinence would be contagious among the rest of the enslaved population if not brought under control. By evoking a fear of slave revolts, Albert Von Frank points out, Saffin was "thereby able to reconstitute himself as the defender . . . of a peaceable and orderly society."[66] Saffin's representation of Adam stands in contrast to other aspects of the legal battle that speak to Adam's compliance. Adam does not attempt to run away from enslavement, even after he discovers that Saffin intends to revoke his indenture. He does not hide when Saffin returns home from business. He confronts him and demands he see Sewall; as most people would who have a grievance with another, Adam seeks arbitration, perfectly willing to abide by the results of that arbitration. When the courts rule for his reenslavement, Adam complies—twice. Furthermore, during his indenture with the Shepards, despite what the deponents claim, Adam must have served some useful purpose, as the Shepards kept him around for years; equally important, Adam *stayed* for years. That he stayed with Shepard, that he stayed with Saffin, that he allowed himself to be reenslaved twice after having been granted his freedom by courts suggests that Adam was not as unruly or threatening as Saffin claimed. The moment of violence on Castle Island perhaps illustrates Adam's frustration over a reneged contract. Adam's intent, then, was not to upset the social order but to restore it by demanding that Saffin deal with him in a manner that was honest and just, moral, consistent with the values of the community at large. He demanded respect and employed the courtroom to achieve those ends. The courtroom was a space inside which Adam's racial difference did not negate a certain degree of equality before the law. At one point, Saffin lamented about Adam's presence in court, "the Negro appeared, where the matter came upon trial, whether the Negro should be free or not, and that he might have all benefits of law as an English man" (8). Adam did finally win his freedom but not the "benefits of law as an English man." As a newly freed man in 1703, Adam would have encountered another set of limitations in the form of laws designed to restrict and track the actions of Blacks in the colony. Those laws, for example, criminalized interracial relationships and prohibited Black Africans from congregating in each other's homes without consent of masters or town authorities.[67] Passage of such laws speaks to the fact that Saffin might have lost the battle with Adam, but perhaps his pamphlet contributed to the general fear of a *dangerous* Black African presence. The dehumanizing rhetoric propagated by texts like Saffin's resonated throughout the eighteenth century, undermining Black African claims to personhood, to liberty. That rhetoric compelled a generation of early Black writers, like Phillis Wheatley and Olaudah Equiano, the subjects of the next two chapters, to deploy respectability tactics to pronounce Black humanity and challenge white supremacist structures.

"THOSE WHO SEEM'D
TO RESPECT ME"

PHILLIS WHEATLEY

AT THE

BORDER OF RESPECTABILITY

PHILLIS WHEATLEY (PETERS) enters this book's discussion about respectability as a seven-year-old girl, maybe eight, facing the slave market,
perceived as the least desirable of human cargo that comes into a Boston harbor on the slave ship *Phillis* in 1761.[1] The ship's captain, despite the explicit
orders of his employer to purchase "prime boys" and men, nonetheless snags
this Black girl and adds her to the stock. The advertisement that announces
the sale of this child speaks to her lack of value.[2]

TO BE SOLD

A Parcel of Likely Negroes, imported from *Africa,* cheap for cash
or short Credit; Enquire of *John Avery* at his House next door to the
White-Horse, or at a Store adjoining to said *Avery's* Distill-House,
at the South-End, near the South market:—Also if any Persons have
any Negro Men, strong and hearty, tho' not of the best moral character, which are proper subjects for Transportation, may have an
Exchange for small Negroes.[3]

The ad is disrespectful on multiple levels. Most obvious is the inhumanity of peddling human beings as chattel. Beyond that is the specific disregard for those Black men sought for purchase, their desirability located in a presumed absence of morality. There is even less regard for those Black children, Wheatley presumably among them, whose youth (and gender) drive their devaluation; they are bartered for able-bodied men of ill-repute. The lack of regard for those enslaved men and children, the disrespect, forms a warped economic logic whereby they are positioned as exchange commodities, of equal (de)value to some prospective buyer(s). At seven years old, Wheatley would not have grasped the import of being exchanged for men of questionable character. At that young age, she would not have understood the economic stakes attached to public perceptions of her Black, female body.

Fast-forward thirteen years to October 30, 1774. Wheatley is a young adult, newly emancipated and mourning the loss of her former enslaver-mistress. In a letter addressed to her spiritual mentor, John Thornton, Wheatley describes the depth of her mourning, "By the great loss I have Sustain'd of my best friend, I feel like One [fo]rsaken by her parent in a desolate wilderness."[4] This sense of isolation is exacerbated, she tells Thornton, by the fact that after Susannah's death "those who seem'd to respect me while under my mistresses patronage . . . have already put on a reserve" (125).

Between 1761 and 1774, through a process of acculturation, Wheatley comes to understand the significance of respectability.[5] She perceives herself as having earned it, although her status as Black and enslaved does not change during most of that time.[6] An infantile perception also follows her into her late teen years. What changes for Wheatley is the fact that she learns to read and write in English. She proves intellectually astute, studying Latin. She converts to Christianity and masters the art of humility. In 1773 she publishes a book of poems in English, the first person of African descent to do so in the early Americas. As a result of her intellectual and literary accomplishments, she moves in the social circles of high-profile political and religious figures on both sides of the Atlantic, including Benjamin Franklin and King George himself. Seemingly, Wheatley achieves the respect denied her upon first stepping onto land from that Boston harbor.

She does not elaborate on how precisely people "seem'd to respect her" when Susannah was alive. Was it in the way that friends and associates of the Wheatleys requested she write elegies to commemorate their sorrow?

Or did she see respect in the willingness of Boston's most elite to sign their names to the front of her one and only published book? Maybe she interpreted respect in conversations had with visitors to the Wheatley home. Or while traveling through England to promote her poetry. Perhaps she believed she had earned their respect, a measure of social acceptance, because she remained meek and humble in the Wheatley household. Or because she espoused Christian virtue in her verses and letters. Perhaps she assumed her white neighbors respected her because she was well-educated and could pen poems in the tradition of Virgil and Homer. She did not consider perhaps that respect was manufactured by proximity to her mistress.

Wheatley censures those who only *seem'd* to hold her in high regard. Perhaps she admonishes, as well, her own naivete in believing that she had achieved respect through her poetry and pious living. With grief comes clarity. She seeks comfort in knowing that God "never forsakes any till they have ungratefully forsaken him" (125). She marks Susannah's death as a moment of social awakening, forcing her to reckon with the ephemerality of respectability. Or its mirage. The letter is striking in its desolate tone. After all her efforts by 1774, she perhaps was no closer to respect than she had been as that little Black girl alluded to in a slave ad thirteen years earlier.

Wheatley's initial sale in 1761 and her letter to Thornton in 1774 mark two defining moments in her entanglement with respectability. Both moments illustrate the ways in which respectability and its absence shaped Wheatley's life. In the previous chapter, I discussed the means by which Adam sought legal remedies to confirm his humanity and demand respect at the turn of the eighteenth century. In this chapter, I examine Phillis Wheatley's very conscious efforts to achieve and maintain respectability, as manifested in her poetry and letters. Wheatley is one of the most often anthologized and studied Black writers from the early American period, and the details of her biography as a self-made woman fit, but perhaps not so neatly, into a narrative of uplift. She rose to become a celebrated poet and obtained her freedom as a result of it. Although we tend to think of Wheatley's literacy achievements as anomalous, she was part of a larger community of Black Africans (we can't know how large) who could read (and write).[7] Jupiter Hammon and Lucy Terry Prince were among her poetic contemporaries. In addition to poetry, Wheatley's archive includes a number of epistles illustrating her interactions with a diverse social network that included free and enslaved Black colonists.[8]

Her poems and letters can tell us a great deal about how she engaged respectability as an expression of her subjectivity and as a coping mechanism. Whereas respectability rhetoric in the hands of an enslaver racialized Adam, it became a means through which Wheatley asserted a sense of self and challenged notions of Black alterity, with the aim of integrating herself, and her Black community at large, into a mainstream British-American imaginary.

For many decades scholars dismissed Wheatley as a serious early American poet because they determined that the assimilationist aspects of her work correlated with a deep-seated hatred of Blackness. We should read her assimilation, though, not as a self-hating gesture but as an act of love for Blackness, understood in the way that bell hooks articulates it as a "revolutionary intervention that undermines practices of domination."[9] A close reading of Wheatley's poems and letters suggest her desire not to remake herself into an image of whiteness but to change public perception of Blackness as a foreign, alien element in the culture, what Samuel Sewall, as mentioned in the previous chapter, called an "extravasat blood." I agree with Will Harris, who notes that "Wheatley's distinctive response to the spirit of her times was to project a reflexively race-conscious presence in her poetry and personal letters."[10] In this way, Wheatley's efforts to incorporate her Black self into a British American mainstream contrast with those notions of assimilation espoused by her contemporaries like J. Hector St. John Crevecoeur, who celebrated America as a melting pot in which immigrants arrived, mixed together, and created a uniquely American character. Through that process of incorporation, according to Crevecoeur, they lost ethnic and cultural particularity as "individuals of all nations are melted into a new race of men."[11]

This is not Wheatley's project. Her work expresses a form of assimilation that embraces mainstream values and norms while also insisting upon the specificity of her racial/ethnic identity. Her efforts anticipate our modern-day understanding of assimilation as, in the words of sociologists Victor Nee and Richard Alba, a process of incorporation whereby a mainstream culture is "made up of multiple interpenetrating layers," which "allows individuals and subpopulations to forge identities out of its materials to distinguish themselves from others in the mainstream . . . in ways that are still recognizably American."[12] Colloquially speaking, Nee and Alba define assimilation as a strategy that enables individuals to eat their cake and still have it. Importantly, this modern conception of assimilation, as Catherine Ramírez reminds us, is "often a two-way process, albeit an uneven one," by which a mainstream is altered by the incorporation of a minority presence.[13] My reading of Wheatley embraces the assimilationist aspects of her work, which I read not as a wish to evade racial difference but as an effort to pronounce Black humanity, to defend it as a respectable subject identity rather than an object of alterity.

Just as Wheatley's assimilationist efforts diverge from those of her contemporaries, her strategy also does not map neatly onto Black respectability politics in the way we understand it today as a means to mute Blackness. Lori Latrice Martin notes with consternation that what began as a politics of respectability in the 1880s has been reduced to respectability politics, which "calls for young people to simply pull up their pants and follow the commands of authority figures, including law enforcement officials, in order to gain the esteem of the dominant racial group in America and to avoid negative—even life threatening outcomes."[14] This formulation, as Martin notes, denies the complexities of a politics of respectability that, in its earliest iterations, was grounded in social protest and a recognition and acceptance of Black particularity.

Martin echoes Higginbotham's observation that Black churchwomen and clubwomen at the turn of the twentieth century "asserted agency in the construction and representation of themselves as new subjectivities—as Americans as well as blacks and women."[15] Acknowledging assimilation as a key element of the movement, Higginbotham maintains, "Their assimilationist leanings led to their insistence upon blacks' conformity to the dominant society's norms of manners and morals."[16] She argues, however, that "such a politics did not reduce to an accommodationist stance toward racism. . . . Nor did it reduce to a mindless mimicry of white behavior."[17] She argues that the movement was compelled by competing impulses that were at once conservative and radical so that the movement "reflected and reinforced the hegemonic values of white America, as it simultaneously subverted and transformed the logic of race and gender subordination."[18] All of this is to say that Wheatley's strategy for assimilation anticipates a key element of a politics of respectability emerging in the late nineteenth century, one that called for Black Americans to model mainstream behaviors but also to assert a distinctly Black experience.

Wheatley's experience, as that of a Black woman poet, forms at the intersection of race and gender. As such, her advocacy for Black humanity complicates the relationship between gender and respectability. Studies of respectability and Black communities in the twentieth and twenty-first centuries often note the gendered bifurcation of respectability politics, with a particular emphasis on the role of respectability in defining Black womanhood. Higginbotham and more recently Brittney Cooper and Victoria Wolcott have discussed respectability politics as a coping strategy for nineteenth- and twentieth-century Black women who either embraced it as a key element in racial uplift or resisted it.[19] Wheatley complicates the notion of respectability as a gendered project. She does not embody respectability to tout the virtues of finer (Black) womanhood. Instead of delineating gender differences, Wheatley collapses those differences in her poetry and through her participation in a public sphere. She operates at what Hortense Spillers has referred to as the ungendered boundary of colonial America. In her groundbreaking 1987 essay "Mama's Baby, Papa's Maybe," Spillers examines the historically problematic relationship between Black Americans and a cis-normative, Western conception of gender. She notes that gender turns on racial difference and argues that historically, Black Americans existed outside the realm of domesticity, subjected to a process of ungendering at the whim of enslavers. I examine this ungendering as a phenomenon that enables Wheatley to adopt a certain measure of gender fluidity through her letters and poetry. Through social modes that are coded as feminine, masculine, and, at times, agender, she portrays herself as a proper model of conduct for both Black men and women.

Reading Wheatley through a lens of respectability adds nuance to critical study of her as a transgressive poet. Traditionally, Wheatley has been a troubling figure in the African American literary canon. As mentioned above, for much of the twentieth century, scholars condemned her work as the product of a racist, hegemonic worldview.[20] Critics based this perspective largely on her often-anthologized poem "On Being Brought from Africa to America." In the poem, Wheatley appears to construct herself as a model Christian convert, a self-avowed African heathen who finds God and salvation in America. In the last thirty-five years or so, scholars have increasingly read her work against the grain, uncovering strains of racial, political, and religious critique. There also has been increased focus on historicizing

Wheatley in order to recover her as an agentive and culture-shaping force in early (and modern-day) America. In other words, the scholarship tends to read for repair and resistance with the endgame of illustrating Wheatley's poetic prowess and genius. It is a critical impulse to correct the record, to rescue Wheatley from decades of critical oversight and misreading.[21] As a consequence, scholars now generally locate her work within a reductive paradigm of subversion that renders her a trickster figure. We are called on to read Wheatley's poetry with the grain or against it, to understand her expressions as sincere or performative. As Samantha Pinto succinctly states it, "Wheatley is either squarely placed in opposition to what is imagined as the black political imaginary, or recovered into a recognizable version of it."[22] My reading of Wheatley moves discussion beyond this binary impulse. Her striving toward respectability infuses her work with a self-conscious energy that gets articulated as cultural accommodation, subversive protest, sincerity, sarcasm. The work also is deeply spiritual, introspective, and a bit fatalistic, as reflected in the letter to Thornton, and also infused with great care for Black humanity. Sometimes her messages are veiled, even playfully so.[23] At other times, she speaks with devastating clarity.[24] Wheatley is more than a trickster figure manipulating verses toward political ends.

I argue in this chapter that Wheatley embraces assimilation as a core strategy to achieve respectability. She offers herself up as a model of virtuous Blackness and in doing so, modifies racial and gendered codes of appropriate behavior. In what follows, I discuss Wheatley's investment in respectability by first addressing her cultural context, focusing in particular on the Enlightenment movement and the proliferation of racialized language that dehumanized Black Africans. The Enlightenment movement added immediacy to the emergence of Wheatley as a Black woman poet and to Black authorship more generally in the latter half of the eighteenth century. Through text, early Black writers deployed respectability rhetoric to model mainstream cultural norms and challenge the exclusion of Black personhood, theorized by Spillers and others, from the category of human in Western culture. I lean in particular on Black feminist scholarship, which has provided valuable theoretical frames for articulating the intersectional politics of Wheatley's life and texts. This discussion reminds us of the stereotypes and obstacles against which Wheatley sought to earn respect. After discussing the cultural context, I offer close readings of select poetry and letters, highlighting Wheatley's strategies for self-constructing as respectable. Those strategies include poetic and spiritual imitation. I end the chapter by considering Wheatley within the eighteenth-century British-American public imaginary, including brief discussion of her marriage to John Peters in 1778. In the eyes of her new husband and a general public, she emerged as a kind of model minority.[25] In the end, however, that did not prevent her from dying young and impoverished. As she learned almost a decade before her own death, respect could be a fickle, fleeting thing, and yet she held out hope, as reflected in poetry and letters even after her mistress's death, that it would pay dividends. That element of hope has given respectability its power over the centuries. Ultimately, as her letter to Thornton communicates, Wheatley's effort to achieve respectability at most produced a façade of social acceptance that failed to insulate her from the degrading, oppressive effects of racism. Nonetheless, her efforts are important for our understanding of how assimilation becomes a prominent feature of respectability politics by the end of the nineteenth century.

THE ENLIGHTENMENT

Scholars have noted the role of the Enlightenment in advancing modern-day racism.[26] As a result of "Enlightened" thinking, those in Europe and the Americas largely shifted their strategies for categorizing (and justifying the categorization of) humans, which was based previously on factors related to cultural traits, such as language, religion, dress, social customs—and behaviors, as illustrated in the previous chapter in the discussion of "Adam Negro's Tryal." As the Enlightenment movement emerged in America in the mid-eighteenth century, race evolved specifically into a scientific system rooted in somatic differences deemed immutable, inheritable, and most important, hierarchical. Therefore, as determined by Enlightenment science, a presumed absence of respectability in a person of African descent corresponded to an inherent, irrevocable deficit. Prominent Enlightenment thinkers questioned the very humanity of Black Africans and at most conceded a place for them at the far end of a human spectrum.[27] In one of the most often excerpted passages from Thomas Jefferson's *Notes on the State of Virginia,* he concludes that "blacks, whether originally a distinct race, or made distinct by time and circumstances, are inferior to the whites in the endowments both of body and mind."[28] This disdain for the intellectual capacities of Black Africans is the context in which Jefferson offers up his famous dismissal of Wheatley's work as more imitative than creative, "below the dignity of criticism."[29] Jefferson's perspective reflects a common assumption of the time that Black Africans were incapable of intellectual pursuits, writing in particular. By extension, they could never exemplify respectability.[30] It also reflects, as Eric Slauter notes, a cultural shift in how people valued the neoclassical style in the latter half of the eighteenth century. According to Slauter, "Wheatley's work emerged in the midst of both a political and cultural revolution, a moment when the imitative model of neoclassical aesthetics began to give way to a new conception of creativity we commonly associate with romanticism." Racist discourses increasingly deemed imitative art proof of intellectual deficiency in Wheatley specifically and in Black Africans in general.[31]

At the same time that Enlightenment thinking rationalized the dehumanization of Black Africans, the movement's rhetoric fueled the American Revolution, manifesting, for example, in Thomas Paine's pamphlet *Common Sense,* which insisted that colonists possessed the rational faculties to rule themselves. That first generation of Black writers grappled with what it meant to be enslaved in a space where its enslaver-inhabitants were deploying the rhetoric of liberty and slavery to justify a revolution. What did it mean to be American? To be *respectable* citizens? Would that rhetoric of liberty apply to Black Africans living in a newly formed United States?[32] Picking up the pen themselves, Black writers employed respectability rhetoric to reposition themselves in relationship to the body politic. They linked respectability rhetoric to discourses about citizenship and belonging. For example, on the eve of war, in 1773 in Massachusetts, an enslaved Black man submitted a petition on behalf of "many Slaves, living in the Town of Boston, and other towns in the Province" for freedom. In the petition, the writer, named Felix, assures the Massachusetts assembly that Black Africans "are virtuous and religious, although their Condition is in itself so unfriendly to Religion." Felix points out the difficulty of maintaining Christian values when enslaved. Yet, he insists, most of them have a strong sense of religious and civic responsibility. "Although some of the Negroes are vicious," he concedes, "there are many others of a quite different Character, and who, if made free, would soon be able as well as willing to bear a Part in the Public

Charges; many of them of good natural parts, are discreet, sober, honest, and industrious."[33] Importantly, Felix links Blackness to piety and respectable behavior, contradicting the racist rhetoric of Saffin at the beginning of the century. What is more, he attaches those virtues to citizenship. He imagines a place in the body politic for Black Massachusetts residents based on virtuous behavior.

Writing in the aftermath of the Revolutionary War, Jupiter Hammon makes an appeal not to white lawmakers but to his fellow "Negroes in the State of New York." Delivered in 1786, the speech is a conduct manual; Hammon advises Blacks living in a newly formed United States to eschew sin, live peacefully, and, for those enslaved, obey their masters.[34] Obedience, he argues, is a Christian imperative. He acknowledges that liberty "is a great thing, and worth seeking for" as whites had just done.[35] Here, he echoes Wheatley's impassioned declaration in a letter to Samson Occom that Black Africans possess a "principle," a "love of freedom" that is "impatient of Oppression, and pants for Deliverance" (120). Notably, however, Hammon's words lack the urgency of Wheatley's. Even as he recognizes the social inequality, he advocates for patience. "By our good conduct," he maintains, masters will be prevailed upon to "set us free."[36] He draws on a Great Awakening sense of egalitarianism to assure the audience that if they live virtuously, then the suffering they endure on Earth will be replaced by joy in the afterlife: "There are but two places where all go after death, white and black, rich and poor: those places are Heaven and Hell."[37] The speech encourages self-policing by urging Black Africans to accept their inferior status or at the very least be patient in advocating for change.[38] All of this is to say that the stakes were particularly high for Black Africans as the Enlightenment rationale for racial difference necessitated that they prove their very humanity rather than having it mediated through the perspectives of others. Writing, according to Henry Louis Gates Jr., became a kind of "commodity" that early Black authors "were forced to trade for their humanity" or, I might articulate more precisely, trade for their freedom.[39]

Early Black women writers especially illustrate the cultural work of authorship, as Katherine Clay Bassard, Frances Smith Foster, and Carla Peterson all note. Focusing in part on Wheatley, Bassard argues, "the women who signed themselves as authors of poetry, fiction, autobiography, essays, and political speeches of this era in African American literary history gather as a collective witness to the importance of the author not just as a function of textuality but as a specific embodiment . . . of a subjectivity that comes into being by virtue of its investment in authorship as a position of agency and empowerment."[40] Bassard notes that through authorship these Black women writers expressed Black womanhood, which echoes Foster's observation that figures like Wheatley "believed . . . their contributions, by their very existence, served as artifacts, physical proof of their intellectual ability to contribute to the western literary tradition."[41] Foster goes on to say they "were testifying to the fact of their existence and insisting that others acknowledge their existence and their testimonies. They were consciously creating new criteria against which the testimonies of others might be judged. And they were testing ways in which the English language and its literature might better serve them as African American women writers."[42] Focusing on the early nineteenth century, Peterson adds the observation that "speaking and writing constituted a form of doing, of social action continuous with [Black women's] social, political, and cultural work."[43] As a "doer of the word," to adapt Peterson's formulation, Wheatley deployed literary forms to establish her own respectability and, with it, a humanity that faced new challenges from the racialized pseudoscience of the Enlightenment, which rejected the very idea of Black personhood.

Importantly, this denial of Black humanity, as Spillers theorizes in "Mama's Baby, Papa's Maybe," depended upon a rejection of Black womanhood, of their bodily experiences. She delineates between the body and flesh to articulate how meaning gets inscribed on enslaved Black bodies. Before the body, Spillers explains, flesh is the "primary narrative," a record of violations/violence, the skin "seared, divided, ripped-apart."[44] The flesh, according to Spillers, is "unseen" or illegible. It is a site of mutilation, "undecipherable markings on the captive body" that "render a kind of hieroglyphic of the flesh whose severe disjunctures come to be hidden to the cultural seeing by skin color."[45] This relationship between the body and flesh, Spillers maintains, points to the "social conceptualization" of Black inhumanity, which undermines the Black body as a "liberated subject," reduces that body to an abject, powerless state.[46] In this way, Black Africans exist in a paradoxical position of being hypervisible and invisible within a mainstream culture. Alexander Weheliye builds on Spillers's ideas to describe this state of being for Black bodies as "not-quite-human," and Charles W. Mills articulates it as "subperson."[47] These formulations are evocative of Frantz Fanon's notion of "epidermalization," the process of dehumanization whereby those of African descent are reduced to skin color and with it a negative set of values that render the "Negro" a "symbol of sin."[48] Dark skin, Fanon argues, encodes "darkness, shadow, shades, nights, the labyrinths of the earth, abysmal depths."[49] According to Fanon, Black Africans, as a result of colonialism, internalize these negative values, developing an inferiority complex.[50]

Importantly for Spillers and central to the present reading of Wheatley, this process of dehumanization is made possible by an ungendering that collapses the differences between Black sexed male and female bodies. The transatlantic slave trade, she argues, "marked a theft of the body—a willful and violent . . . severing of the captive body from its motive will, its active desire." As a result, she maintains, "we lose at least gender difference in the outcome, and the female body and the male body become a territory of cultural and political maneuver, not at all gender related, gender specific."[51] That is to say, enslaved female bodies are subjected to the same kind of physical and psychological violence as their male counterparts. Bodily differences matter not in terms of socialization and ordering human relations but in terms of property value. Spillers uses the example of the cargo hold of a slave ship where enslavers allocate less room to accommodate Black female bodies. This move, Spillers notes, is not an acknowledgment of gender differences but a consideration for cargo space and efficiency.

Spillers insists on the liberatory potential of this kind of ungendering as Black women exist "out of the traditional symbolics of female gender." She insists, then, that society accommodate this ungendered figure, "make a place for" a "different social subject," and in doing so "rewrite . . . a radically different text for a female empowerment."[52] The potentiality Spillers explicates, produced by social exclusion and marginalization, evokes what Carla Peterson notes about the mobility afforded those at the margin. In her study of Black women writers of the North in the nineteenth century, Peterson observes that "if positions at the center tend to be fixed, such is not the case for locations on the periphery, which can move and slide among the circumference."[53] This speaks to a certain kind of freedom. Peterson and Spillers understand mobility as a consequence, indeed an advantage, of marginalization. The mobility is a by-product of disregard; that very disregard for Black women allows them to move at the borders of society, surveilled only to ensure they remain at the margins. Spillers and Peterson, together, foreground the bidirectional nature of mobility, as both lateral and upward movement for Black communities. That is to say, early Black women writers, like Wheatley, gravitated toward respectability on the promise that it would provide upward mobility, which would be called racial uplift in the nineteenth century, and specifically for Wheatley, she moves, I argue shortly, at the margins of society as an ungendered Ethiop, an Afric muse operating as part of what Peterson calls a "community sphere," a liminal space neither public nor private and yet both.[54]

Today, we would recognize Wheatley's identity politics as intersectional, based on the formulation first articulated by Kimberlé Crenshaw in 1989.[55] In many ways, her Black womanhood, her intersectionality, renders her both invisible and hypervisible. She becomes what Samantha Pinto calls a "celebrity." In her study of "infamous bodies," Pinto examines the lives and afterlives of several Black women from early America, including Wheatley, who rose to celebrity status, defined for Pinto as public visibility. That status, or fame, in turn, Pinto argues, rendered Black women's bodies as sites of a public cultural and political tension. Noting that discussions about Wheatley in particular often centered on concerns about her enslaved status and freedom, Pinto argues that Wheatley functioned as a "public mediator between race and rights—the first black celebrity and an origin story of Western human rights."[56] Among her contemporaries and among those who study her in subsequent generations, Pinto argues, "Wheatley is repeatedly imagined as a site of the trials and failures of freedom, yoking the invention of blackness to its relationship, even in political philosophy and especially in the formation of modern law in the West, to the domain of culture (here literature and literacy) and positing that relationship as the scene of freedom, so to speak." Pinto observes that Wheatley's celebrity status is the grounds on which American culture has grappled with discourses of race and rights, collapsing the categories of culture and politics. "The political" she argues, "is made through rather than against [black] feminine embodiment."[57] She argues that Wheatley stands as the "epitome of black fame, . . . a literary celebrity in her time and beyond, whose name and figure often signal the very stakes of antiracist thought as well as the fraught promises of liberal humanism. . . . Her race, her gender, her age, her literacy, and her enslaved status were the currency of her fame."[58] In her work, Pinto makes clear the gendered significance of Wheatley's Black woman's body, which "encapsulates the ways the black female body in the spotlight in the post-rights (civil, individual, human) era has been imagined: criminalized, vulnerable, precarious, performative, resistant, exception and example, victim and hero, victim as hero."[59] The point here is that gender, as part of Wheatley's intersectionality, circumscribes her life experiences and cultural, political output. Still yet, her aesthetic choices in her poetry and letters respond to that aspect of gender that erases Black humanity, as theorized by Spillers. Importantly though, as Spillers notes, Black women, from their liminal position beyond social borders, have the opportunity to transcend the restrictions of gender, to escape the confines of patrilineal distributions of property, of power. Throughout her poetry and letters, Wheatley seldom adheres to modes of conduct coded specifically as feminine or female. She most often deemphasizes gender differences, which positions her to advocate for Black men and women alike.[60] Her Black, woman's body stands in for a universal Black humanity. She strips this ungendering process of its dehumanizing power by pronouncing Black humanity through respectability rhetoric.

THE POETICS OF A MODEL MINORITY

To ascertain something of Wheatley's concerns for respectability, one obvious place to look is the frontispiece for her published volume. The image of Wheatley as a young woman garbed in hair bonnet, her hand resting contemplatively against her chin, has garnered quite a bit of critical attention as an early image of a Black woman in the act of writing. Scholars have asked the source of the frontispiece, with circumstantial evidence pointing to the young African painter Scipio Moorhead.[61] Others speculate about the commission of the artwork used for the frontispiece; is this Wheatley actively attempting to shape her public image, or is the piece the result of co-optation by her community of white supporters?[62] What does the hand-and-chin gesture mean? Melancholy? Contemplation? Poetic creativity? Intelligence? Several studies link her image and pose to her benefactress Selina Hastings, the Countess of Huntingdon, or note that it is anomalous.[63] The most telling detail, besides her dark skin, that marks her cultural alterity is the ribbon of text that encircles the image, which labels Wheatley a "Negro," a servant, the possession of John Wheatley. As a gesture toward respectability, the image reflects Wheatley's acculturation, through the typical dress, the stock pose, and the accoutrements of literacy that surround her, including a writing desk, book, quill, paper, and ink.

A second obvious place to look for information about Wheatley's investment in respectability would be her elegies, which comprise a third of *Poems on Various Subjects.* As Joanna Brooks and Eric Slauter have already noted, Wheatley claims a great deal of spiritual authority by censuring the grieving behaviors of her white neighbors.[64] She expresses respectability in terms of Christian values. That is to say, Wheatley endeavors to achieve a certain level of visibility, or respect, by espousing Christian virtue and doing so within the poetic form of the elegy. She purports a mode of proper grief, of comportment rooted in Christian ideals about faith, Divine sovereignty, and a heavenly afterlife. In one elegy to the parents of a deceased five-year-old, for example, she follows a typical pattern in elegies of characterizing death as transcendental. She tells the parents, "FROM dark abodes to fair etherial light / Th' enraptur'd innocent has wing'd her flight" (60). She encourages them at the end of the first stanza to display proper sentiment, to turn their "sorrows into grateful praise." In the next stanza, she commands, "Restrain your tears, and cease your plaintive moans." If they cannot praise their daughter's ascendance into Heaven, Wheatley insists in the same stanza, they should at least "Let hope [their] grief control, / And check the rising tumult of the soul" (60). In another elegy, she instructs a grieving widow, "cease thy tears, bid ev'ry sigh depart, / And cast the load of anguish from thine heart" (62). In yet another, she challenges a widower, "Say in thy breast shall floods of sorrow rise? / Say shall its torrents overwhelm thine eyes?" (73). Instead of longing for the return of his wife, she encourages the husband to strive toward the same heavenly elevation. She says, "no more with grief retire, / Let grief no longer damp devotion's fire, / But rise sublime, to equal bliss aspire" (74).

Although Wheatley encounters grief, on a traumatic scale, at a very early age, most of the elegies are not explicitly self-referential.[65] Instead, she mostly assumes the role of expert observer, a kind of spiritual adviser for her white counterparts, there to remind them that death is a transition, release from a captive state, which enables the deceased to live in Heavenly peace. If they insist on mourning, rather than celebrating the passing of a loved one, she counsels, they should at least focus that grief on an anticipated reunion in a spiritual realm. At one point she admonishes the grieving mother (and her surviving children) of a deceased boy, "Still do you weep, still wish for his return? / How cruel thus to wish, and thus to mourn? / No more for him the streams of sorrow pour, / But haste to join him on the heav'nly shore" (86). She is, as Astrid Franke calls her, "a dramatist of mourning."[66]

Wheatley is not unique in her use of elegies to commemorate and regulate grief. As an assimilative gesture, she models the poetic form of the day. It is not incidental, though, that these elegies are the creation of a young, Black poet. The effort is exceptional if for no other reason than Enlightenment racism dictated that she should not be able to produce such verses. She is writing against sociopolitical exigencies that her white contemporaries do not. As a form of assimilation, then, her poetic efforts should modify the mainstream by changing their perceptions of the intellectual capacities and morality of Black Africans. It's the same reason assimilation is a key element of respectability politics today. Black communities strive to conform to mainstream standards with the expectation that doing so will shift mainstream perceptions of their worth.

The spiritual authority Wheatley claims, then, inherently speaks for the ability of Black Africans to possess Christian virtue and, by extension, respectability. To make this point explicit, Wheatley offers herself as a model of proper sentiment in an elegy for her pastor Joseph Sewall, a minister at Old South Church in Boston and the son of Samuel Sewall. In "On the Death of the Rev. Dr. SEWELL," she points out, "I, too, have a cause this mighty loss to mourn, / For he my monitor will not return. / O when shall we to his blest state arrive? When the same graces our bosoms thrive" (58). She writes herself into the same context as her white counterparts, insisting that proper Christian virtue is not solely the purview of her white, colonial neighbors. It probably is the case, as others have argued, that Wheatley wrote so many elegies because it was a popular form of the day and because she could claim a spiritual authority and because her white neighbors commissioned such poems.[67] Those elegies also are an element in her efforts to deploy assimilation as a strategy to transform public perception of Black Africans.

To be sure, Wheatley's assimilationist aims were not confined to the elegies, as illustrated in her other poems and letters. Consider, for example, the very first poem in the 1773 volume, "To Maecenas," which pronounces her poetic mastery of Western artistic traditions. In the poem, she calls on Maecenas, the ancient Roman patron of the arts, to support her poetry. She imitates an aesthetics that would have been familiar and acceptable to her white, reading audience. In other words, she crafts a *respectable* poem. She does this through certain poetic conventions. She, for example, invokes the muses, employing a neoclassical style.[68] She also, as Astrid Franke points out, dons a posture of melancholy, a "poetic expression" that was "highly convention- alized by the eighteenth century."[69] Her reliance on these stock poetic moves reflects the same energy as the frontispiece, designed to disprove, Frances Smith Foster notes, "arguments for black intellectual inferiority."[70] Her stylis- tic choices are a nod to her education, her progression from the "benighted" state referenced in "On Being Brought from Africa to America." Wheatley (and her advocates) build her subjectivity around her intellectual abilities, her poetic skillfulness. It was the case, as Mary Catherine Loving argues, that "Wheatley's move into literary and intellectual circles hinged on her ability to produce written work acceptable to an audience not invested in her intelli- gence; thus, the poet had to prove herself. Therefore, she carefully mimicked the forms, including language and stereotypes regarding enslaved Africans, which she inherited."[71] Education for centuries has been a signature aspira- tion among Black communities seeking racial uplift and cultural integration.

Wheatley signals her intellectual aspirations in "To Maecenas." The speaker insists in stanza three that with Maecenas's patronage

> O could I rival thine and Virgil's page,
> Or claim the Muses with the Mantuan Sage. (lines 23–24, page 53)

She links her poetic potential to Virgil (and Homer earlier in the poem). With Maecenas's help, she muses,

> Soon the same beauties should my mind adorn,
> And the same ardors in my soul should burn:
> Then should my song in bolder notes arise,
> And all my numbers pleasingly surprise. (lines 25–28, page 53)

She entertains notions of grandeur, of being, as Foster articulates it, "not just a poet, but a great poet."[72] Her imagination collides with reality at the end of this third stanza, where the poem turns on a couplet:

> But here I sit, and mourn a grov'ling mind
> That fain would mount and ride upon the wind. (lines 29–30, page 53)

The "But" that begins line 29 is tantamount to a brick wall that divides the speaker's imagination from reality. It presents the reader with an image of the would-be poet in the present moment of the poem, seated and mourning. Here, Wheatley offers the competing images of a body that both sits and grovels. As Franke notes about the image of the speaker sitting, "it . . . refers back to the frontispiece and its thoughtful, melancholic pose. In that moment . . . the poem leaves behind the tumultuous events of a different time and place to inhabit a calm, domestic setting in the present."[73] The melancholic pose that Franke notes and the passively sorrowful gesture it evokes belie the inner turmoil of the speaker, represented by a "grov'ling" mind that beseeches, complains, critiques. The image suggests a level of frustration, disenchantment, as noted in the next stanza of the poem:

> But I less happy, cannot raise the song,
> The fault'ring music dies upon my tongue. (lines 35–36, page 53)

Her poetic longings assume a material quality here as articulated through the competing images of the body and a mind destined for poetic greatness. Even as she mimics mainstream poetic traditions, she challenges the social invisibility that Spillers, Fanon, Mills, and others have argued defined the Black experience by embodying Blackness through references to the speaker's body and the mind. The speaker reconciles the disjuncture between mind and body two stanzas later with a reference to the African poet Terence:

> The happier Terence all the choir inspir'd,
> His soul replenished, and his bosom fir'd. (lines 37–38, page 53)

The happiness of Terence contrasts the "less happy" state of the speaker. Terence experiences the poetic greatness that threatens to evade the speaker. She questions the muses,

> But say, ye Muses, why this partial grace,
> To one alone of Afric's sable race;

> From age to age transmitting thus his name
> With the first glory in the rolls of fame? (lines 39–42, page 53)

The reference to Terence stages the poem's ultimate argument. This ancient Roman poet, of African birth (which Wheatley glosses in a footnote), benefited from the same resources that the speaker seeks. With patronage and the muses on her side, the speaker insists, she, too, can achieve the fame of not just Virgil and Homer but, even more important, of Terence. This is the more significant comparison because of what it suggests about the presumed intellectual deficiency of Africans. She "flaunts her lineage," L. Lamar Wilson argues, "as unapologetically African and equal" to Western poetic traditions.[74] Many scholars gravitate toward line 21, where the speaker references her "grov'ling mind," to argue that Wheatley accepts intellectual inferiority.[75] To the contrary, the image of a mind "grov'ling" seems more an indictment of those social conditions that have reduced the speaker to such circumstances, articulated in the poem as the "partial grace" of the muses, who have denied her the same resources granted to Terence.[76] Rather than understanding the reference to Terence as a "negative comparison," as Helen Burke asserts, we can see Wheatley here contemplating an African poetic tradition with Terence and herself as representatives of that tradition. More to the point, racial excellence is made manifest in the figure of Terence; the speaker represents Black potentiality. I do agree with Burke that the "insertion of a black literary predecessor into the Western tradition demands recognition by the tradition for her own black voice, a right she reemphasizes constantly by identifying her writing persona with her ethnic background, as 'an Ethiop'. . . . 'Afric's muse.'"[77] Notably, Wheatley employs racial, not gendered, markers to articulate that persona. It should be noted, too, that the reference to Terence tells us something about how Wheatley understood racial difference. She articulates a racial connection between herself and Terence based on geographical commonalities, not somatic ones. He is not a *Black* poet or an *Ethiop* but an African, perhaps Wheatley's acknowledgment of historical accounts, which are repeated by her contemporaries like Thomas Jefferson, that claimed Terence was of North African ancestry and therefore swarthy or white in color. What matters for Wheatley is that she and her poetic predecessor hail from the same "dark abode." "Wheatley has found," as Marsha Watson notes, "in western literary history an African poet whose 'soul possesses the sacred flame,' and rewrites that history to create an artistic community in which, as an African herself, she may now claim an inheritance."[78]

More a challenge to Maecenas than a plea, "To Maecenas" can be read as a racial critique and defense of the intellectual faculties of people of African descent. It is, as Paula Bennett notes, "a bitter and angry poem from a poet reputed for generosity and mildness."[79] By directing the reader's attention to the poetic achievements of Terence, Wheatley illustrates that her desire for poetic greatness is not a lofty, impertinent, or ridiculous aspiration of one lacking intellectual capacity. She "forces the nonblack world," Wilson notes, "to face its foundational lie: Black voices, minds and flesh . . . [are] more, not less, capable of making impactful art of language."[80] Wheatley ends the poem on a defiant note, insisting in the final stanza that she will keep striving

> As long as Thames, in streams majestic flows,
> Or Naiad's in their oozy beds repose,
> While Phebus reigns above the starry train,
> While bright Aurora purples o'er the main,
> So long, great Sir, the muse thy praise shall sing,
> So long thy praise shall make Parnassus ring.
> Then grant, Maecenas, thy paternal rays,
> Hear me propitious, and defend my lays. (lines 48–55, page 54)

The speaker demands visibility, acceptance. This posture, perhaps, mirrors her strategy for securing the signatories whose attestation prefaces the volume. In a sense, those eighteen white men "hear" her "propitious" and "defend" her "lays" and yet they do not see her. They authenticate the poetry of "a young Negro Girl." The descriptive marker infantilizes Wheatley and marks her gender. Joanna Brooks speculates that Wheatley constructed the attestation (thereby referring to herself as a "Negro Girl"), which suggests, as Lucia Hodgson and Jennifer Thorn argue, that Wheatley leaned into public perceptions of herself as an infantile girl poet.[81]

Hodgson reminds us of the importance of considering childhood when examining the intersectional nature of Wheatley's subjectivity and her poetic persona: "Wheatley's writing and marketing tapped into the eighteenth-century recognition of childhood as a status distinct from adulthood with its own unique set of weaknesses and strengths. The child figure of the early 1770s was simultaneously affiliated with varied and contradictory—yet primarily positive—characteristics, including malleability, obedience, and faith in authority. This constellation of attributes enabled Wheatley's literary child persona to speak to her social superiors about family, religion, and politics while mitigating the threat associated with her wronged and enslaved African body."[82] Hodgson argues that Wheatley's youthful appearance muted negative connotations evoked by her Black body. We can extend Hodgson's observations by complicating even more Wheatley's manipulation of childhood rhetoric and its relationship to Black adulthood. Drawing from social contract theory and the seventeenth-century ideas of John Locke, Hodgson argues that children in early America existed in a "prepolitical" state, what she calls the "Lockean Child," a state in which they were perceived as "imitative and not yet fully developed . . . a stage of apprenticeship toward conformity to existing literary and social conventions."[83] In this way, childhood was a space of potential, and children were viewed as nonthreatening, harmless, according to Hodgson. As Charles Mills points out, however, the social contract derived its efficacy from racial exclusion, so that children might have existed in a "prepolitical" state, but they did not exist in a preracial one. The child imagined under Lockean theory was white. Wheatley, then, built a public audience not only because she could appear nonthreatening as a child but also equally important because her racial classification deemed her a novelty worth spectatorship. If anything, Wheatley's youth and race (not to mention gender and enslaved status) were coconstitutive elements in her poetic profile.

Regardless of the source of the attestation at the front of Wheatley's volume, there is a notable contrast between that youthful, diminutive description and the erudite, mature, voice of the Afric muse who inhabits "To Maecenas," whose racial identity—by association with Terence—ennobles her in a way that her gender cannot. More often than not, when Wheatley references herself in her poems, she adds a racial rather than gender marker. She is the "Afric' muse" or "Ethiop." In a typical heteronormative, patriarchal society, (white) man is the default subject position. In other words, unless otherwise stated, a subject is assumed to be white and male. Wheatley challenges this assumption through her omission of a gender reference. Her Black woman's body, expressed as a "Negro Girl" in the volume's preface, is the Black body of the ungendered Ethiop in "To Maecenas."

Besides poetic imitation and the claiming of kinship with classical writers, Wheatley employs spiritual rhetoric to build a persona of respectability. In her charge to Harvard students in her poem "To the University of Cambridge in New-England," she embraces stereotypes about the absence of virtue in Black Africans to derive spiritual authority and exhibit what Antonio Bly has called "sass."[84] She is able to "rebuke without necessarily appearing rebuking" in her censure of students.[85] Also, there is a certain tension in the poem as the speaker marks both her similarity with and difference from her audience. In the first stanza of the poem, she reminds readers of her immigrant status:

'Twas not long since I left my native shore
The land of errors, and *Egyptian* gloom:
Father of mercy, 'twas thy gracious hand
Brought me in safety from those dark abodes. (lines 3–6, page 55)

She mimics the common perception of Africa as a dark continent and describes her capture and transport to America as a "fortunate fall."[86] She implies some residual darkness that might still linger within her given that she "not long since" left. This seemingly self-deprecatory opening echoes that of "On Being Brought from Africa to America." In this case, the opening stanza establishes a contrast between the speaker, and her connection to a "land of errors" and of "Egyptian gloom," and those students she addresses in the poem. They exist in a much more privileged state, as she notes in the second stanza:

Students, to you 'tis giv'n to scan the heights
Above, to traverse the ethereal space,
And mark the systems of revolving worlds. (lines 7–9, page 55)

She remarks on the educational advantages of these "sons of science" who have access to a formal training denied her based on both her race and gender. She does not dwell on those differences, though, quickly linking herself and the students through a Christian discourse of mercy. The same "Father of mercy" who delivered her out of "those dark abodes" of Africa is the same one who sends a savior, a "Son of God," whose "matchless mercy" has redeemed them all. She employs again the idea of mercy in salvation. This time she conceives of the entirety of humankind as the beneficiaries of God's mercy, not just "benighted" Black Africans, proclaiming:

> When the whole human race by sin had fall'n
> He deign'd to die that they might rise again,
> And share with him in the sublimest skies,
> Life without death, and glory without end. (lines 17–20, page 55)

In the third and final stanza of the poem, the speaker sermonizes to the students, imploring them:

> Improve your privileges while they stay,
> Ye pupils, and each hour redeem, that bears
> Or good or bad report of you to heav'n. (lines 21–23, page 55)

She further encourages them to eschew evil and sin:

> Let sin, that baneful evil to the soul,
> By you be shunn'd, nor once remit your guard;
> Suppress the deadly serpent in its egg. (lines 24–26, page 55)

Importantly, the speaker derives credibility and authority for her sermonic insistence by referencing her racial difference:

> Ye blooming plants of human race divine,
> An *Ethiop* tells you 'tis your greatest foe;
> Its [sin] transient sweetness turns to endless pain,
> And in immense perdition sinks the soul. (lines 27–30, pages 55–56)

The emphasis on the speaker's alterity is ironic, invoking as such the Christian association between Blackness (signaled by *Ethiop*) and the sin referenced in the next line. The speaker seems to intimate that an Ethiop is especially positioned to warn an audience about the pernicious and seductive nature of sin. She embraces a racial stereotype to claim authority for her sermonic charge.[87] As Adélékè Adéèkó has observed, "Because [Wheatley's] placement on the fringe does not allow her to directly command her privileged addressees to follow the righteous path, she focuses on her lowly self."[88] She delivers a pious message about gratitude, salvation, and virtue to an audience of young, white, male students who will either squander their privilege or maximize it to God's glory.

Wheatley touts a form of respectability that challenges mainstream stereotypes about Black Africans by emphasizing Blacks as having the capacity to embody the same virtue as their white counterparts. Consider her most oft-discussed poem, "On Being Brought from Africa to America." At the outset, the speaker in the poem appears a model Christian convert, a self-avowed African heathen who finds God and salvation in America. The poem signals her assimilation by describing her enslavement as a divine mercy.[89] The first four lines read like a rudimentary catechism, a profession of faith and recognition of personal depravity:

> 'Twas mercy brought me from my *Pagan* land,
> Taught my benighted soul to understand
> That there's a God, that there's a *Saviour* too:
> Once I redemption neither sought nor knew. (lines 1–4, page 56)

With the poem's opening couplets, Wheatley accommodates the expectations of white readers and perhaps articulates her own sincere gratitude about her spiritual transformation. She expresses appreciation and respect for her earthly saviors—the Wheatleys. In the second set of couplets, she ventriloquizes and seemingly concedes the widespread stereotypes about Black Africans bearing the cursed mark of Cain:

> Some view our sable race with scornful eye,
> "Their colour is a diabolic die."
> Remember, *Christians, Negros,* black as *Cain,*
> May be refin'd, and join th' angelic train. (lines 5–8, page 56)

As current Wheatley scholarship points out, we cannot read this assimilationist display as a wholly hegemonic recital of Black degradation; the fact that she distances herself from the stereotype by using quoted speech suggests she disagrees with the viewpoint. Alternatively, though, there is the danger of overreading the turn in line five if one simply deems it subversive. Wheatley both accommodates the status quo by highlighting Black stereo-types and resists it by pointing out that Black Africans, even if "black as Cain," can indeed be redeemed; Wheatley is living proof. Contrary to what an enslaver like John Saffin might think about the incompatibility of Black Africans and respectability in 1701, as discussed in the previous chapter, Wheatley embodies the possibilities.

As the elegies and other poems illustrate, Wheatley combats mainstream stereotypes and anti-Blackness by embodying Christian morality and man-ners, which constitute respectability in her eighteenth-century context. To some extent, Wheatley upholds herself as representative of Black virtue rather than an exception as she acknowledges those traits in other Black Africans, as well. She illustrates this in her poem addressed to a young Black painter and in letters to her close friend Obour Tanner. In "To S.M. a Young *African* Painter, on Seeing His Work," Wheatley marks a connection be-tween two Black artists based on the idea of virtue. Conventional readings of "To S.M." emphasize Wheatley's celebration of Black art. The speaker recognizes a kinship between the poet and the painter, both empowered by imagination to create and therefore transcend the mundane. Wheatley, as Rafia Zafar notes, "goes beyond scripturally delivered affirmations of African freedom and equality to hail the dignity, artistic worth, and future immortality of Scipio Moorhead, a fellow slave."[90] The speaker muses in the first stanza:

> Still may the painter's and the poet's fire
> To aid thy pencil, and thy verse conspire!
> And may the charms of each seraphic theme
> Conduct thy footsteps to immortal fame! (lines 9–12, page 100)

The speaker celebrates the artist while also instructing him on proper be-havior. Like her charge in "To the University of Cambridge," in this poem, Wheatley seems drawn to the youth of the artist and appeals to his virtuous potential. After praising his talents, the speaker cautions the painter:

> Still, wond'rous youth! each noble path pursue,
> On deathless glories fix thine ardent view. (lines 7–8, page 100)

She reminds him of the ephemerality of the world: "No more to tell of Damon's tender sighs, / Or rising radiance of Aurora's eyes." He should, instead, anticipate the "nobler themes" and "purer language on th' ethereal plain" (100). The poem assumes a more intimate tenor, one that suggests that Wheatley's connection to Scipio Moorhead goes beyond a shared artistry. She mentors the young painter on proper comportment. In this way, she serves the role of a patron. This is one of the last poems in the volume and offers an ironic echo of "To Maecenas." Whereas she began the volume by challenging a white patron to appreciate her work, she ends it by praising the artistic virtues of another Black artist, who in many ways reflects the potential for Black excellence that was realized in Terence so many centuries earlier. She even describes Scipio's progression toward the same "immortal fame" she insists was Terence's due. Recognizing the poem's "African American agenda," Zafar notes Moorhead's inclusion in a volume that also highlighted prominent white, male figures, such as George Whitefield and the Earl of Dartmouth, and argues, "For Wheatley to include an African American servant with the highest of white males, to invoke his talents as though he were the most renowned of painters, and to speak of his immortality and spiritual nobility, claims for black people the neoclassical mode in poetry and an equal place in society."[91] Zafar goes on to say that "Wheatley participates in a white, Western, largely male tradition at the same time she fashions it into an expressive, 'black' vehicle."[92] All of this is to say that the creative output and the potential for future output of Wheatley, Terence, and Scipio embody Black humanity by showcasing their intellectual and virtuous capacities, rendering them respectable. For Wheatley, and the others discussed in this book, respectability was an integrationist tool. They endeavored to embody the artistic and spiritual values of a mainstream culture, sometimes in transgressive ways, to prove their humanity against Enlightenment rhetoric that insisted they were inhuman.

Wheatley's letters also reflect her investment in respectability as a survival mechanism. This is especially true of her correspondence with Obour (or Arbour) Tanner, who lived in Newport, Rhode Island. Based on the seven extant letters we have to date, all from Wheatley to Tanner, it is apparent that the women were friends. They shared the personal, intimate details of their lives—about ailments, finances, death, and, of course, spiritual matters. Tara Bynum argues that these letters "document a collective worship and reveal a bond that asks us to consider what pleasure and friendship might look like to two enslaved women in New England."[93] I would add to Bynum's observations that the letters illustrate for us the early attempts on the part of Black Africans to assimilate with the aim of shifting mainstream racial attitudes.

Alongside the sentimental expressions of friendship in the letters exists a subtext about respectability. For example, in a letter dated July 19, 1772, Wheatley writes to Tanner of her poor health and then reminds Tanner of the glory that awaits on the other side of death. "How happy that man who is prepar'd for that Nig[ht] wherein no man can work!" Wheatley writes. "Let us be mindful of our high calling, continually on our guard, lest our treacherous hearts should give the adversary an advantage over us" (36). Not only does Wheatley aim to regulate their behavior, but she also reminds Tanner what is at stake if they do not model proper Christian sentiment—they make themselves vulnerable to an "adversary."

At times the letters read almost like a Bible study. Wheatley constantly evokes Scripture to shore up her and Tanner's faith. On October 30, 1773, upon her return from a six-week trip to London to promote her book, Wheatley responds to a letter she received from Tanner. Apparently, Tanner offered her thoughts about the Old Testament figure Esau. Wheatley responded to Tanner's observations: "What you observed of Esau is true of all mankind, who (left to themselves) would sell their heavenly Birth rights for a few moments of sensual pleasure whose wages at least . . . is eternal condemnation. Dear Obour let us not sell our Birth right for a thousand worlds, which indeed would be as dust upon the Ballance" (111). Of note here is Wheatley's insistence again that there is a single human race, all the members of which are susceptible to vice—willing to sell their "heavenly Birth rights." All people are alike in that regard. But she imagines herself and Tanner in a virtuous alliance to avoid that mortal weakness. They were mirrors for each other, modeling the godly behavior that was key to Heavenly salvation and respect among their earthly neighbors. It seems that Wheatley recognizes God as the ultimate judge of her and Tanner's holiness, their worthiness. Yet, there is a clear sense that she aims to achieve regard among her neighbors by the insistence that she and Tanner conduct themselves in a manner to prevent the censure of their "adversaries." This latter awareness drives Wheatley's concern for respectability. The spiritual language that permeates the letter exchange between them constitutes, in Bassard's words, a "rhetorical meeting place" where they build community, claim self-empowerment, and theorize about selfhood, which they articulate in terms of virtue and proper comportment.[94] This commitment to godly behavior perhaps made it especially difficult for Wheatley to accept that the respect she thought she had earned from friends of the Wheatleys by 1774 had been "put on a reserve."

In general, Wheatley's correspondence with others reveals her preoccupation with Christian virtue, including the quality of humility. When writing to Tanner of the warm reception she received during her six-week tour of England, Wheatley says: "Their Benevolent conduct towards me, the unexpected, and unmerited civility and Complaisance with which I was treated by all, fills me with astonishment, I can scarcely Realize it,—This I humbly hope has the happy Effect of lessning me in my own Esteem" (111). Her anxiety about remaining humble in the face of newfound adoration and fame echoes the warning she received from Thornton just weeks before Susannah's death. In a letter dated February 1774, Thornton tells Wheatley, referring to her visit to England, "I feared for you when here, least the notice many took of you, should prove a snare. . . . [P]raise is agreeable to corrupt nature; and the consequence is, we . . . become proud of our graces, the power of grace gradually dwindles away, and little more than the empty name and profession remains" (117). He understands Wheatley to have garnered a certain measure of "respect . . . paid to [her] uncommon genius" (117). In the letter she pens to Thornton some eight months later, remarking on the loss of respect she experienced in the wake of Susannah's passing, she also confirms her struggle with vanity. Mournful and jaded, she writes, "The World is a severe Schoolmaster . . . for its frowns are less dang'rous than its Smiles and flatteries, and it is a difficult task to keep in the path of Wisdom" (125).

As her letters make clear, Wheatley understood the stakes inherent in her efforts to remain humble and embody virtue. She accepts that she functions as a member of her "Nation" and frequently speaks on behalf of Black Africans as her poetry gains her an audience with prominent political and religious figures. Repeating the idea espoused in her poetry that Africa is a dark continent populated by benighted souls, she beseeches Tanner in a letter to rejoice with her in their mutual deliverance from a "land semblant of darkness . . . and where the divine light of revelation (being obscur'd) is as darkness" (32). Importantly, though, she imagines a spiritual deliverance for Black Africans. In a letter to the congregationalist minister Samuel Hopkins, who advocated for Black repatriation and mission programs to Africa, Wheatley lends her support to such efforts, calling Africa her "benighted Country" suffering from a "Spiritual Famine" (119). Black Africans, she insists to Hopkins, are ripe for conversion as "their minds are unprejudiced against the truth therefore tis to be hoped they would receive it with their Whole heart" (119). She predicts optimistically that "Ethiopia Shall Soon Stretch forth her hands Unto God" (119). Perhaps echoing the idea of salvation for all races pronounced in her poems like "On Being Brought from Africa to America," she proclaims in a letter to Thornton dated December 1, 1773, that God "is no respecter of Persons: being equally the great Maker of all." She insists he is "the Father of Humble Africans and Indians; though despised on earth on account of our colour, we have this Consolation, . . . 'That God dwells in the humble & contrite heart.'" Rehearsing her desire for humility, she prays that she will be "directed by the immediate influence of the divine spirit in my daily walk & conversation" (113). When she receives news of the failed missionary efforts of the Black evangelist Philip Quaque in 1774, she doubles down on her optimism about African conversion by attributing the failure to Quaque. In a letter to Hopkins, she suggests, "Possibly, if Philip would introduce himself properly to them . . . he might be more Successful." She offers the advice tentatively, using the conditionals "possibly" and "if." She also recommends, more assertively, that Quaque set "a good example which is more powerfully winning than Instruction" (124). The idea of setting a good example is quintessential respectability rhetoric. One is encouraged to set a good example not only for the sake of other members of one's minoritized community but also for the sake of those outside the community who observe and judge the conduct of the individual as representative of the whole. Wheatley's advice to Quaque, for sure, is presumptuous, maybe even accusatory.[95] It also speaks to the political stakes she understands are attached to setting a good example.

A MODEL MINORITY

Wheatley's emphasis on Black character, both hers and others', was part of a larger discourse surrounding her poetry and communal interactions. Her contemporaries were just as apt to remark on her intellect and Christian virtue as they were to speak of her poetic aesthetics, upholding her as emblematic—or exceptional—of (Black) humanity. As Marsha Watson notes, "When looking over the history of Wheatley's critical reception, one finds that virtually any non-derogatory comment on Wheatley's work has coincided with observations about the 'unusual' mental abilities of the poet."[96] To her contemporaries, she was, in Hilene Flanzbaum's words, an "anthropological test case."[97] The ardent British abolitionist Thomas Clarkson, for example, wrote of Wheatley, "if the authoress was designed for slavery, (as the argument must confess) the greater part of the inhabitants of Britain must lose their claim to freedom."[98] He went on to say that if Wheatley was a genius or prodigy as many viewed her, she was not an anomaly but like any other with the "same opportunities of acquiring knowledge . . . and the same expectations in life to excite . . . genius."[99] In other words, she was representative of humanity, not an exception to it. The Philadelphia physician Benjamin Rush articulates a similar conclusion in a pamphlet condemning slavery in 1773. In a footnote, he observes, "There is now in the town of Boston a free Negro girl, about eighteen years of age, who has been but nine years in the country, whose singular genius and accomplishments are such as not only do honour to her sex, but to human nature."[100] Among Wheatley's contemporaries, white women were especially instrumental in shaping and propagating her public image. Several scholars, Joanna Brooks and Wendy Raphael Roberts among them, have examined the extent to which Wheatley, in Brooks's words, "built her career with support from both black and white women." Brooks maintains that "white female agents and audiences," especially, "asserted a definitive influence over the content of her poems."[101] Roberts examines specifically the antislavery poetry of Ruth Barrell Andrews and her amplification of Wheatley's intellectual abilities.[102]

Focusing more on virtue than intellect in a letter to the Countess of Huntingdon, Richard Cary, one of those eighteen signatories who authenticated *Poems on Various Subjects,* determined about Wheatley during a visit to Boston that "The negro girl of Mrs. Wheatley's, by her virtuous behavior and conversation in life, gives reason to believe, she's a subject of Divine Grace—remarkable for her piety."[103] Perhaps Cary witnessed behavior like that described by Margaretta Matilda Odell, a purported niece of Susannah Wheatley. In 1834, Odell published a memoir about Wheatley. She portrays Wheatley as a submissive and humble servant in the Wheatley household.

In the memoir, Odell, who says she was "familiar with the name and fame of Phillis from her childhood,"[104] writes that Susannah Wheatley was drawn to Phillis immediately because of the girl's "humble and modest demeanor."[105] According to Odell, celebrity did not alter Wheatley's personality. After the poetry was published, among frequent visits by "clergymen, and other individuals of high standing in society," Odell notes, "notwithstanding the attention she received, and the distinction with which she was treated, she never for a moment lost sight of that modest, unassuming demeanor."[106] As an example, Odell recalls that "whenever [Wheatley] was invited to the houses of individuals of wealth and distinction, (which frequently happened,) she always declined the seat offered her at their board, and, requesting that a side-table might be laid for her, dined modestly apart from the rest of the company. We consider this conduct both dignified and judicious."[107] As a source of biographical information about Wheatley, Odell's memoir tells us less about Wheatley's poetry than it does about cultural perceptions of her comportment—her respectability.

In his 2005 biography of Wheatley, Vincent Carretta warns readers to approach Odell's memoir with a healthy dose of skepticism. He maintains that "much of the information in [the] account is either unverifiable, unreliable, demonstrably incorrect, or apparently intended to serve Odell's" larger aim of suggesting that "enslavement [was] preferable to the unpredictability of freedom for people of African descent."[108] The reliability of Odell's account notwithstanding, her emphasis on Wheatley's behavior and character tells us something about the value placed on how Black Africans conducted themselves in early America.

Even among her Black African contemporaries, a rhetoric of respectability cloaks Wheatley. In his praise of her work, Ignatius Sancho proclaims that her poetry improves the moral sensibility of its readers. "I could wish that every member of each house of parliament had one of these books," he writes, "—And if his Majesty perused one through before breakfast—though it might spoil his appetite—yet the consciousness of having it in his power to facilitate the great work—would give an additional sweetness to his tea."[109] Here, Sancho anticipates that Wheatley's work will have the transformative effect that is the intent of assimilation, to move the mainstream. In a poem he wrote paying homage to Wheatley, "An Address to Miss Phillis Wheatly [*sic*], Ethiopian Poetess," Jupiter Hammon praises her conduct. The poem's speaker begins by proclaiming Wheatley a "pious youth" and echoes her description of her enslavement as a fortunate fall. In the first third of the poem's twenty-one stanzas, Hammon mostly responds to Wheatley's "On Being Brought from Africa to America" by confirming her religious ethos. In the first stanza, the speaker calls on Wheatley:

> O come you pious youth! adore
> The wisdom of thy God,
> In bringing thee from distant shore,
> To learn His holy word.[110]

Like Wheatley, Hammon emphasizes the sovereignty of God as the mechanism by which Wheatley was taken to the Americas. Enslavers, including the Lloyd family that enslaved Hammon, and the Wheatleys, are agents enacting God's will rather than perpetrators of inhumane crimes. In the second stanza, he also imitates her strategy for representing the African continent as a "dark abode" from which "God's tender mercy" delivered her. Through the eighth stanza, the poem's speaker reflects upon that tender mercy, which extends salvation to all humans. In this way, Hammon celebrates with Wheatley, who, as discussed above, expressed her joy in correspondence with Thornton that God "is no respecter of Persons: being equally the great Maker of all."

Although the first eight stanzas of Hammon's poem seem to align with Wheatley's religious outlook, in the ninth stanza the poem transitions. It assumes a more anxious tone as the speaker implores Wheatley:

> Come you, Phillis, now aspire,
> And seek the living God,
> So step by step thou mayst go higher,
> Till perfect in the word.[111]

No longer celebrating Wheatley's piety and salvation for all races, now the speaker endeavors to guide *Phillis,* much like Wheatley sought to guide a young Scipio Moorhead down a path of righteousness. Here, though, the guidance would seem superfluous, given the acknowledgment of Wheatley's piety in the opening lines of the poem. Nevertheless, Hammon endeavors to mentor Wheatley, calling on her in the eleventh stanza to worship with him:

Thou hast left the heathen shore;
Thro' mercy of the Lord,
Among the heathen live no more,
Come magnify thy God.[112]

Anticipating that she will encounter spiritual crises, he warns her in the thirteenth stanza:

Thou, Phillis, when thou hunger hast,
Or pantest for thy God;
Jesus Christ is thy relief,
Thou hast the holy word.[113]

Hammon assumes the role of spiritual mentor for Wheatley, invested in regulating her behavior and shoring up her faith. The poem, which she may or may not have read, is a kind of instruction manual that builds on the public persona of virtue and grace that she had established and—by her own recognition in that 1774 letter to Thornton—lost by the time Hammon published these verses in 1778. Of course, the poem is not really about Wheatley. The Wheatley persona mediates Hammon's own relationship to respectability. The poem allows him to espouse proper Christian sentiment, speak with Christian authority and, like Wheatley, advocate for a God of all.

BEYOND THE BOUNDS OF GENDER

The characterization of Wheatley by her contemporaries was decidedly atypical for the day. Like Adam, who Saffin argued was inherently violent and lazy, Black women were seen as naturally incapable of embodying the virtues of (white) womanhood. So, Wheatley stood against the raced, gendered expectations of colonial American society that stereotyped Black women as promiscuous and in other ways degenerate.[114] Harriet Jacobs bemoans this fact in her slave narrative *Incidents in the Life of a Slave Girl* (1861). She explains to the "virtuous reader," white women in the North, her choice to initiate a sexual relationship with a white lawyer, Mr. Sands, in her rural North Carolina community, as means to thwart the sexual advances and harassment of the enslaver Dr. Flint. She claims sexual agency by denying Dr. Flint while sacrificing her chastity to Mr. Sands. She then begs of the reader, "Pity me, and pardon me. . . . I know I did wrong. No one can feel it more sensibly than I do. Still, in looking back, calmly, on the events of my life, I feel that the slave woman ought not to be judged by the same standard as others."[115] Jacobs points out that the model of Victorian virtue to which (white) women aspired in the nineteenth century was inaccessible to enslaved Black women. Similarly, in the seventeenth and eighteenth centuries, Black women, those enslaved and free, encountered assumptions about their sexuality and degeneracy.[116]

Specifically focused on the plight of enslaved Black women in the North, Jennifer Thorn argues that northern enslavers viewed sexuality and reproduction negatively with regard to enslaved Black women.[117] Wanting to avoid the expense of caring for additional bodies, according to Thorn, enslavers in colonial New England often posted ads announcing the sale of enslaved women who were *too* fertile. This attitude of enslavers, or "anti-reproductivity," meant that enslaved women's reproductive and sexual lives were devalued, and in the case of Wheatley, suppressed.[118] Thorn argues that Wheatley's "status as the first African-American, and the second American woman, to publish a book—exists on a continuum with her typicality as a Northern bondswoman. The effacement of her sexuality, and, in particular, her reproductivity, was crucial to her success."[119] Unlike her counterparts in the South and the Caribbean, Wheatley provided very little in the way of manual labor for the Wheatleys; nor did she provide the labor of childbirth (augmenting their slave stock).[120] Rather, her intellectual production was the basis for her commercial value and social respectability. Her marginalized status afforded Wheatley a certain freedom of movement to participate in both public and private realms. Wheatley could speak on political matters, insinuate herself into a public sphere, manage the circulation of her poetry, and try to earn a living without the charge of impertinence or without impropriety because her Black body, as Spillers has so eloquently ruminated, existed beyond the heteronormative confines of Western culture.[121]

Walt Nott and Phillip M. Richards both examine Wheatley's presence in an early American public sphere. Nott notes Wheatley's transformation from a child perceived as an "uncultivated barbarian" into a "poetical genius." This "authorial metamorphosis,"[122] as he terms it, is encapsulated in her book, which "represents her conspicuous participation in the 'public sphere'—the eighteenth-century network of rational discourse whose formation and operation aimed at the acquisition of political power through the control of an emerging public opinion."[123] Importantly, he understands *Poems on Various Subjects* as a "manifestation of her power to call into question the conceptual assumptions that both formed the foundation of the public sphere and justified the American/European enslavement of Africans."[124] In other words, by virtue of writing and functioning in public, Wheatley challenged the very nature of such spaces and the exclusion of Black Africans from those spaces.

Richards argues that Wheatley writes from a position of self-consciousness that is driven by the fears of an American colony perceived of as "provincial." That self-consciousness, even more importantly, Richards notes, is informed by Wheatley's racial position as a marginalized body within the provincial context of America. Like Notts, Richards notes the power Wheatley claims as a writing subject, constructing a public persona: "Identifying her own poetic voice and its limitations with the checked aspirations of her [white American] audience, Wheatley asserts herself as the circumscribed voice of a culturally aspiring colonial society."[125] Simultaneously, she challenges the image of America as provincial and the image of Black Africans as intellectually inferior. Nott and Richards both acknowledge the anomalous nature of Wheatley's raced body participating in an Anglo(-American) public sphere.[126]

We can extend and complicate their observations by considering more fully Wheatley's intersectional positionality as Black and as woman participating in a public sphere. Kirstin Wilcox gestures toward the significance of Wheatley's intersectionality. In her study of the marketing strategies Wheatley and others employed in order to sell her books, Wilcox notes, "For Wheatley to become known, her multifaceted marginality had to be reformed into a print persona shaped by the racialized and gendered parameters of eighteenth-century authorship."[127] Wilcox argues that "publication itself implied a degree of self-authorization and expressive subjectivity inherently incompatible with servitude."[128] *Poems on Various Subjects,* then, "open[ed] a channel between Wheatley" and a reading public; it created a space for her in the public sphere that otherwise would have "denied her as a slave, an African, and a woman."[129]

I would add to Wilcox's observations that Wheatley is yet another example of how and why the private/public binary through which we tend to think about gender and social relations in earlier periods cannot apply to enslaved Black women, who necessarily maintained vexed relationships to concepts like family, home, and domesticity, not to mention chastity.[130] This is not to say that enslaved Black women did not strive to construct and maintain those structures for which their labor provided stability.[131] Once her owners free her in 1773, Wheatley does in fact marry, and, according to Odell, she births three children, all of whom die in infancy.[132] She dutifully assumes the last name of her husband, John Peters, signing her poems after 1778 as Phillis Peters.

John Peters has been a troubling figure in Wheatley studies. A common thread of scholarship has dismissed him as a ne'er-do-well, a drain on Wheatley's meager resources and a major contributor to the infant deaths and declining health that led to the poet's early death.[133] Thanks to the recent revision work of Cornelia H. Dayton, among others, a more complex image of Peters emerges, one that suggests Wheatley might well have gravitated toward him as a suitable partner because of his own pursuit of respectability.[134] Unlike his wife, John Peters was born into slavery in the Massachusetts town of Middleton, some twenty miles from Boston. In her biographical sketch of Peters's life, Dayton maps a trajectory of upward mobility in which Peters rises from enslavement through means that are not exactly clear. He settles at some point in Boston and becomes a grocer, or shopkeeper. He owns this business when he and Wheatley meet in the 1770s.

Through a series of negotiations with his previous enslaver and then with the widow of that enslaver, Peters becomes a landowner and caretaker for the estate on which he was formerly enslaved. He styles himself a yeoman, and in 1780, two years after he and Phillis marry and perhaps with an infant in tow or with Phillis in the final months of a pregnancy, the couple moves to Middleton. Dayton articulates Peters's sociopolitical climb from chattel to "urban and itinerant retailer of groceries and dry goods to owner-manager of orchards, fields, pasturage, and woodland."[135] Peters sought respectability as suggested in how he conducted himself as a landowner and estate manager. Documents outline Peters's management style. He sought to control who could and could not visit the estate, and he made aesthetic changes particularly to the receiving rooms in the main house to "reflect current architectural genteel styles," according to Dayton. He also restricted which members of the household could eat at the formal dining table, reserving that privilege specifically for himself, his wife, and the estate's widow, his former mistress. A Black woman named Dinah Cubber who worked as a servant or enslaved domestic in the home was excluded. As Dayton argues, Peters "aspired to a gentleman's life and status" and "would have seen his wife as a gentlewoman."[136] Further illustrating this point, is the fact that Peters dictated that his wife be spared the labor of cooking and other household chores, according to Dayton, presumably to free up her time to write. This move further complicates Wheatley Peters's relationship to domesticity and the private sphere.

Peters's sociopolitical and economic aspirations were foiled, ironically, by his efforts to achieve a certain level of regard among his Middleton neighbors. He and Wheatley Peters were evicted from the estate some four years after they arrived and just months before Wheatley Peters's death. The eviction was orchestrated by the estate's widow, who took specific exception to the idea that Wheatley Peters would not cook or perform other household duties. With the help of neighbors, the widow registered a series of charges against Peters that included mismanagement of the estate, neglect in his role as her caretaker, and a violent disposition. In court depositions, the widow, along with her Black counterpart Cubber, testified that Peters failed to provide for the widow adequately. Cubber, in particular, testified to Peters's disrespectful carriage, claiming that he used "saucy language" toward his enslavers and even once threatened the life of his master when he grabbed him "by the Throat & push'd him backwards upon a bed."[137] Neighbors offered similar testimony. A court sided with the widow, terminating the contracts binding the lands and estate to Peters.

The story of John Peters, in many ways, echoes that of Adam. Through a series of legal entanglements, Peters endeavors to make others take him seriously as a landowner, as a neighbor, as a human being. Even before his move to Middleton, Peters was no stranger to court proceedings and lawsuits. He himself sued business associates, sometimes successfully, to enforce the terms of business transactions. Just as often he found himself on the losing end, as was the case in Middleton. Despite his failed efforts in Middleton, John Peters's actions illustrate a desire to achieve not simply an economic elevation but one tied to respectability. That striving was an ambition with which Wheatley Peters certainly could have identified and very well might have admired and respected in her choice of a life mate.

Perhaps the cruelest irony of Wheatley's life is that for all her efforts, she did not achieve financial stability or maintain the renown that respectability promised. She died impoverished in her early thirties, having failed to publish a second book. "The details of Wheatley's later life," Flanzbaum argues, are "much less frequently recounted than her rapid rise to fame" and confirm "the precarious nature of even the minimal personal control she eked out."[138]

Although we honor her life and legacy today in academic circles, Phillis Wheatley is a salient reminder of the cruel trappings of respectability that have not immunized Black Africans against the traumas of enslavement and other forms of racial oppression. Wheatley embodies a Black consciousness and respectability through her strategies to assimilate; she understands her poetic and life efforts as working on behalf of Blacks in America. She offered herself up as a model, even if mainstream culture interpreted her as an anomaly, the exception that proved the rule. She is vital in discussions about respectability politics in an early Black Atlantic because she illustrates the ways in which assimilation mattered for early Black Americans as they demanded respect, visibility in the face of racial subjugation. In addition, she disrupts the ways that gender overdetermines how we have come to understand respectability as a coping strategy for Black communities. She occupies that ungendered space as a feature of cultural assumptions that do not accept (enslaved) Black women's bodies within a gendered matrix. For all the slippage in Wheatley's gender politics, Olaudah Equiano leans into gender differences in the autobiography he constructs about his experiences. He embodies the image of the self-made man, made respectable through education, spiritual conversion, and business acumen. For all his personal success, Equiano also acknowledges the impossibility of Black uplift under Western mechanisms that conspire to ignore Black humanity, impede racial progress. In the next chapter, I examine the ambivalent tenor of Equiano's respectability rhetoric.

(S O M E)

BLACK LIVES MATTER

OLAUDAH EQUIANO

AND THE

~~SOCIAL~~ RACIAL CONTRACT

IN MANY WAYS, the late eighteenth-century abolitionist, author, and merchant Olaudah Equiano epitomizes respectability. In 1756, at the age of eleven, he was captured from his home in Essaka in present-day Nigeria and sold into slavery across the Atlantic.[1] For about a decade, he endured enslavement in England and the Americas, including the West Indies. While enslaved, Equiano learned to read and write. He studied accounting, commerce, and ship navigation and fought in the Seven Years' War alongside the man who enslaved him. In 1766, when he was twenty-one, Equiano purchased his freedom for forty pounds sterling by saving the profits he earned from trading goods in the Caribbean. As a free man, he continued to earn a living through overseas trade and traveled around the world—to Italy, Spain, Turkey, the Arctic. Along the way he converted to Christianity. He served a brief stint in 1786 as commissary for the Sierra Leone resettlement plan that relocated hundreds of Black Africans from London and Nova Scotia to the coast of Sierra Leone and became an outspoken advocate for the abolition of the slave trade.[2] In 1792, he married an English woman, with whom he had two daughters. One of those daughters survived into adulthood; to her he left a small fortune upon his death in 1797. By most standards, Equiano lived a successful life.

The way he crafted that life is the subject of the autobiography he published in 1789, *The Interesting Narrative of the Life of Olaudah Equiano, or Gustavus Vassa, The African, Written by Himself.* The narrative was immensely popular in the decades immediately following its publication. Within five years, it went through some nine editions, plus several translations, including Dutch and German. Equiano's narrative took center stage in British debates about the slave trade in the 1790s. In addition to outlining the horrors of the transatlantic slave trade, the narrative details Equiano's social and economic elevation with a particular emphasis on his character, education, and industriousness. Transforming from commodity into human subject, an individual who owns property of his own, Equiano embodies what we would call in the next century bourgeois liberalism. As Rafia Zafar articulates it, he is "the earliest of Anglo-African success narrators."[3]

Equiano's social and economic rise supports the efficacy of respectability. It is no accident that Equiano includes as a frontispiece for the first edition of his narrative a self-portrait that styles him learned and successful. He lifts himself up from slavery, to borrow Booker T. Washington's phrasing from a century later. However, this narrative of personal responsibility and agency exists alongside Equiano's critique of those larger systems of oppression, rooted in white supremacy, that impede Black African achievement. Equiano's success is exceptional rather than representative, a point he makes in the narrative through representations of his encounters with and observations of other Black Africans who do not experience a similar level of success, such as his younger sister who is kidnapped alongside him in 1756 and Black companions he befriends in the Caribbean who endeavor but fail to achieve the same kind of mercantile success as he.[4] Notably, Equiano shifts between identifying with the struggles of other Black Africans and reporting on those struggles as an allied but detached observer.

The Black African figures who suffer at the margins of Equiano's narrative—and Equiano himself—point to the insidious nature of respectability, revealing its chimeric qualities. Black Africans experience a social exclusion, enacted through law and custom, that stifles their potential. In this way, Equiano illuminates for readers the mechanics of what Charles W. Mills has termed the "racial contract." In his influential study of social contract theory, Mills rearticulates the Enlightenment notion that societies cohere based on a social contract whereby individuals form governments through mutual consensus in order to protect their natural, God-given rights to life, liberty, and property. The social contract espoused equality and prioritized the preservation of individual rights. According to Mills, this social contract was founded upon an unacknowledged racial exclusivity. Equiano, through his emphasis on the social invisibility of Black Africans, illustrates the racist underpinnings of the social contract, which Mills argues should more properly be called a "racial contract."[5] More than a theory or prescription for government, the racial contract, Mills argues, is a historical fact.

In this chapter, I argue that Equiano's narrative illuminates the racial contract that circumscribed his eighteenth-century experiences. The narrative tests the limits of respectability as a coping strategy to combat that racist social order. To make this argument, I begin with a brief overview of Mills's notion of a racial contract in order to highlight important elements of Equiano's critique of eighteenth-century British slavery culture. I then discuss the critical tradition of Equiano's narrative. Most critics attend to issues of subjectivity in the text, understanding it as an account of personal growth. My approach emphasizes more the communal nature of the text by positioning Equiano within the context of those other Black Africans about whom he writes. Reading the text from the margins in this way nuances our understanding of Equiano's abolitionist critique, which is embedded in respectability rhetoric. He condemns specifically unrespectable forms of slavery by, in part, romanticizing the practice in West Africa.[6] My discussion then turns to a close reading of Equiano's narrative to emphasize several points. First is the fact that he establishes a link between place and morality. He most often associates unrespectable slavery practices with the West Indies, marking the region as ground zero for his abolitionist cause. What is more, he upholds his own conduct as a standard against which to measure the inhumane, brutal actions of enslavers and white islanders. In other words, Equiano establishes himself as respectable through a process of negation and opposition. Second, a close reading illuminates Equiano's emphasis on the invisibility of Black Africans by identifying specific abuses committed against them, which undermines any claims about the effectiveness of respectability as a coping mechanism. Finally, a close reading reveals the extent to which Equiano, himself, struggled to navigate the racial politics of a social contract in order to achieve some measure of respect. Ultimately, Equiano relies upon respectability to tout the possibilities for Black achievement while simultaneously critiquing the inability of respectability to overcome a social order compelled by white supremacy.

MILLS AND THE RACIAL CONTRACT

As a political theory and an aspiration, the social contract featured prominently in seventeenth- and eighteenth-century Enlightenment political philosophy. Guided by prominent thinkers, including John Locke, Thomas Hobbes, Jean-Jacques Rousseau, and Immanuel Kant, the theory describes a movement of the individual from a "natural" state of being, characterized by unchecked freedom and passions, into a "civil" state, characterized by laws agreed upon and applicable to all. People sacrifice only as much of their freedom as is necessary to safeguard their own well-being and property. They consent to be governed. What emerges out of this theory is the *liberal subject*, the individual who inherently possesses certain rights that government cannot (or should not) take away. Although the concept of a social contract did not originate during the Enlightenment, in this era philosophers popularized the theory to advocate for what they deemed acceptable forms of government. Their ideas shaped in crucial ways political revolutions sweeping through England, France, Haiti, and the American colonies in the seventeenth and eighteenth centuries. Particularly important for an understanding of early Black Atlantic literature and respectability politics is the rise of that liberal subject. As I argue shortly, Equiano (like other Black Africans discussed throughout this book) contemplates respectability as a means to make legible Black humanity and his natural rights to life, liberty, and property.

In an ideal world, the social contract purports equality, which contradicts the historical mechanics of imperial and colonial regimes that have implemented oppressive and violent policies designed to relegate or exterminate certain populations. The apparent contradiction between idea and practice, Mills argues in *The Racial Contract*, results from the fact that the social contract as imagined by Enlightenment thinkers was embedded in racial difference so that the contract was limited only to those deemed "white" (and male). It is, in fact, a racial contract, Mills asserts, which is a term he uses "not merely normatively, to generate judgments about social justice and injustice, but descriptively, to explain the actual genesis of the society and the state, the way society is structured, the way the government functions, and people's moral psychology."[7]

The social contract, as Mills notes, turns on the creation of two categories of people—those deemed persons and those deemed, in Mills's words, "subpersons." "Subpersons," he asserts, "are humanoid entities who, because of racial phenotype/genealogy/culture, are not fully human and therefore have a different and inferior schedule of rights and liberties applying to them. In other words, it is possible to get away with doing things to subpersons that one could not do to persons, because they do not have the same rights as persons."[8] Importantly, for Mills, subpersons exist, by opposition, to clarify the natural rights of persons. In the eighteenth-century Atlantic world through which Equiano circulated, he repeatedly encountered the limitations of his designation as a subperson, which followed him even after his legal status changed from enslaved to free. He employs respectability rhetoric in his text to challenge his social standing and undermine the chief mechanism of the social contract—race.

EQUIANO, THE CRITICAL TRADITION

Although *The Interesting Narrative* enjoyed great popularity in the decades following its initial publication, once England banned the transatlantic slave trade in 1807 and then emancipated those enslaved in its colonies several decades later, Equiano's narrative lost its cultural appeal. For the late nineteenth- and early twentieth-century reader, Equiano's was an obscure eighteenth-century text. In the mid-twentieth century, several scholars, among them the Harlem Renaissance writer Arna Bontemps, revived the narrative as a subject of critical literary study.[9] Today, most critics focus on Equiano's subjectivity, his sense of personhood. One central question has been, how does Equiano understand himself, and how/why does he employ narrative to communicate that understanding to the reader?[10] Susan Marren, for instance, identifies a transgressive element in Equiano's subjectivity, arguing that he embodies a subjective "I" that crosses racial and national boundaries in order to elicit sympathy from white, English readers and critique the transatlantic slave trade.[11] Other scholars find Equiano's mercantile activities, which occur primarily in the West Indies, as especially formative in how he comes to understand himself as an African transplant, Afro-Briton, Englishman, or hybrid national.[12] From this perspective, the narrative is, in the words of Elizabeth Jane Wall Hinds, a "tale of fiscal growth."[13] Houston A. Baker Jr. argues that the narrative is Equiano's effort to come to terms with his "commercially deportable status" as an enslaved being in the Americas.[14] "The mercantile endeavors of the autobiographical self in *The Life*," Baker maintains, "occupy the very center of the narrative."[15] Scholars, too, have concerned themselves with Equiano's spirituality. In the latter part of *The Interesting Narrative*, he embeds a conversion narrative relating his spiritual awakening and conversion to Methodism. For these critics, Christianity shapes Equiano's sense of self—accounting for how he understands his background in West Africa, his mercantile activities, his condemnation of the slave trade, and his travels across the globe.[16] Other critics, speaking of travel, ask questions about how mobility shapes Equiano's identity.[17] Critics also examine issues of voice. Who speaks in the text and when? Valerie Smith, for instance, notes a double voice through which Equiano both praises and condemns British society. That quality of doubleness, she maintains, "symbolizes [Equiano's] allegiance to both his African heritage and his European acculturation . . . it allows him . . . to adopt a critical stance toward the capacity for savagery of a society he otherwise admires."[18] In addition to subjectivity, critics have been interested in the political exigencies circumscribing the narrative—an emerging British abolition movement, the Enlightenment, nationalism movements and revolutions, commercial transformations on the West African coast resulting from the slave trade, and the Great Awakening.[19] In this way, critics excavate the sociopolitical world of Equiano.

Some literary scholars, in particular, address questions of genre. Cathy N. Davidson, for example, suggests somewhat tongue-in-cheek that Equiano's narrative ushers in an early American novelistic tradition, and Valerie Smith examines it as a conversion narrative.[20] Rafia Zafar emphasizes the text's hybridity, "a book that folds conversion, captivity, and picaresque together into a genuine New World document."[21] Noting the book's "heterogenous nature," Vincent Carretta suggests that it contains elements of historical fiction.[22] For his part, John Bugg argues that the narrative defies generic categorization through its use of "trifles," or "odd vignettes" Equiano scatters throughout the text that seemingly break from the main narrative. In those trifling moments, Bugg argues, Equiano constructs a counternarrative that allows him to speak the unspeakable, to go beyond the conventions of the abolitionist writing of the day.[23] Ramesh Mallipeddi labels the text a senti-mental narrative that emphasizes human relationships and Equiano's efforts to re-create human bonds in the wake of his traumatic separation from fam-ily.[24] Scholars also interrogate the narrative's relationship to a larger tradition of early Black Atlantic writing. Is it simply Black autobiography? Should we consider it a slave narrative, what Hinds calls a "master rubric," Henry Louis Gates Jr. calls a "prototype," and Geraldine Murphy calls a "palimp-sest," that anticipates the nineteenth-century accounts of U.S. plantation slavery, written by the likes of Frederick Douglass and Harriet Jacobs?[25] Is it part of an early African American literary tradition, although Equiano spent very little time traveling through or living in the United States?[26] How does his affinity for England—he swears off the West Indies and the British American mainland after experiencing a number of cruelties while traveling there—determine the literary category of his writing?[27]

In short, how does one categorize Equiano's narrative given that it is, as Davidson articulates it, "(in unequal parts) slave narrative, sea yarn, military adventure, ethnographic reportage, historical fiction, travelogue, picaresque saga, sentimental novel, allegory, tall tale, pastoral origins myth, gothic ro-mance, conversion tale, and abolitionist tract, with different features com-ing to the fore at different times, and the mood vacillating accordingly"?[28] These questions grow more complicated when we consider the debate in-volving Equiano's birthplace. Over the decades some critics have questioned whether Equiano was actually born in West Africa, as he claims, or whether he fabricated those chapters of his narrative. This question about his birth became more pronounced in 1995, when documents materialized, including a baptism record, that list his birthplace as South Carolina, forcing schol-ars to think through what it might mean—and what it does not mean—in terms of how we read Equiano's narrative as a historical document and as a literary one.[29]

A few studies think about Equiano as a representative figure construct-ing a narrative that speaks on behalf of Black Africans by condemning the slave trade and advocating for Black African humanity.[30] Ronald Paul, for example, argues that the narrative is a "unique personal testimony of the collective existential trauma of Blacks in White society."[31] These approaches deemphasize Equiano's selfhood to understand the ways in which he employs his voice to gain access to a public sphere and affect communal ends. My own understanding follows mostly this vein. I do attend to aspects of Equiano's subjectivity, but I am more interested in how and why Equiano speaks on behalf of a larger community of Black Africans, both enslaved and free, living daily under the oppressive regime of white supremacy. Despite the exceptionalism of his experiences, Equiano, as Andrew Kopec notes, "looks beyond the actualization of the self and, consequently, toward the actualization of a future aggregate of Africans" who are liberated and equal to their white counterparts. For Kopec, Equiano expresses this vision of equality through commerce. Equiano insists at the end of his narrative that, as a substitute for the slave trade, England and West Africa can enter into a mutually beneficial trade relationship, a "most immense, glorious, and happy prospect" (178). The narrative adopts an "optimistic worldview," Kopec maintains, that imagines "a collective [Black African population] transformed by commerce."[32] Kopec ascribes a prophetic vision to the narrative, one in which Black Africans and Europeans construct a kind of commercial utopia. My approach to the text emphasizes more the single obstacle that impedes the realization of that utopic vision—white supremacy. Defined simply as the idea that the racial category white is superior to all other racial categories, the ideology undergirded the transatlantic slave trade and excluded Black Africans from the social contract, denying them those legal and social protections fundamental to the interracial trade and commercial relationships Equiano envisioned. As Hinds points out, the law operated in Equiano's world "as a rather monolithic body of representations—legal 'fictions' designed not only to protect Whites, but also specifically to withhold protection of Blacks from all nations."[33] Hinds points to the legal tropes present in the narrative, which reveal the mechanics of a racial social order that I argue Equiano sought to disrupt.

Despite the narrative's explicit antislavery and antiracist aims, scholars remain perplexed by a key contradiction in Equiano's narrative and life. On several occasions, this abolitionist participated in slaving voyages and at one point worked as a plantation overseer. As Zafar notes, Equiano's "simultaneous holding of what we today consider incompatible views complicates our understanding of Equiano as a 'black writer.'"[34] I would add that the contradiction also complicates our understanding of him as an abolitionist who was focused specifically on ending the slave trade and bringing attention to the racism fueling it.[35] Racism, he notes repeatedly, keeps Black people in bondage, even when they are *legally* free. I read Equiano's slaving activity as at once subversive and accommodationist—his efforts to live out the terms of the social contract while also pointing out his exclusion from that contract. What scholars today identify as a contradiction might not have been a contradiction at all for Equiano but an expression of his complex subject position, one that exists both within and outside of the community's social order.

To illuminate those complexities, Equiano constructs a self through negation. That is to say, he sets himself up as an ideal citizen of a body politic that has deemed him all but invisible. He insists on his inclusion, visibility, by embodying certain virtues—industriousness, piety, loyalty, integrity, intelligence. Even as he "reflects and affirms" what Caldwell calls an eighteenth-century English "perception of self" and Marren describes as the "personification of the best qualities of the British nation," Equiano renders himself in contradistinction to his white counterparts, many of whom lack virtue, in particular those living in the West Indies.[36] Keith Sandiford observes, "Jostling daily among men given to drunkenness, swearing, and bloodthirsty threats, [Equiano] stood out as a model of virtue and industry."[37] This representation through opposition is the context in which Equiano relates his role as an overseer on Irving's plantation, a point on which I elaborate later in this chapter.

The work of Peter Jaros and Lisa Lowe has been particularly instructive for my understanding of Equiano's respectability strategies and the social contract. Both Jaros and Lowe note the narrative's engagement with Lockean notions of liberalism and the language of natural rights. In his essay "Good Names: Olaudah Equiano or Gustavus Vassa," Jaros argues that Equiano uses his narrative to articulate a paradox, a kind of double bind in which Equiano claims personhood, in the form of a liberal subject with good moral character or integrity, while also conceding his status as human commodity, a conflicting mode of being that turns character into the financial realm of credit. In other words, the narrative reflects an existential tension between character and credit, a tension endemic among Black Atlantic subjects in general, Equiano in particular. Jaros argues: "The economy of character, the

93

economy of credit, and the slave as the unit of fungible and speculative value coalesce into a microcosm of Equiano/Vassa's Atlantic world. . . . He appears simultaneously as creditable person and sound investment property."[38] Consequently, Jaros maintains, "*The Interesting Narrative* destabilizes the liberal identification of the legal person, the possessive individual, and the human being by highlighting the disparate, even incommensurable, grounds of identity."[39] He argues that Equiano articulates this paradoxical form of personhood through his choice to list both Olaudah Equiano and Gustavus Vassa on his book's title page. Jaros illuminates the difficulties inherent in Equiano's efforts to articulate self-possession and moral value beyond the financial terms and objectification of slavery. From his perspective, the narrative is Equiano's struggle to reconcile conflicting aspects of personhood "through his singular assertion of good names."[40]

Jaros offers vital nuance for our understanding of what character meant in Equiano's eighteenth-century context; however, his argument stops short of engaging the actual racial mechanisms driving Equiano's paradoxical notions of personhood. Besides struggling to articulate a coherent sense of self, Equiano challenges the legal invisibility and social subordination of Black Africans, both enslaved and free. Importantly, the islands of the West Indies are a staging ground for his critique as his experiences in the region reveal the problematics of a Lockean social contract that denies Black African humanity. The critique is amplified by the failures of respectability strategies to inoculate Equiano and other Black Africans from violence and other forms of oppression even as the rhetoric illustrates Black African humanity and potential. In general, Equiano's interactions in the West Indies are marked by the duplicitous, violent actions of white plantation owners and islanders whose inhumane behavior toward Black Africans enjoys the protection of law, of the social contract. Largely through his representations of the West Indies, Equiano renders himself a model of respectability and asserts the "natural" rights of Black Africans, challenging the limits of the social contract.

Like Jaros, Lowe reads Equiano's narrative as a deeply conflicted text resulting from the emergence of a "liberal modernity" that was based on political, social, and economic freedom and individualism, goals predicated on the unacknowledged subjugation of colonized peoples.[41] In her book *The Intimacies of Four Continents,* Lowe examines the connections, or the mutually constitutive nature, among an emergent European liberalism, settler colonialism in America, the transatlantic slave trade, and East Indies/China trade beginning at the end of the eighteenth century. Lowe articulates liberalism as an "economy" that "civilizes and develops freedoms for 'man' in modern Europe and North America, while relegating others to geographical and temporal spaces that are constituted as backward, uncivilized, and unfree."[42] In other words, communities of people of color in Africa, Asia, and America mediate, through their exclusion, the ideals that are the cornerstone of European liberalism, ideals including freedom, economic improvement, and national citizenship. In this way, Lowe dialogues with Mills by emphasizing empire and nation building as racially exclusive processes that produce social inequalities and erasure.

Lowe argues specifically about Equiano that his narrative embodies a central contradiction of the autobiography, which she calls the "genre of liberty," designed to advance narratives of freedom and individual progress.[43] "The canonization of Equiano's autobiography," she argues, is "the quintessential narrative of progress, which suggests that the slavery of the past is overcome and replaced by modern freedom."[44] The problem for Equiano, Lowe points out, is that slavery is never fully in the past. Instead, it looms large over the narrative, compromising Equiano's efforts to construct a true narrative of progress: "Equiano becomes a liberal cosmopolitan subject of globalization, a mobile world citizen. . . . Yet his race is the remainder of the colonial slavery that was not dissolved by legal emancipation, constituting the limit and critique" of European liberal ideals.[45] Lowe characterizes the contradiction in Equiano's text as a problem that Equiano struggles to reconcile, insisting that his "relationship to freedom is forever haunted by his former status as property within transatlantic social relations."[46] Although my reading of Equiano's narrative also emphasizes its contradictory elements, mainly resulting from a discourse of liberalism that characterizes his rise to a state of quasi-freedom, I posit that Equiano actually leans into the contradiction. As I will argue shortly, in those contradictions reside his critique of liberalism, of the social contract. For my purposes in this chapter, Jaros's and Lowe's readings are most valuable for what they tell us about how liberalism shaped Equiano's literary imagination. I extend their approaches by applying to Equiano's narrative the concept of respectability as a heuristic, a kind of racialized logic or lens that illuminates Equiano's efforts to embody liberal notions of individualism while simultaneously critiquing a social order that denies the possibility of Black liberal subjectivity, a denial reflected in Equiano's representations of himself and other Black Africans, particularly in the West Indies.

THE INHUMANITY OF THE WEST INDIES
AND A SOCIAL CONTRACT

In condemning the slave trade, eighteenth-century English abolitionists pointed to the West Indies as an especially problematic driving force of that trade. Expansive and profitable sugar plantations in Barbados and elsewhere demanded large workforces, and the labor to produce sugar was especially grueling. The work conditions resulted in high death rates for enslaved Black Africans. Enslavers in the West Indies needed a constant, steady supply of new bodies to work their fields. Given this, it makes sense that abolitionists, Equiano among them, would center their critique of the slave trade on the West Indies. To stage his specific argument, Equiano employs respectability rhetoric by spatializing morality, noting its lack in the West Indies.[47]

In his first encounter with the region, Equiano describes the horrors of a slave market in Barbados, where he arrives as an eleven-year-old boy.[48] With youthful innocence, he articulates his wonder and surprise about the sights and sounds on the island—flying fish, clouds on the horizon that look like land, men riding on horseback. "I was now more persuaded than ever that I was in another world, and that every thing about me was magic," he says (42). That wonder soon gives way to dismay when he witnesses his first slave market, where "without scruple are relations and friends separated, most of them never to see each other again." He notes the "eagerness visible in the countenances of the [white] buyers," which contrasts the expressions of "terrified Africans." He points out the hypocrisy: "O, ye nominal Christians! might not an African ask you, learned you this from your God, who says unto you, Do unto all men as you would men should do unto you?" Pointing to an anomalous quality in how this Barbados slave market separates families, he insists, "Surely this is a new refinement in cruelty, which, while it has no advantage to atone for it, thus aggravates distress, and adds fresh horrors even to the wretchedness of slavery" (42). As Ramesh Mallipeddi argues, "A distinctive feature of New World slavery is its willful, unremitting assault on the slave's biological family."[49]

Having been snatched away from his own family just months before, Equiano here alludes to personal trauma. He addresses that trauma overtly in the narrative's prefatory letter, where he condemns the slave trade that tore him "away from all the tender connexions that were naturally dear to [his] heart" (7). He says about his separation from family, "I was quite oppressed and weighed down by grief" (33). For Equiano, according to Wilfred Samuels, "Essaka meant bonding, security, and aggregation," and "slavery meant separation, alienation, and liminality."[50] Equiano was first kidnapped alongside a sister who, a day later, was "torn" from him, leaving him in "a state of distraction not to be described" (33). He "cried and grieved continually" and starved himself for days (33). Several months later, he encounters his sister again on the seacoast. Upon seeing each other, Equiano says, "Neither of us could speak; but, for a considerable time, clung to each other in mutual embraces unable to do any thing but weep" (35). The reunion, however, is short-lived. The next day, they are separated again, permanently, which causes Equiano anguish anew. "I was now more miserable, if possible, than before," he says (36).

As an adult narrator reflecting back on the moment, Equiano writes grimly of the fate he presumes was his sister's lot. He fears that her "youth and delicacy" long ago fell "victim to the violence of the African trader, the pestilential stench of a Guinea ship, the seasoning in the European colonies," and the "lash and lust of a brutal and unrelenting overseer" (36). He does not imagine a narrative of uplift like his own. Black women, as Equiano notes repeatedly, were subjected to particular sexual atrocities, including rape, in addition to other modes of physical and psychological abuse. For a moment he breaks from the narrative to address his sister directly: "Though you were early forced from my arms, your image has been always rivetted in my heart, from which neither time nor fortune have been able to remove it" (36). He prays for his sister's soul "To that Heaven which protects the weak from the strong" (36). Through his sister, Equiano acknowledges implicitly the exceptionalism of his own fate; because he is gendered male, he finds himself in situations that enable him to take advantage of mobility, apprenticeships, and mercantilism, opportunities less likely to have been available to enslaved women. His sister, who is never named in the text, reminds readers of the anomalous quality of Equiano's own outcome even as she represents the familial ruptures wrought by the slave trade.

While describing the emotional trauma of his initial capture, the familial separation, Equiano does not condemn African enslavers. He calls them "sable destroyers of human rights" but then acknowledges "that I never met with any ill treatment, or saw any offered to their slaves, except tying them, when necessary, to keep them from running away" (35). The quasi-apologetic tone contrasts his deep censure of those in the West Indies. "How different was their condition from that of the slaves in the West Indies" he proclaims (26). Apparently, he does not consider the forced separation of families in West African slave systems as especially cruel and inhumane. In fact, he notes the compassion of those enslavers who allow him and his sister to sleep next to each other and draw comfort from each other's proximity. "When these people knew we were brother and sister they indulged us together," he says (35).

For sure, slavery in West Africa could be equally as brutal as its American counterpart. Equiano, though, propagates a myth, embraced by his abolitionist contemporaries and by some modern-day scholars, that African slavery was a gentler, kinder form of captivity, one based on a model of incorporation by which enslaved people over time were absorbed into the kinship networks of their captors. Essentially, they became family. This perspective was made popular in the 1970s by Igor Kopytoff and Suzanne Miers.[51] Over the subsequent decades, the idea that West African slavery was more humane has been contested by a number of historians and anthropologists, among them Frederick Cooper, Paul Lovejoy, Mohammed Bashir Salau, and, most recently, Lisa Lindsay, who argues that "like forms of American slavery, African slavery in various contexts derived its characteristics from constellations of cultural background, state power, and market forces." Lindsay cautions historians and others to "resist the assumption that African slavery . . . was more benign than slavery in the Americas. . . . Fundamentally, the degree to which enslaved people were absorbed or their cultural lives were transformed was about power—the power of slave owners and merchants."[52] As a paradigm of power, then, West African slavery came with its own set of violent, brutal practices that reduced human beings to chattel, to property.

The fact that Equiano mutes the crueler aspects of the African slave trade, creating a distinction between the two kinds of enslavement he experienced, speaks to his narrative design, his effort to isolate the West Indies as uniquely horrendous. Therefore he proclaims that the slave market in

Barbados is a "*new* refinement in cruelty" (43, emphasis mine). The West Indies is distinct for Equiano in that it is populated with "buyers" who engage in the slave trade with "eagerness" and are motivated by "lust of gain" and "avarice" rather than compassion (43).

Throughout the narrative, Equiano describes in vivid detail the horrors inflicted upon enslaved Black Africans in the West Indies. "It was very common," he says, "in several of the islands, particularly in St. Kitt's, for the slaves to be branded with the initial letters of their master's name; and a load of heavy iron hooks hung about their necks" as punishment (79). In chapter 5 of the narrative, he catalogues a series of heinous abuses committed by island enslavers and traders: bodily mutilation, murder, rape of enslaved women and girls. "The small account in which the life of a negro is held in the West Indies," he says, "is so universally known" (81).

He relates the specific story of one Black companion, his "countryman." This man, Equiano explains, "was very industrious, and, by his frugality" managed to save up enough money from hiring out his time to buy a boat that he could rent out to move cargo around the islands. The man endeavors to carve out a space for himself in the West Indies market. His efforts, importantly, do not result in a narrative of uplift even though he, like Equiano, embodies core tenets of respectability as hardworking and thrifty. As property who owns property, he is thwarted by white counterparts, like an island governor who rents the man's boat to transport his sugar cargo. Rather than compensating the man for the use of the boat, this unnamed governor "would not pay the owner a farthing," understanding it to be a "negro-man's boat" (76). Adding insult to injury, the man is unable to find redress with his owner, who becomes enraged upon discovering that his *property* claims to own property. According to Equiano, the Black boat owner "was damned very heartily by his master, who asked him how dared any of his negroes to have a boat" (76). Through examples like this, Equiano points to the inability of Black Africans to assert property ownership. This boat owner enters the public market sphere; however, he cannot participate fully in that sphere—even though he seems to embody virtues of respectability as exhibited through his frugality and industriousness—because his legal status marks him as invisible, or a subperson beyond the protections of a social contract. Equiano makes it clear that this one example is representative of the ways in which slavery in the West Indies denies Black Africans financial self-determinacy. "It is a common practice in the West Indies," he notes, "for men to purchase slaves though they have not plantations themselves, in order to let them out to planters and merchants at so much a piece by day" (75). These enslavers claim sole right to the wages and allot "what allowance they chuse out of this produce of . . . daily work" (75). It is often the case, Equiano argues, that the allowance is scant or nonexistent: "Many times have I even seen these unfortunate wretches beaten for asking for their pay" (75). The observations here matter because they illustrate the extent to which enslaved Black Africans exist outside of the bounds of a social contract, a state of existence resulting not from an inherent depravity—again the boat owner was frugal and hardworking—but from social and legal codes.

The cruelty to which enslaved Black Africans are subjected in the West Indies is so overwhelming, Equiano argues, that it "often drives these miserable wretches to despair, and they run away from their masters at the hazard of their lives" (76). Pointing out the hypocrisy, he says that these acts often are inflicted by *Christian* masters. Slavery, Equiano argues, "violates that first natural right of mankind, equality and independency, and gives one man a dominion over his fellows which God could never intend!" (83).

Equiano points to the West Indies as an extreme example of the corrupting effect of slavery on the humanity of whites and Blacks alike. "Such a tendency has the slave-trade to debauch men's minds, and harden them to every feeling of humanity," he says. "Surely this traffic cannot be good, which spreads like a pestilence, and taints what it touches" (83). Those participating in the slave trade, who otherwise might be "generous" and "tender-hearted," Equiano argues, become "unfeeling, rapacious and cruel" through the practice of slavery. Not only does it corrupt the morality and common sense of white enslavers, but it also denies Black Africans the opportunity to develop into virtuous beings. "When you make men slaves," Equiano insists, "you deprive them of half their virtue, you set them in your own conduct an example of fraud, rapine, and cruelty" (83).

He directly refutes the Enlightenment notion that Black Africans lack a natural ability to reason, which makes them inferior and, therefore, well suited for enslavement. This is an instance where he seeks to undo the designation of Black Africans as subpersons who, in Mills's words, are "deemed cognitively inferior, lacking in the essential rationality that would make them fully human."[53] Their perceived inferiority, Equiano argues, is not a natural state but a product of the cruelties they experience through enslavement. At one point, he directly addresses enslavers, imploring them to adopt more humane practices:

> You stupify [*sic*] them with stripes, and think it necessary to keep them in a state of ignorance; and yet you assert that [Black Africans] are incapable of learning; that their minds are such a barren soil or moor, that culture would be lost on them; and that they come from a climate, where nature, though prodigal of her bounties in a degree unknown to yourselves, has left man alone scant and unfinished, and incapable of enjoying the treasures she has poured out for him!—An assertion at once impious and absurd. Why do you use those instruments of torture? Are they fit to be applied by one rational being to another? And are ye not struck with shame and mortification, to see the partakers of your nature reduced so low? But, above all, are there no dangers attending this mode of treatment? Are you not hourly in dread of an insurrection? . . . But by changing your conduct, and treating your slaves as men, every cause of fear would be banished. They would be faithful, honest, intelligent and vigorous; and peace, prosperity, and happiness, would attend you. (83–84)

There are several points worth noting in this passage. First, Equiano does not push for an end to the practice of slavery; he advocates for its more humane administration. Second, he challenges the rational faculties of enslavers by pointing out the sheer illogic of holding a people in bondage and treating them so cruelly. Third, he relies on respectability rhetoric to appeal to avarice; he points out that by reforming their practices, they create a labor force of enslaved people who would be "faithful, honest, intelligent, and vigorous"; they would embody virtues that could improve the financial outlooks, the "prosperity," for enslavers. As Willie James Jennings articulates it, Equiano knew that "'character' existed for black flesh in the New World as an aspect of use-value, of commodification itself."[54] So he exploits an association between respectability and utility in order to advocate for enslaved Blacks.

Finally, and this is perhaps the most significant point of the passage, Equiano points to the exclusion of Black Africans from the social contract and its deleterious effect, namely the potential for violent uprising. In moments like this, as Yael Ben-Zvi argues, Equiano challenges a "Eurocentric rights discourse that excludes enslaved and colonized subjects despite Enlightenment promises of universal entitlement, and . . . advocates universal human rights."[55] What is more, because slavery denies the natural rights of Black Africans, Equiano suggests that Black Africans are bound to act toward their self-interest, governed by an innate impulse to preserve their lives and freedom. This impulse toward self-preservation is the natural state of individuals, what Thomas Hobbes calls the "Right of Nature."[56] The social contract acts as a mechanism to protect individuals from the violent impulses of others and vice versa. The way slavery is administered in the West Indies, Equiano argues, forces Black Africans to exist in a natural state rather than a civil one. Perhaps channeling Locke, Equiano argues that Black Africans are compelled "to live . . . in a state of war" with enslavers (83).[57] Put another way, the cruelties practiced in the West Indies and the exclusion of Black Africans from the social contract have triggered a survival response in Black Africans, which has stymied their intellectual and moral development and compromises the safety and stability of the region.

THE POTENTIAL OF BLACK RESPECTABILITY

To illustrate for readers the potential for Black African intellectual and moral growth, Equiano upholds himself as a model. In general, he portrays himself as intelligent, industrious, and virtuous. He learns to read and write from multiple sources. His owners teach him about accounting, which enables him to develop his mercantile skills. With money he saves from trading goods, he pays other sailors to teach him sea navigation. In England, he converts to Christianity. In chapter 10, he details the long, emotional process of his spiritual conversion. He says of the moment of his awakening, "It was joy in the Holy ghost! I felt an astonishing change; the burden of sin, the gaping jaws of hell, and the fears of death, that weighed me down before, now lost their horror" (144). Afterward, he proclaims, "I was enabled to praise and glorify his most holy name" (145).

Others attest to Equiano's respectability. When one of his former owners, Captain Doran, sells Equiano to another enslaver, he assures Equiano that he endeavored to find him the "best master he could" because Equiano "was a very deserving boy" (73). The new owner, a Quaker named Robert King, likewise refers to Equiano's good character when explaining that "the reason he had bought [Equiano] was on account of [his] good character; and, as he had not the least doubt of [Equiano's] good behaviour, [he] should be very well off" with King (74). Recognizing the importance of a good reputation, Equiano reflects, "I was very grateful to Captain Doran, and even to my old master [Pascal], for the character they had given me; a character which I afterwards found of infinite service to me" (74). According to Frank Kelleter, Equiano values a good reputation for the economic benefits; it is a means of extracting better treatment and regard from his various owners. "Fully aware of his economic value," Kelleter maintains, Equiano "offers [his owners] competence and dependability to receive in return what he calls a character (and what later generations will simply name reputation): an authorized public persona."[58]

Besides the testimonials, Equiano also produces documents attesting to his character that, in Peter Jaros's words, "reiterate [his] reputation for integrity."[59] After Equiano buys his freedom from King in 1766, King provides him a reference letter, or "certificate of behaviour," that confirms Equiano "always behaved himself well, and discharged his duty with honesty and assiduity" (123). After working for about a year as overseer on a plantation on the Mosquito shore (the east coast of present-day Honduras and Nicaragua) in 1767, Equiano secures a reference letter from the plantation owner, the English physician Charles Irving, that testifies to the fact that Equiano served him "with strict honesty, sobriety, and fidelity. . . . I do hereby certify that he always behaved well, and that he is perfectly trustworthy" (159). Equiano reproduces both reference letters in the narrative, part of what Hinds calls a "trope of documentation" that was "everywhere in eighteenth-century writing, non-fiction and fiction alike, designed to shore up 'factuality.'"[60] The inclusion of these character letters, then, helps to establish Equiano's respectability as a matter of fact.

Respectability, I would argue, even governs Equiano's work on Irving's plantation. Irving seeks out Equiano for the role of overseer because he trusts Equiano "with his estate in preference to any one" (153). Equiano accepts the offer with the idea that "the harvest was fully ripe in those parts." He articulates the job as a missionary venture that would allow him to "be the instrument, under God, of bringing some poor sinner to my well beloved master, Jesus Christ" (153). In this way, Equiano sees enslavement as what

Vincent Carretta has called a "fortunate fall," a term describing the attitude adopted by some early Black Atlantic writers that "the discomfort of the slaves' present life was overcompensated by the chance given them of achieving eternal salvation."[61] Equiano, then, accompanies Irving to Jamaica "to purchase some slaves to carry with us, and cultivate a plantation" (155). Without irony, he says, "I chose them all my own countrymen" (155), displaying what Marion Rust calls an "imperialist economic ethics."[62]

Ross Pudaloff notes an "absence of self-consciousness, much less guilt" in Equiano's role on Irving's plantation.[63] I see the opposite. Equiano is very much conscious of how his actions might be perceived as illustrated in the fact that he differentiates his actions from the brutality and inhumanity of white overseers and enslavers in the West Indies. He carries out his overseer duties in a manner he sees as compassionate and humane. "I had always treated them with care and affection, and did everything I could to comfort the poor creatures, and render their condition easy," he says (160). The way Equiano articulates his actions tells us something about what he imagines might be respectable versus unrespectable forms of enslavement. For Pudaloff, Equiano's approach to slavery is informed by his understanding of commerce and commodification. He argues that Equiano thinks about slavery through its potential for exchange, and the process of exchange as a route to freedom. He notes that Equiano "gains his freedom by purchasing himself and implies that the exchange of money for self can lead to a new and better identity."[64] What is more, according to Pudaloff, this process of exchange has the potential to create "new subject positions by virtue of exchange relationships that produce formal and discursive equality with Europeans."[65] So that "being a commodity was not only the opposite of being human . . ., it could also be a means of becoming human," according to Pudaloff.[66] He insists that Equiano "celebrates commerce and exchange" as predominant models of social relations as they "make the self a product of exchange."[67] In this way, those laboring on Irving's plantation are not merely enslaved. They also are brimming with human potentiality.

Pudaloff's reading is useful for highlighting some of the complexities of Equiano's stance on slavery as a practice. More than anything he points out Equiano's mastery of this particular kind of commercial exchange. Problematic, though, is the idea that Equiano "celebrates" the necessity of having to purchase his own freedom—which should be his as a natural right—or that a formerly enslaved person somehow comes out of that process with a "new and better identity." We should not ascribe too triumphant a meaning to Equiano's willingness to participate in these systems of exchange, which, yes, at times make him complicit in the slave trade. It seems more likely that Equiano accepts it as illustration of the vicissitudes of life, a circumstance to be endured (not celebrated) and negotiated to the best possible ends that one can manage. His participation in European commercial exchange systems or his insistence at the end of his narrative that Europe and West Africa enter into trade agreements, what Fichtelberg calls a "hegemonic solution," does not mean that Equiano "celebrates" this brand of commercialism.[68] The exchange model is a major source of contention for Equiano as he constantly finds his property and person under assault in the marketplace, a point I discuss in the next section of this chapter. Quite often, it is by the intervention of well-meaning whites, and on occasion by threat of violence, that he succeeds in his business transactions.

The representation of Equiano's work on Irving's plantation, then, does not illustrate Equiano's ringing endorsement or celebration of the potentiality of commercial exchange. Nor does it contradict the narrative's larger abolitionist aims. The moment in the narrative helps to sharpen Equiano's slavery critique. I agree with Eileen Razzari Elrod, who notes that the "narrative is not an unequivocal anti-slavery polemic. Rather, Equiano expresses specific opposition to the violence of slave masters."[69] He attacks the execution of slavery. Amplifying this point, Equiano offers a kind of coda for his involvement on the Mosquito Shore plantation. A bit later in the narrative, he recounts the consequences on the plantation of his having left:

> I now learned that after I had left the estate which I managed for this gentleman on the Musquito shore, during which the slaves were well fed and comfortable, a white overseer had supplied my place: this man, through inhumanity and ill-judged avarice, beat and cut the poor slaves most unmercifully; and the consequence was, that every one got into a large Puriogua canoe, and endeavoured to escape; but not knowing where to go, or how to manage the canoe, they were all drowned; in consequence of which the doctor's plantation was left uncultivated, and he was now returning to Jamaica to purchase more slaves and stock it again. (165)

It is yet another instance of white inhumanity, represented by a "white over-seer," who "beat and cut the poor slaves most unmercifully." The inhuman-ity of this overseer contrasts the humanity of Equiano, who left the enslaved Black Africans "well fed and comfortable." They die by drowning while trying to escape the cruelty of their new overseer. Presumably, if Equiano had stayed on, the enslaved Africans would have still been alive. He is, as Fichtelberg points out, "the ironic cause of their destruction."[70] Equiano does not comment on this irony. Instead, he narrates their fate as a matter of fact, the chief difficulty being that Dr. Irving's "plantation was left uncul-tivated," which necessitated a return to "Jamaica to purchase more slaves" in order to replenish the "stock." In this moment, Equiano does not rail against the process of buying humans and coercing them to work for free. Those dead Black Africans that Equiano personally hand-picked and the new Black Africans that Dr. Irving presumably will choose to replace those who died (whether they will suffer under the same cruel white overseer or another, Equiano does not say) are finally reduced to "stock," of which there is a seemingly endless, unproblematic, generic supply.

Equiano seems to acknowledge the objectifying nature of slavery, but he does not condemn it.[71] He condemns instead the actions of that white overseer who in a very short time ran into the ground what he helped Dr. Ir-ving build. The representational binary that Equiano constructs in moments like this, Susan Marren argues, illustrates a racial cross-dressing that makes Equiano's self-presentation especially transgressive. "In eighteenth-century English discourse," Marren argues, "whiteness . . . denotes skin color but comes to signify civilization, Christianity, nobility, justice, industry, intel-lect, truth. While Equiano allows the word white to reverberate in the text on every customary semantic level, he ascribes its concomitant virtues to himself and . . . attributes" to white islanders and enslavers the "savagery and irrationality that Western culture associates with dark-skinned peoples."[72] Marren understands Equiano's racial negation as a process of assimilation in which he embodies a white, English identity, suggesting fluidity in racial categorization. I argue the opposite about that process of negation. By em-bodying the perceived virtues of whiteness, Equiano does not—indeed, he cannot—mute his Blackness; he remains vulnerable to bodily, psychological, and economic violence, as do other Black Africans, like (we are to presume) his sister and his unnamed "countryman" mentioned earlier, who saved up his coins to buy a boat and was cheated and harassed for his efforts. Through Equiano and these other marginal Black figures, we can see the failure of respectability to inoculate Black bodies or to allow a racial cross-dressing.

Rather than a break from Equiano's larger rhetorical project, the scene on Mosquito Shore further elucidates the narrative's racial politics and antislavery stance as it defends Equiano's humanity and, by extension, that of Black Africans in the face of a social contract that has rendered them subhuman. It is in response to the actions of men like that white overseer that Equiano petitions Queen Charlotte in 1788 to have "compassion for millions of my African countrymen, who groan under the lash of tyranny in the West Indies" (175), where the practice of slavery is carried out by white enslavers, men of the "worst character of any denomination of men" (78).

EQUIANO, HIS VIRTUE AND NATURAL RIGHTS

Equiano's description of the West Indies establishes the character of place and provides context for the kinds of encounters to which he is subjected as both an enslaved sailor and a free man traveling among the islands. In challenging the racial exclusivity of the social contract, he offers several examples of his own efforts to assert his natural rights. One of the most striking examples is his refusal to be sold by a naval lieutenant named Henry Pascal, who purchased Equiano from a Virginia planter in 1757, when Equiano was eleven or twelve years old. Equiano serves Pascal for some five years. During that time, he learns to read and write in English; he is baptized in England, and he serves Pascal as a valet and gun powder runner during the Seven Years' War. Equiano describes his time with Pascal in positive terms. "He always treated me with the greatest kindness," Equiano says, "and reposed in me an unbounded confidence; he even paid attention to my morals (68). He also enjoys emotional attachments with his shipmates, including a teen named Richard and an older spiritual mentor named Daniel Queen, whom Equiano "loved with the affection of a son" (68). In his study of sentimentality in Equiano's narrative, Ramesh Mallipeddi argues that an enslaved Equiano models "social relations [aboard ship] upon those of kinship, inventing a sequence of familial figures to counter the social death unleashed by enslavement."[73] Although enslavement under Pascal is bearable for Equiano, he still expects that Pascal one day will free him. "For though my master had not promised it to me, yet besides the assurances I had received that he had no right to detain me," Equiano says, he enjoyed a great deal of "tenderness" from Pascal (68). He understands his enslavement as a choice, a source of agency, and as proof of a familial bond (like that of a father and son) between himself and Pascal. "I had never once supposed," Equiano says, "in all my dreams of freedom, that [Pascal] would think of detaining me any longer than I wished" (68).

Equiano's favorable view of Pascal and of his legal status transforms in December 1762. While sailing down the Thames, near Gravesend in England, Pascal accuses Equiano of plotting to run away from him and resolves to sell him off. When Equiano, who neither confirms nor refutes Pascal's suspicions, hears of Pascal's plans, he says, "I told him I was free, and he could not by law serve me so" (69).[74] James Doran, the ship captain who would become the new enslaver, questions Equiano's refusal to be sold. "I have served [Pascal] many years," Equiano explains, "and he has taken all my wages and prize-money, for I only got one sixpence during the war; besides this I have been baptized; and by the laws of the land no man has a right to sell me" (69).[75] Equiano exhibits a keen cultural (and legal) literacy, gleaned, in part, from overhearing the conversations of "lawyers and others at different times" (69). The problem for Equiano, though, is that he assumes the protection of law that does not extend to him as an enslaved person. Hinds makes the point that Equiano's legal suppositions are right; based on statute law and natural law, Equiano should be free. She notes that Doran even concedes the validity of Equiano's claims by not attacking the veracity of his statements. Instead, he criticizes Equiano's education and linguistic skills by quipping that Equiano "talked too much English" (69). He accuses Equiano of impertinence. Doran finds Equiano's behavior especially offensive because it is, as Willie James Jennings points out, "an attempt to offer a rational argument against slavery," which "was ridiculous from the captain's vantage point. What was also unseemly was English in the mouth of a slave, not to mention a slave speaking to white men as though he was their equal."[76]

In terms of respectability, Doran's criticism is ironic indeed. Language, the way one speaks, has been a cornerstone of the assimilative behaviors that Black communities have employed over the centuries in the effort to appear more respectable.[77] The same is true for the acquisition of knowledge, education. The elements of respectability Equiano apparently displays in the exchange, importantly, do not result in an improved situation for himself.

Instead, his behavior provokes threats of bodily violence from Doran, who declares that Equiano is actually too refined.[78] The outcome of Equiano's protest challenges the maxim that *knowledge is power*. His assimilation—he learns English, he becomes a Christian through baptism, he learns something of English statute (and common) law—is ultimately ineffective. As Hinds notes, "*Effective* law, in this case, is the law of force and the absence of refuge Equiano has in statute law."[79] She maintains that the episode with Doran is important as illustration of Equiano's "juridical understanding of his rights—along with an understanding of his legally unprotected status."[80] I would add that the moment is an equally important illustration of the limitations, and failures, of respectability to inoculate Equiano's Black body against the inhumanity of the slave trade, against racism. Equiano is forced to concede failure. When Doran threatens him to "be quiet or he had a method on board to make" him, Equiano submits. "I was too well convinced of his power over me to doubt what he said," Equiano writes (69). After acquiring Equiano, Doran heads for the West Indies, where he promptly sells Equiano to Robert King in Montserrat.

While in the West Indies, Equiano repeatedly attempts to assert, with mixed results, what he perceives are his rights as a merchant engaged in overseas commerce. As Pudaloff argues, Equiano represents himself as a "rational and civil" member of society through his commercial exchanges.[81] Following the example of his new enslaver King, Equiano trades goods among the islands to earn money. King allows Equiano to purchase his freedom for forty pounds sterling. After four years, in 1766, he had saved up the money. In this way, as Lowe asserts, "Equiano claims his individual productivity out of the barbarism of unwaged slavery, proposing in a Lockean manner to sell the fruits of his 'free labor' to become [Adam] Smith's economic man."[82] The social dynamics of Equiano's commercial exchanges is nowhere better illustrated than in the moment when he presents King the money to redeem himself:

> When I went in I made my obeisance to my master, and with my money in my hand, and many fears in my heart, I prayed him to be as good as his offer to me, when he was pleased to promise me my freedom as soon as I could purchase it. This speech seemed to confound him; he began to recoil; and my heart that instant sunk within me. "What," said he, "give you your freedom? Why, where did you

get the money? Have you got forty pounds sterling?" "Yes, sir," I answered. "How did you get it?" replied he. I told him, very honestly.
The Captain then said he knew I got the money very honestly and
with much industry, and that I was particularly careful. On which
my master replied, I got money much faster than he did; and said
he would not have made me the promise he did if he had thought
I should have got money so soon. "Come, come," said my worthy
Captain, clapping my master on the back, "Come, Robert, (which
was his name) I think you must let him have his freedom; you have
laid your money out very well; you have received good interest for it
all this time, and here is now the principal at last. I know Gustavus
has earned you more than an hundred a year, and he will still save
you money, as he will not leave:—Come, Robert, take the money."
My master then said, he would not be worse than his promise; and,
taking the money, told me to go the Secretary at the Register office,
and get my manumission drawn up. (104–5)

This passage is striking for several reasons. First worth noting is that the
moment begins with Equiano's "obeisance" and "fears." Although his forty
pounds sterling gains him access to the public sphere of the marketplace,
he does not enter that space as King's equal. He also does not enter that
space alone. He takes with him his companion and ally Captain Thomas
Farmer, who serves the dual role of advocating on his behalf and witnessing
the exchange. Noteworthy, too, is the fact that King hesitates to honor his
promise. He is a reluctant partner in this exchange, bound not by the forty
pounds sterling that Equiano has to offer but by the risk of damaging his
good character if he reneges on the promise. More to the point, Equiano is
called on to defend his own character, assuring King that he "got the money
very honestly and with much industry." Money is not enough to compel the
exchange. It also turns on the good reputation of the parties involved, and
it depends upon the mediatory presence of Captain Farmer, who provides
the necessary perspective, both moral and financial, that motivates King to
complete his part of the transaction.

I agree with critical readings of this moment that determine it is an illustration of the "link between the market and a civilized society," in Pudaloff's words.[83] Pudaloff argues that King's promise, as a concept, "authorizes

each party as an active agent and thus a free individual."[84] Kelleter argues that Equiano functions within a civil context whereby he "not only stakes a claim for his liberation but does so by using liberalist tools for their intended purpose: making self-ownership possible."[85] Seemingly, he exists within the bounds of the social contract. Jaros argues that the moment is an essential element in Equiano's effort to transition from a commodity to a liberal subject.[86] Houston Baker, too, notes that Equiano, "having been reduced to property by a commercial deportation, . . . realizes . . . that only the acquisition of property will enable him to alter his designated status *as property.*"[87] This scene, then, according to Baker, marks the "ironic transformation of property by property into humanity."[88] I might point out, though, that Equiano does not actually participate in this exchange as a *free individual,* and although he might deploy *liberalist tools* to buy his freedom, he does not enjoy the status of a liberal subject. Even after King agrees to honor his promise, Equiano defers to him as a subordinate; he genuflects rather than flexes his newly liberated muscles. "I most reverently bowed myself with gratitude," he says, "unable to express my feelings." Then, he says he "left the room, in order to *obey* [his] master's joyful *mandate* of going to the Register Office" (105, emphasis mine). While at the Register Office, Equiano reflects on the exchange and does seem to acknowledge that he has "become [his] own master," declaring himself "completely free" (105). Yet, he finds that he is still bound to King, in whose employ he remains for another year although "the bent of [his] mind was towards London" (106). In what he describes as a "struggle between inclination and duty," duty prevails (107). As Elizabeth Maddock Dillon notes, freedom "operates" in a "range of discursive fields" in Equiano's narrative.[89] That is to say, freedom means a lot of different things for Equiano; it is always relative and situational. Dillon offers the crucial nuance that Equiano in this moment is not a free man but a "free *black* man in the Atlantic world who is therefore never unproblematically guaranteed the right of legal freedom to which whites have access. . . . Being a 'free man' is shorthand for being black and constantly subject to the threat of violence and captivity, particularly while on land in America."[90] Equiano does not enjoy the rights and privileges of a Lockean liberalism.

As his commercial exchanges throughout the narrative illustrate, Equiano finds himself constantly negotiating the boundaries of the social contract and its racist underlay. "Over and over again," as Lowe points out, "*The*

Interesting Narrative exposes the historically specific relationship between racial slavery and capitalism, and yet Equiano's story suggests that he might achieve political freedom through the mastery of that economy."[91] He proves himself an adept sea merchant, but he plies the trade under duress as he frequently is the target of white sailors and enslavers, or "Europeans," who rob him of his goods or in other ways conspire to compromise his livelihood. "I experienced many instances of ill usage, and have seen many injuries done to other negroes in our dealings with Europeans," he writes. "They without cause, have molested and insulted us" (86). They commit these acts largely with impunity. As Jaros notes, "Equiano/Vassa's complaint—being cheated by white customers—is neither signified nor signifiable under the laws of the West Indies or U.S. slave states."[92]

One notable episode involves Equiano and a Black companion endeavoring to sell bags of fruit—oranges and limes—in St. Croix. The two bags belonging to Equiano constitute his "whole stock, which was about twelve bits' worth" (87). As soon as they arrive on the island, two white men steal their bags. In a desperate attempt to retrieve their goods, Equiano and his companion pursue the men, "begging of them" to return the fruit. According to Equiano, "We told them these three bags were all we were worth in the world" (87). They plead in vain; the men refuse to return the bags, promising instead to "flog" Equiano and his partner. "They even took sticks to beat us," Equiano says. When they fail to retrieve their property from the men, Equiano and his partner appeal to the men's commanding officer but "obtained not the least redress: he answered our complaints only by a volley of imprecations against us, and immediately took a horse-whip, in order to chastise us, so that we were obliged to turn out much faster than we came in" (87). In a last desperate attempt to salvage their trading venture, Equiano and his partner go back to the men who stole their bags and "begged and besought them again and again." Finally, a couple of onlookers intervene on their behalf to help them retrieve two of the three bags, those belonging to Equiano. This enables Equiano finally to make a profit on the sale of his portion of the fruit. As an act of mercy, he splits the profit with his companion, who otherwise would have walked away empty-handed. Afterward, to minimize his risk, Equiano mobilizes the authority of his captain, who, he says, "frequently used to take my part, and get me my right, when I have been plundered or used ill by these tender Christian depredators" (88).[93] Because Black Africans are not protected by law, Equiano's economic survival, in part, depends upon the goodwill of his white associates. The survival of his business companion in the scene above is even more precarious as he must rely upon Equiano's compassion.

This unnamed companion is one to whom Equiano refers earlier in the narrative as a "poor creole negro" (82), who bemoans his enslaved state mainly because it undermines all his efforts toward self-possession. According to Equiano, the companion is an industrious man who spends his days working for a master and then employs his scant leisure hours fishing in order to earn a few coins for himself. Like Equiano and the boat owner discussed earlier, this fisherman is subject to the whims of white buyers who sometimes compensate him properly for his fish but often do not. His situation is exacerbated by a capricious master who sometimes intervenes on the man's behalf but who is just as likely to claim the man's fish and profits for his own. In a state of hopelessness, the man muses to Equiano one day: "Sometimes when a white man take away my fish I go to my maser, and he get me my right; and when my maser by strength take away my fishes, what me must do? I can't go to any body to be righted . . . then I must look up to God Mighty in the top for right" (82). Equiano ventriloquizes the man's speech, rendering it in a pidgin English, in precisely the kind of English that has for centuries marked Black Americans as intellectually inferior, inhuman.

At first glance, Equiano's linguistic choice seems to belie respectability. It is not, however, through language that Equiano establishes the Black fisherman as respectable but through the honesty and emotion of the man's musings. This is an "artless tale," Equiano tells us, one without artifice or manipulation, a simple tale of one man's sincere frustration, bemusement, and resignation about his lot in life (82). Equiano ventriloquizes the man's speech, then, as a self-effacing move that hides his mediating presence to shorten the distance between his companion and the reader. This man's struggles rather than Equiano's relative successes are the common fate of Black Africans in the Americas; it is not just enslavement that causes this kind of existence. It's the particular brand of enslavement that is executed in the West Indies.

To emphasize the social and civil invisibility of Black Africans in the West Indies, he points to a law in Barbados that permits a slaveholder to maim or kill an enslaved Black person if the act is done as punishment for running away "or any other crime or misdemeanor" (81). If the injury or death of a Black person is the result of "wantonness, or only of bloody-mindedness, or cruel intention," the perpetrator gets away with paying a simple fine—into the public treasury. "Is not this one of the many acts of the islands which call loudly for redress?" Equiano says. "And do not the assembly which enacted it deserve the appellation of savages and brutes rather than of Christians and men?" Again, Equiano insists that the system of slavery necessarily degrades white perpetrators and Black victims alike, rendering both inhuman. He condemns the laws in the West Indies that conspire to deny Black Africans their natural rights and dehumanize them.

As Equiano learns, they cannot escape that degradation, even once they are free, because they still suffer under a racist regime. Much to his consternation, the state of legal, of civil, invisibility does not change once he becomes a free man. He relates another incident that occurs five years after he purchases his freedom, in 1771, in Grenada in which a white buyer refuses to pay him and several others for purchases made. Equiano and his companions complain to a justice of the peace on the island. "But being Negroes, although free," Equiano says, "we could not get any remedy" (129). Failing a legal solution, Equiano seeks the man out at his home and, along with several other white sailors who also had been swindled by the buyer, threatens the man bodily harm. The show of force works to help Equiano recuperate some part of what was owed him. The course of action emphasizes Equiano's earlier warning to slaveholders that by excluding Black Africans from the social contract, violence is a natural consequence. He laments the pitiable state of free Black Africans, insisting it is a worse condition than being enslaved. "I had thought only slavery dreadful," he reflects, "but the state of a free negro appeared to me now equally so at least, in some respects even worse, for they live in constant alarm for their liberty; and even this is but nominal, for they are universally insulted and plundered without the possibility of redress; for such is the equity of the West Indian laws, that no free negro's evidence will be admitted in their courts of justice" (90). West Indian laws render Black Africans mute. As Kelleter notes, "after having literally 'earned' his freedom, the black self-made man must discover that his legally and financially certified self-ownership does not amount to much in a racist world." As a free man, Kelleter points out, "[Equiano's] situation becomes even more precarious . . . because he is now more exposed to exploitation, being no longer protected white property rights."[94]

Equiano's business ventures are no less vexed in the British mainland colonies, especially Georgia. Initially, he understands the mainland, specifically Savannah and Charleston, as another country and looks forward to escaping the harsh landscape of the West Indies. His travels soon divest him of that misconception about difference. More than a corner of the British American mainland, Georgia is an extension of the West Indies in Equiano's Atlantic context. He trades goods and travels often between Georgia and the islands. He does so at great risk. On several occasions, unscrupulous men attack him or, once he is free, threaten to capture and sell him back into slavery. During his first trip to Savannah, in fact, he is nearly beaten to death by a drunken enslaver and an overseer. Equiano relates the incident, which occurs at the end of the year in 1764:

We soon came to Georgia, where we were to complete our lading; and here worse fate than ever attended me: for one Sunday night, as I was with some negroes in their master's yard in the town of Savannah, it happened that their master, one Doctor Perkins, who was a very severe and cruel man, came in drunk; and, not liking to see any strange negroes in his yard, he and a ruffian of a white man he had in his service beset me in an instant, and both of them struck me with the first weapons they could get hold of. I cried out as long as I could for help and mercy; but, though I gave a good account of myself, and he knew my captain, who lodged hard by him, it was to no purpose. They beat and mangled me in a shameful manner, leaving me near dead. I lost so much blood from the wounds I received, that I lay quite motionless, and was so benumbed that I could not feel any thing for many hours. Early in the morning they took me away to the jail. As I did not return to the ship all night, my captain, not knowing where I was, and being uneasy that I did not then make my appearance, he made inquiry after me; and, having found where I was, immediately came to me. As soon as the good man saw me so cut and mangled, he could not forbear weeping; he soon got me out of jail to his lodgings, and immediately sent for the best doctors in the place, who at first declared it as their opinion that I could not recover. My captain on this went to all the lawyers in the town for their advice, but they told him they could do nothing for me as I was a negro. (96)

Presumably, Equiano includes this moment as yet another illustration of the wanton, arbitrary violence to which Black bodies are susceptible in the West Indies and now Savannah. The moment also illustrates the failure of respectability to shield Black Africans from that violence. Equiano makes it clear that he has done nothing to precipitate the attack—beyond being a "strange negro" in the yard of Dr. Perkins. He provides the doctor "a good account" of himself, a general reference to his character and demeanor that lets the reader know he complied with standard codes of conduct. And because his own character is not enough to recommend him, he depends upon his association with his captain to protect him from the doctor's hostility. Despite his compliance, despite the supplication—he "cried out . . . for help and mercy"—no amount of proper behavior can prevent the beating, from which Equiano spends some four weeks recovering. What is more, he cannot pursue prosecution against his attackers because, as colonial lawyers remind him and his captain, Equiano "was a negro," which is to say invisible before the law.

After so many degrading and brutalizing encounters in the West Indies and in Savannah, in July 1767 Equiano departs the region, intending never to return (although he does multiple times). "I bade adieu to the sound of the cruel whip," he declares, "and all other dreadful instruments of torture! adieu to the offensive sight of the violated chastity of the sable females, which has too often accosted my eyes! adieu to oppressions (although to me less severe than to most of my countrymen!) and adieu to the angry howling dashing surfs!" (124).

Equiano characterizes life for Black Africans in the West Indies as a constant assault on life, liberty, and property. Rooted in an ideology of white supremacy, the violence that he witnesses and experiences illuminates for readers the status of (non-)existence for Black Africans. Denied their natural rights, they are forced to live in a state that cripples their moral, social, and economic development. He points to all the ways that the slave trade and its concomitant racism prove the mythological dimensions of liberalism, at least where Black people are concerned. Success, his narrative argues, is not simply a matter of hard work, determination, and good character—or personal agency. Repeatedly, respectability fails to shield Equiano from a racism that constantly threatens his well-being and that of his Black counterparts. Nevertheless, he relies upon a narrative of respectability, showcasing his own good character, integrity, and industry, to illustrate for white readers the potential for Black African achievement. His life example, then, is the exception that both illuminates the general perception of Black degradation and challenges it. Like Equiano, those Black settlers who immigrate to Sierra Leone at the end of the eighteenth century in order to eke out a better quality of life must navigate the exclusionary effects of the social contract. They test the limits of a rhetoric of respectability deployed to define their sociopolitical experiment on the west coast of Africa, which is the focus of this book's final two chapters.

"MY POOR LITTLE
ILL-THRIVEN
SWARTHY DAUGHTER"

GRANVILLE SHARP

AND THE

RESPECTABILITY OF DEPORTATION

TO PROVINCE OF FREEDOM

OVER THESE NEXT two chapters, I examine respectability through British efforts to establish a settlement in Sierra Leone at the end of the eighteenth century. In the wake of the American Revolutionary War, England experienced an influx of formerly enslaved Black Americans, those who had fought on the side of the British and gained their freedom by doing so. Many of those new immigrants ended up destitute on the streets of London in the 1780s. To relieve their plight—and to rid Britons of a perceived public nuisance—English philanthropists created a settlement on the coast of Sierra Leone in 1787 where the population they termed the "Black Poor" could start over.[1] This back-to-Africa plan extended conversations about resettlement that had been ongoing for decades on both sides of the Atlantic. As early as 1700, Samuel Sewall, in his oft-discussed pamphlet *The Selling of Joseph,* which condemned slavery, argued that Black Africans were an "extravasat blood" and suggested removing them from the American body politic.[2] In 1780 in Newport, Rhode Island, free Blacks formed the Free African Union Society with a back-to-

Africa agenda, which was supported by the Rev. Samuel Hopkins, a prominent Congregationalist minister.[3] A number of British and American Quakers also supported the movement of Black Americans to Africa, including John Fothergill and Anthony Benezet, in his 1771 *Some Historical Account of Guinea.*

In the nineteenth century, emigration movements were even more prevalent with the establishment of a free and independent Haiti in 1805 and the creation of the American Colonization Society in 1816, which formed colonies next door to Sierra Leone that would become the country of Liberia. As the first sovereign, all-Black nation in the Western Hemisphere, Haiti's nascent leadership beckoned to diasporic Black Africans, particularly those living in the United States, to immigrate to Haiti. Sierra Leone, itself, benefited from an influx of some 1,200 Black Africans from Nova Scotia and 550 maroons from Jamaica at the turn of the nineteenth century. In addition, once Britain banned the slave trade in 1807, Black Africans they recovered from confiscated slave ships were resettled in Sierra Leone. The initial experiment in Sierra Leone, while relatively small in terms of the number of settlers, provided crucial context for sociopolitical conversations in the nineteenth century about the feasibility of resettling Black Americans.

Granville Sharp, an abolitionist and early supporter of such movements, named the Sierra Leone settlement Province of Freedom; its inhabitants also referred to it as Granville Town, in honor of Sharp's advocacy. By 1787, Sharp had become one of the most outspoken critics of the transatlantic slave trade. A self-avowed "friend to Blacks," he involved himself in several high-profile legal battles, including the Somersett Case, which resulted in the 1772 ruling that English law did not permit slavery.[4] Sharp and other abolitionists saw the settlement as a corrective to the slave trade. "If Africans," as Michael J. Turner points out, "could be shown to be capable of useful cultivation, social organization and legitimate trade . . . and all in a state of freedom," then Britain would be forced to acknowledge African humanity and cease the slave trade.[5] The resettlement plan also was a religious mission, an effort to spread Christianity into parts of Africa to halt the spread of Islam. Alongside his abolitionist work, Sharp helped to found a number of religious organizations, including the British and Foreign Bible Society and the Protestant Union. He also belonged to the Clapham Sect, a London-based group of evangelical Anglicans who advocated for social and moral reform in England. With backing from the British government and the Committee for the Relief of the Black Poor, Sharp brought to bear on the settlement of Province of Freedom the full weight of his reputation, plus all the financial resources he could muster, including his own savings.[6]

Not purely a philanthropic endeavor, Province of Freedom was mostly a hybridized experiment with moral and commercial aims. Although supporters of the effort more commonly termed it a settlement or province, it functioned much like a colony, a base from which the British Empire could exploit the resources of sub-Saharan Africa. In one regard, it mirrored British colonization efforts in early America in the seventeenth and eighteenth centuries and anticipated the nineteenth-century expansion of the British Empire into West Africa. That is to say, supporters of the plan saw an opportunity to strengthen overseas trade by creating a conduit, in the form of a British-backed settlement, through which they could dominate trade on the coast and gain mercantile access to the African interior.[7] In another regard, the settlement plan promised a radical departure from the precepts of colonization by touting a more altruistic goal of correcting the evils of the transatlantic slave trade by facilitating the return of Black Africans to their ancestral homelands. They also sought to develop a market economy and overseas commerce that was not dependent upon the slave trade. Abolitionists like Sharp, Thomas Clarkson, and William Wilberforce catalogued the region's material resources—camwood, cotton, etc.—to illustrate the commercial possibilities.[8] The settlers also existed in an ambiguous state. They were settler colonists whose ancestors (and themselves) had been colonized.[9] Most of them had never lived in any part of Africa, but their *return* to the continent perhaps was just as much a deportation as it was repatriation. The Sierra Leone resettlement project was further complicated by the proliferation of racist ideologies, given credence through that same Enlightenment movement to which Equiano and Wheatley responded in their respectability efforts discussed in the previous chapters. Detractors questioned whether a settlement peopled by what they deemed quasi-human beings, at best, could be civilized and economically successful. What is more, some supporters of resettlement, among them Black Africans, questioned the true nature of freedom when it was granted and overseen by a British imperial structure. They wondered, as Isaac Land notes, whether freedom was "the mere removal of enslavement" or whether "emancipation require[d] meaningful economic and political self-determination as well as social equality?"[10]

As it turns out, the settlement did fail. In 1789, the leader of a nearby Temne town waged war on Province of Freedom; its residents scattered, some seeking asylum at a neighboring slave factory. Under the auspices of a newly formed trade consortium, the Sierra Leone Company, abolitionists pursued settlement a second time in 1790 and emphasized respectability as key to its success. This emphasis on respectability mirrored conversations that were unfolding in the United States and abroad centered on questions about emancipation and Black virtue, as I have pointed out in my discussions of Wheatley, Equiano, and Adam. Here, then, I am most interested in how those conversations show up in the pamphlets, letters, reports, and slave biographies written in and about Sierra Leone between 1786 and 1800. Those documents illustrate the extent to which respectability rhetoric shaped the colonizing enterprise of Sierra Leone and informed the cultural ambitions of the region's inhabitants.

Ultimately, my goal over the course of this chapter and the next is to show how respectability happens as a kind of cross-pollination whereby Black Africans bring their experiences in the United States and Britain to bear on what happens in Sierra Leone and vice versa. This challenges our understanding of the African diaspora as a unilateral movement away from Africa. We can think about it as a circular movement that fully integrates Africa into the circulation of ideas and cultural production. To make this case, I discuss in this chapter the rhetoric that Sharp and Black settlers propagate about the establishment of Province of Freedom. For his part, Sharp produced a number of letters, reports, pamphlets, and treatises in defense of the settlement idea. The plan's success, he insisted, depended upon the medieval concept of frankpledge, a system of government whereby families were grouped into units of ten and one hundred; they voted for representatives to act on their behalf. With power invested in the people, frankpledge operated by communal policing. Members of the community ensured the conformity and civil behavior of other members. Frankpledge's policing apparatus was an early form of the respectability politics that would more overtly guide the settlement in subsequent iterations.

Sharp's ideas for Province of Freedom existed alongside, indeed were complicated by, the material reality or lived experiences of those Black African settlers tasked with the responsibility of realizing his vision. Mainly through letters exchanged with Sharp, the settlers apprised him of the settlement's progress, petitioned for more resources from Britain, and attempted to secure positions of power for themselves in the newly formed town. They did all this while convincing Sharp of their respectability, a necessary rhetorical move as onlookers—those mostly white slavers living at nearby slave trading forts and ship captains—represented them as the antithesis of respectable. Letters were a primary vehicle through which Black settlers engaged in respectability rhetoric. At stake—their autonomy and dignity. My discussion in this chapter begins with a historical overview of colonization in Sierra Leone. Then I discuss Sharp's understanding of frankpledge and its relationship to respectability. I end with an examination of those letters exchanged between Sharp and Black settlers; the letters reveal the ways in which settlers embodied notions of respectability while engaging Sharp's rhetoric to both advance and impede his vision. Settlers at Sierra Leone more squarely reflect the kind of respectability politics that Higginbotham identifies among Black churchwomen and clubwomen at the turn of the twentieth century. These settlers strive for respect as a strategy to assert themselves and combat racism.

THE HISTORY OF SIERRA LEONE COLONIZATION

The idea of Sierra Leone as a commercially viable region was not new in 1786. The earliest written accounts of English voyages to Guinea (or West Africa), in 1553 and 1554, describe the region as a space peopled by Black exotics and teeming with natural resources and wonders.[11] In 1555, the scientist and travel writer Richard Eden, after declaring that inhabitants in Guinea are a people of "beastly living" who walk around "naked," marvels at the immense displays of wealth.[12] He notes that "many of them and especially their women in maner [adorn themselves] with collars, braslettes, hoopes, and chaynes eyther of golde, copper, or Ivery," each piece weighing more than two pounds.[13] He marvels, too, that even their dogs wear chains and collars of gold. They enjoy an abundance of drink and food; fish is plentiful as are root vegetables, beans "as bygge as chestenuttes," and fresh sources of water.[14] He offers an extended discourse on wheat and bread-making as evidence of the land's "frutefulnesse."[15] "They haue," he writes, "very fayre wheate, the ere whereof is two handfulles in length and as bygge as a great bulrusshe, and almost foure ynches abowt where it is biggest. The steme or strawe, semeth to be almost as bygge as the little finger of a mans hande, or little lesse. The grayness of this wheate are as bygge as owr peason: round also, and verye whyte and sumwhat shynynge lyke perles that have lost theyr colour."[16]

Subsequent accounts of the merchant William Towerson confirmed Eden's descriptions. Towerson undertook three voyages to Guinea between 1555 and 1558. During stops specifically along the Melegueta Coast, which includes present-day Sierra Leone, Towerson describes an abundance of spice, or pepper, available for trading and observes that the landscape is full of "strange trees . . . with great leaues like great dockes, which bee higher then any man is able to reach the top of."[17] Peason, growing right beside the seashore, is "very long." One stalk, he estimates, was "27 paces long," and the soil is so fertile that the pea plant sprouts up right out of the sand along the coast.[18] In addition, Towerson notes that the "trees and all things in this place grow continually greene."[19] Wild game is plentiful, too. The people, Towerson writes, "might gather great store of graines" with minimal effort. However, he concludes, "they give themselves to seeke out nothing" due to their "wilde and idle" disposition.[20] Towerson's observations coincide with those of Europeans traveling to the Americas where they made similar conclusions about Natives. Of course, the rhetoric is imperialistic and self-serving, fueling the drive for conquest and colonization in the Americas and Africa alike.

Towerson's descriptions and those of Eden are crucial here because they remind us that in the English textual imagination, West Africa was a desirable, lucrative market for a century before England began its slave trade in earnest in the mid-seventeenth century. The English even contemplated the possibilities of establishing a physical presence in the region as early as 1560, when sea captain and merchant John Lok planned to establish a fort just east of Sierra Leone.[21] Lok based his plan on news brought back from previous voyages that the king of a rich, large kingdom on the Gold Coast wanted the English to build a fort there to facilitate trade.[22] Lok canceled the venture, though, complaining about the poor quality of ships for the travel, turbulent weather, and rumors of an armed Portuguese fleet waiting to attack the English off the Guinea coast.[23] England established its first permanent fort on the Gold Coast at Kormantin in 1631, southeast of Sierra Leone. In subsequent decades, they built posts all along the west coast. In 1660, some British merchants formed the Company of Royal Adventurers Trading to Africa. Not incidentally, the prized trade commodity was gold, at least initially.

After a few years, they developed a slave trade and expanded their charter in 1672 under a new name, the Royal African Company. This all speaks to the fact that Sierra Leone (with its material resources) was well within the commercial and imperial imagination of Britain by the eighteenth century.[24]

Alongside the material bounty, Europeans saw Sierra Leone—all of sub-Saharan Africa—as a deadly place, particularly for Europeans. In the same text where Eden noted the riches of Guinea in 1553 and 1554, he also noted the high rate at which Englishmen died on the voyages. That first voyage began with 140 men of whom only 40 returned; most of them perished, according to Eden, from the "extreme heate" in West Africa. He describes the hot, humid climate of Guinea as corrosive; it is a "smotherynge heate with close and cloudy ayer and storming wether of suche putryifyinge qualitie that it rotted the cotes of[f] theyr backs."[25] He postulates about the effect of a tropical climate on English bodies, "men that are borne in hotte regions may better abyde coulde, then men that are borne in coulde regions may abyde heate, forasmuch as vehement heate resolveth the radicall moisture of mens bodies, as could constreyneth and preserveth the same."[26] Towerson, too, attributed the heavy losses he experienced on his third expedition to the climate. He returned with "not above thirty sound men," so few he was forced to scuttle a ship in his fleet for want of manpower to navigate it back to England.[27]

Their anxieties reflected an idea dating back to antiquity that the nature of a place dictates the cultural and bodily constitutions of the life forms that reside in it. To some extent, Columbus's voyages through the Caribbean at the end of the fifteenth century challenged climate-based theories of human difference. He noted with some bemusement that the Taino and Arawak he encountered did not have kinky hair and dark skin, as was expected given similarities in climate between the Caribbean and sub-Saharan Africa. Nevertheless, accounts like Eden's and Towerson's seemed to validate climatological determinism, stoking English fears about traveling to the tropics of West Africa. By the eighteenth century, those fears still were ever-present in English discourses about travel and settlement in the region.[28] For that reason, the Committee for the Relief of the Black Poor considered other locations for its resettlement plan, including Nova Scotia and the Bahamas, locations to which some African American Loyalists from the United States were already immigrating.

Sierra Leone benefited from the campaign of advocates like the botanist Henry Smeathman, who produced a pamphlet in 1786 espousing the virtues of a settlement in Sierra Leone. He had spent time there in the 1770s. Smeathman, in fact, not Sharp, was the prominent figure in the early days of the resettlement plan. After his death, Sharp assumed the role as leading advocate, using Smeathman's vision as the basis for his own. In 1771 Smeathman traveled to the Banana Islands, off the southwest coast of Sierra Leone, under the auspices of the Royal Society, to study flora and fauna for four years.[29] While there, he observed the landscape and customs of the people. He also married the daughter of a local king, who later played a key role in the establishment of Province of Freedom. He wrote several texts about his experiences, including a 1786 pamphlet, *Plan of a Settlement to be made near Sierra Leone, on the Grain Coast of Africa*. With the pamphlet, Smeathman advertised a plan for the "happy establishment of Blacks and People of Colour" in a region with "a most pleasant fertile climate" and where land could be had for cheap.[30] To ensure the success of repatriation, settlers would be given three months' worth of bread, beef, spices, and other food, which, according to Smeathman, "is as long a time as will be necessary for their safe establishment."[31] Smeathman promises settlers easy living. "Such are the mildness and fertility of the climate and country," he insists, "that a man possessed of a change of cloathing, a wood axe, a hoe, and pocketknife, may soon place himself in an easy and comfortable situation. . . . [A]nd it is not necessary to turn up the earth more than from the depth of two or three inches, with a slight hoe, in order to cultivate any kind of grain."[32] The climate is so pleasant, he insists, that men won't need to build "compact or durable" houses.[33] Simple huts will suffice "that a company of ten or twelve men may erect . . . for themselves and their families in a few days."[34] Likewise, they would not need to trouble themselves with elaborate dress: "All the cloathing wanted is what decency requires."[35]

Not only can they secure their necessities with little trouble, but also, with some "moderate labour," Smeathman writes, they can enjoy a few comforts or excesses. He catalogues the wildlife. "Such provisions as fowls, hogs, goats, and sheep, are very cheap, being propagated with rapidity unknown" in England and other cold climates. There are also great quantities of fish that "may be caught with the utmost facility; the forests abound with venison, wild fowl, and other game."[36] Those material resources combined

with the "peaceable temper of the natives" leads Smeathman to conclude
that in Sierra Leone, England could build a "safe and permanent establishment of commerce": "The numerous advantages resulting from the quiet
cultivation of the earth, and the exportation of its valuable productions . . .
may be exchanged to great advantage for the manufactures of [England]."[37]
Smeathman anticipates the thinking of abolitionists like Sharp when, in a
letter to a doctor associate in 1783, he writes, "My plan would tend to eman-
cipate and to civilize every year, some thousands of slaves, to dry up one
great source of that diabolical commerce [the slave trade]."[38]

To be sure, Smeathman's observations about Sierra Leone are not ob-
jective, disinterested commentary. He returned from Sierra Leone in debt.
To earn money he proposed to escort Black Africans to Sierra Leone at a
charge of four pounds per person.[39] What is more, his positive assessment of
the land in 1786 reverses an assessment he offered just a year before to the
House of Commons; he claimed then that the region's brutal climate posed
a significant health risk to English colonization.[40] Then, he was speaking on
the unsuitability of the region for the establishment of a penal colony comprised of white Englishmen. This, as Emma Christopher notes, illustrates
the racializing nature of the Sierra Leone project. Smeathman's perspective
was informed by beliefs about the differing constitutions of white and Black
bodies. As Christopher points out, Smeathman presumed that "black men
could survive Africa far more than their white counterparts."[41] He echoes
the thinking of Anthony Benezet, who insists that the climate in West Africa
"agrees well with the Natives; but [is] extreamly unhealthful to the Europeans."[42] Climatic determinism, as Ikuko Asaka argues, was a cornerstone of
Britain's "doctrine of a racially organized empire."[43] Besides the racial presumptions, though, the prospective Black settlers themselves insisted upon
immigrating to Sierra Leone after having been told by a native of the region
that the people there would "receive them joyfully."[44]

In addition to Smeathman, the retired naval officer John Matthews published a pamphlet lending credence to the viability of Sierra Leone settlement, *A Voyage to the River Sierra-Leone, on the Coast of Africa,* published
in 1788. Matthews traveled through Sierra Leone between 1785 and 1787
as a fledgling merchant. In his narrative, he includes maps of the coast and
river ways. He discusses the flora and fauna, though not with Smeathman's
meticulous, scientific eye. He names the myriad natural resources, which

include rice, camwood, sugarcane (like that grown in the West Indies), and indigo, which he writes is the best "in the world, if we may judge from the deep indelible blues the natives give their cloths."[45] He speaks hyperbolically about the land's resources. "No country produces more variety of excellent and beautiful timber," he says, "fit for every purpose."[46] Like Towerson two centuries earlier, Matthews observes that the natives lack the wherewithal to appreciate fully the natural bounty. "The vallies near the sea are inhabited," he writes, "but few or any of the natives reside in the interior part of the mountainous country; which, if properly cleared and cultivated, would in my opinion, be equal in salubrity, and superior in productions, to any of the West India islands."[47] Ultimately, he concludes about Sierra Leone, "Nature appears to have been extremely liberal, and to have poured forth her treasures with an unsparing hand: but in most cases the indolence of the natives prevents their reaping those advantages, of which an industrious nation would possess themselves."[48] Sierra Leone joined a wider transatlantic discourse of discovery whereby European travelers post-1492 characterized American and African spaces in Edenic terms. The imperial potential was boundless.

Beyond identifying the natural resources, Matthews discusses at the end of the narrative the logistics of the slave trade. Determining that the trade is "of essential importance to the naval interests of Great Britain," he outlines the means by which Black African nations in the region enslave each other—mostly through religious wars. Citing the practice of some nations that put to death captives taken in war, Matthews argues that transatlantic slavery offers a better option—saving captives from execution. Furthermore, abolishing transatlantic slavery, he argues, would not end the practice of slavery. "Let us suppose," he writes, "that the slave trade was abolished by every nation in Europe, would it abolish it in Africa, or would it in any measure add to the happiness of the natives of that country? That it would not abolish it in Africa is an incontrovertible truth to those who are at all acquainted with the state of the interior country," as Matthews, himself, is.[49] Unlike Smeathman, then, Matthews sought to foster the slave trade, not stymie it. His text had the added effect, though, of resurrecting images of Sierra Leone as a space ripe for trade in material goods. As I will argue shortly, Sharp and later Thomas Clarkson and the members of the Court of Directors for a newly created Sierra Leone Company cite those very same natural resources to prove that England could enjoy lucrative trade in Sierra

Leone without the slave trade. The idea was that a so-called *legitimate* trade in material goods would supplant the *illegitimate* trade in humans. Early Black Atlantic writers, including Olaudah Equiano, shared this perspective. In his autobiography, Equiano insists that commerce without slavery is "trading upon safe grounds. A commercial intercourse with Africa opens an inexhaustible source of wealth to the manufacturing interests of Great Britain, and to all which the slave trade is an objection."[50] By establishing a successful, free Black settlement in the heart of the slave trade, abolitionists could attack slavery at the root, providing, as Land notes, "redemptive closure" and bringing Black Africans full circle back to Africa.[51]

RHETORIC OF COLONIZATION

Granville Sharp understood the taint of the slave trade as both a religious sin and an economic burden. He and others sought to halt the trade and reshape the moral and spiritual landscape of West Africa. Sierra Leone also was a mediatory tool he employed to regulate a kind of socioeconomic morality in Britain. He imagined the settler experiment as a microcosm for British society. He presents that vision most explicitly in a 1786 treatise titled *A Short Sketch of Temporary Regulations (Until Better Shall Be Proposed) for the Intended Settlement of the Grain Coast of Africa, near Sierra Leona* that details, like Smeathman's pamphlet, the logistics for a Sierra Leone settlement. Importantly, Sharp bases his ideas—initially—on medieval concepts of civil and social order. Specifically, he advocates for the resurrection of frankpledge.[52] In addition, like Smeathman and Matthews, Sharp employs the rhetoric of discovery and plantation to make visible his vision for a landscape defined by more humane methods of social interaction and commerce. In this next section, I discuss the importance of medieval culture in Sharp's efforts to construct a respectable settlement on the coast of West Africa that would be by extension applicable in all corners of Great Britain's empire.

Because Smeathman died shortly after publishing his colonization pamphlet in early 1786, Sharp picked up the mantle and published his own *A Short Sketch* in July of that same year. Sharp's plans, more idealistic than practical, far exceeded those of Smeathman, illustrated, for example, in his insistence that a system of frankpledge was the most appropriate form of governance for the colony; it provided, to Sharp's mind, "the greatest security" against crime and vice.[53] Frankpledge worked by bonding men of a tithing unit together so that the behavior of one man in the unit reflected upon the behavior of all men in that unit; women and children were excluded. If one man committed a crime, for example, the tithing unit, led by the unit's elected tithingman, ensured the suspect stood trial and, if necessary, faced punishment. Otherwise, the consequences fell on the entire unit.

Meticulously, Sharp explicates the mechanics of dividing the would-be settlers into tithing units and hundreds, led by a hundreder, and outlines the process for electing representatives to act on behalf of those units, but he adds one slight modification. He divides the settlers into dozens rather than tens to accommodate an organizational structure with which the settlers were already familiar.[54] As an extension of his medieval ideas, Sharp mandates Saturday for leisure time and "folkmotes," or medieval-style courts. In addition, he imagines that every man in the settlement at least sixteen years old will comprise a thirteenth-century-style "watch and ward," system to maintain peace and guard the community. He allows for the creation of poorhouses, a hospital, a militia, and a prison to be managed and funded in common. It is no accident that Sharp begins his eighty-eight-page treatise and ends it with discussions of frankpledge. The governance style came into popular use with the eleventh-century Norman invasion of England, emerging out of systems of accountability that linked members of a family together in relationships of surety. Prior to frankpledge, members of families or clans, whether they wanted to or not, were responsible for controlling the criminal impulses of individual members. An important distinction with frankpledge was that it bonded people not through blood ties but through voluntary will and necessitated the civil exercise of voting for representation. Frankpledge remained a dominant system for two centuries and resonated in some minor aspects in English culture through the nineteenth century.[55] Much to Sharp's chagrin, by the end of the eighteenth century, frankpledge had fallen out of favor, replaced, Sharp notes, by "a much less eligible plan, formed on the model of the arbitrary system of government in France, commonly called *police.*"[56]

Sharp's support of medieval-style civil systems matters for two reasons. First, it indicates for us what Sharp sees as key to establishing a successful, respectable community—a stable system of law and order that derives its efficacy from communal policing. Frankpledge places responsibility for civil order in the hands of members of the community. Put another way, all those Black bodies that people Province of Freedom will surveil other Black bodies. At the end of the essay, he insists that frankpledge is the best way to foster morality and peace in a community because its self-policing powers are "extended to the *minutest immoralities,* and *negligences,* in order to render the peace and regularity of society as perfect as possible."[57] The second reason these medieval ideals matter is that they allow Sharp to critique the English status quo so that Sierra Leone becomes a conduit through which Sharp suggests reform in England—beyond the abolition of the slave trade.

In a Jeremiad-like lament, Sharp notes at the very beginning of his essay that the concept of frankpledge "is now unhappily neglected, and consequently crimes abound and increase; so that notwithstanding the horrible increase also of bloody laws to intimidate offenders, yet there is no effectual security from violence and robbery, either in our streets or roads, or even in our chambers."[58] The effective implementation of frankpledge in Sierra Leone, then, would be a reminder to English onlookers of the system's efficacy. It was, to be sure, part of a much larger sociopolitical strategy for Sharp. His advocacy for frankpledge was a reaction to what he saw as the growing disfranchisement of commoners in eighteenth-century England as Parliament increasingly was being controlled by the will of a few powerful towns as representatives to Parliament were apportioned according to land size rather than population numbers. Under frankpledge, representation was based on population, which meant that each man's vote counted equally. "The Kingdom," he argues, "has lost the means of expressing the sense of the people in parliament, and the king has been deluded by majorities of alternate factions; factions, which, falsely calling themselves the commons of England, have plunged the nation into desperate measures and enormous expences."[59] Frankpledge, then, according to Sharp, was "the shortest and most easy mode of restoring to all the householders of this realm their ancient right of voting," that is to say, one person, one vote.[60]

His written works—both manuscripts and published texts—repeatedly expound upon the virtues of frankpledge. For example, in a 1789 letter to the French revolutionary and abolitionist Jacques-Pierre Brissot de Warville, Sharp urges France to adopt frankpledge, insisting that "Frankpledge alone can invest the great Body of the masters or Heads of Families throughout the Nation with so compleat a share both of civil and military power, as to render them superior to any unjust force that can ever be opposed to them."[61]

Likewise, in a letter to a skeptic companion in 1788, Sharp assures the companion that Sierra Leone colonization would work so long as frankpledge is the "basis of all the Regulations proposed for the new Settlement; being thoroughly persuaded that every Place must, of course, be a free Settlement, whenever Frank Pledge . . . is maintained; and that colonies, or even Kingdoms and Monarchies may be rendered perfectly free and happy by this glorious Patriarchal System of Frankpledge."[62] As a more extended discussion, he publishes a treatise on the history, implementation, and benefits of frankpledge in 1784, with a second edition in 1786, which he titles *An Account of the Constitutional English Polity of Congregational Courts.* In that text, he links the system not only to England's Anglo-Norman past, a time period when the system was so effective that Sharp hyperbolically claims it "immediately" eradicated "all robbery and violence," but he also links it to biblical, Hebrew law by pointing out that Moses divided the Israelites into tithes and hundreds.[63] Believing frankpledge "an institution thoroughly consistent with the most perfect state of Liberty that Human Nature is capable of enjoying," he advocates for its implementation throughout the British Empire.[64] In the appendices to his *Congregational Courts,* Sharp argues that Britain's holdings in the Americas and East Indies would be especially well suited to the system.[65]

Also in the appendix to that treatise, he includes a memorandum he wrote in 1784 in response to an African settlement plan; this was two years before Smeathman published his *Plan for Settlement.* It could be the case that Sharp was responding to a manuscript version of Smeathman's text.[66] In his memorandum, Sharp argues for the efficacy of frankpledge in Africa on the grounds that its policing powers would curb any reprobate, degenerate tendencies in the individual. "Wherein every individual," he argues, "however violent or morose in himself, is prevented from injuring others, by having his person and his property rendered answerable for all damages, which he either occasions by his own rapacious violence or caprice, or which he does not endeavor to prevent in others, as a member of the tithing wherein any violence or offence is committed."[67] Frankpledge derives its efficacy not from the strength of character of individuals but from the policing apparatus of the collective.

To the minds of many of his contemporaries, Sharp proposed the impossible, a settlement off the coast of West Africa that did not depend upon the slave trade for its viability. It would be a space where men were all equal and had an equal stake in the settlement's success, bonded together by the ancient notions of frankpledge that guaranteed the respectability of the settlement's inhabitants through communal policing. Like Wheatley and Equiano, Sharp writes and advocates on behalf of Black Africans amid Enlightenment-inspired racial discourses that proclaimed Black Africans lacked the rational faculties to exercise liberty and participate in civil government. Sharp, too, relies on the energy of the Enlightenment to claim the reverse about Black African humanity. In general, beliefs about the natural rights of man and natural laws form the basis of his attack on the slave trade and slavery and provide proof for the feasibility of establishing a Black utopia in West Africa. He argues in *A Short Sketch* that the inhabitants of Province of Freedom would "gradually improve that natural faculty of reason or knowledge which is inherited by all men from our first parents and may have their understandings exercised by habit to discern both good and evil."[68] This is why he insists that "as soon as a slave shall set his foot within the bounds of the new settlement, he shall be deemed a free man, and be equally entitled with the rest of the inhabitants to the protection of the laws, and to all the natural rights of humanity."[69] Sharp's understanding of frankpledge, as John Peterson notes, was more "the product of the fertile enlightened imagination of its eighteenth-century author rather than anything from the ages past."[70] Sharp publishes two editions of his *A Short Sketch* in the same year; he comes to see very quickly the vast gulf that exists between the idea of a thing and its execution.

THE EXPERIMENT: IN WORDS AND DEEDS

Literary imagination, political rhetoric, and material reality all collided in 1787. At the outset, the settlement plan looked hopeful. Some seven hundred people signed on for the journey. Lending credibility to the plan, in November 1786 Equiano agreed to serve as a commissary for the expedition, in charge of managing provisions. He held Sharp in high regard as evident by a letter dated December 15, 1787, that was addressed to Sharp and signed by twelve Black Londoners, including Equiano (signed as Gustavus Vassa) and Ottobah Cugoano. In the letter, the men affirm their esteem and gratitude for Sharp's efforts on behalf of enslaved Blacks: "And we must say, that we, who are a part, or descendants, of the much-wronged people of Africa, are peculiarly and greatly indebted to you, for the many good and friendly services that you have done towards us, and which are now even out of our power to enumerate."[71] Not incidentally, in March 1783 Equiano first sought out Sharp to intervene in the aftermath of the *Zong* massacre.[72]

Despite Equiano's respect for Sharp, he soured quickly on the settlement plan. He accused the expedition's leaders, Joseph Irwin, who was the man appointed to succeed Smeathman, and Patrick Frazer, a Presbyterian pastor appointed as the settlement's chaplain, of mismanaging the funds for the expedition and poorly providing for the care of the Black African settlers. He writes that the accommodations for the settlers "were most wretched; many of them wanted beds, and many more cloathing and other necessaries."[73] Months into his post, Equiano was fired. In his autobiography, he writes of his "dismission" that he was forced out because of his efforts to hold the expedition's administrators accountable. Sharp suggests that Equiano was fired because he fomented racial tensions that threatened to undermine the settlement's success. In a letter to his brother John, Sharp writes that once "Mr. Vasa and two or three other discontented persons had been left on shore" back in England, "[the settlers Black and white] had been very orderly."[74]

Whatever the reasons for Equiano's dismissal, he was not alone in voicing his concerns. Some Black Londoners worried that the resettlement plan was a trick to reenslave them. Sharp recounts in a letter to his brother in January 1788 that, prior to departure in 1786, "many [Black settlers] came to consult me about the proposal: sometimes they came in large bodies together" seeking reassurance.[75] It did not help to assuage their suspicions any that the ships designated to transport them to Sierra Leone docked in Portsmouth alongside ships destined for Botany Bay, a penal colony in Australia.[76] Add to this that slave factories operated in the same area of the proposed settlement, making prospective Black settlers particularly vulnerable to kidnapping. In his criticism of the relocation scheme, Cugoano questions, "Can it be readily conceived that government would establish a free colony for them nearly on the spot, while it supports its forts and garrisons, to ensnare, merchandize, and to carry others into captivity and slavery?"[77] Like Equiano, Cugoano supported the idea of resettlement but also possessed a strong measure of cynicism about its execution.

Of the seven hundred Black Africans who initially signed on for the expedition, about four hundred actually boarded the ships over the course of three months beginning just before Christmas in 1786. While the settlers waited to depart, many fell sick and died, which Sharp attributed to intemperance, ship overcrowding, and a poor "diet of salt provisions."[78] Equiano blamed the deaths on "sickness, brought on by want of medicine, cloaths, bedding, &c," proof of mismanagement.[79] In the end, three ships, the *Atlantic, Belisarius,* and *Vernon,* set sail on April 8, 1787, carrying 411 passengers, a number that included up to 70 whites, most of whom were described alternatively in records as wives of Black settlers, prostitutes, or "women of the lowest sort, in ill health."[80] The naval sloop *Nautilus,* under the command of Captain Thomas Thompson, escorted the ships. The settlers arrived at Sierra Leone on May 9, many still sick. Once there, organizers brokered a land treaty with a Temne headman named King Tom to secure twenty square miles of land on the peninsula.[81] Because the expedition left later than planned, they arrived at the start of the rainy season. The wet conditions exacerbated their already weakened physical states.[82] Within four months of their arrival, the settlers had been reduced by more than one-third: 50 died in Plymouth, before departing; 34 died during the passage; and 86 died in Sierra Leone shortly after arrival.[83]

One of the Black settlers, Abram (also spelled Abraham) Elliot Griffith, summed up the pitiable state of the colony in those first months.[84] "It is quite a plague seems to reign here among us," he writes to Sharp in July 1787 (two months after arrival). He complains about the quality of the soil and the situation of the settlement atop a hill. "We are settled upon the very worst part" of it, he insists. "There is not a thing, which is put into the ground, will grow more than a foot out of it." He goes on to despair about civil and social chaos in the colony: "Neither can the people be brought to any rule or regulation, they are so very obstinate in their tempers. It was really a very great pity ever we came to the country, after the death of Mr. Smeathman." He offers the grim prediction that "this country does not agree with us at all; and, without a very sudden change, I do not think there will be one of us left at the end of a twelvemonth." He concludes his letter by plotting a course of action that must have troubled Sharp greatly. "At the first opportunity," Griffith tells Sharp, he will abandon the settlement and "embark for the West Indies."[85] Perhaps initially seduced by the enticing rhetoric of Smeathman, Matthews, and Sharp, Griffith processed a measure of cognitive dissonance, exacerbated by the high number of deaths upon his arrival in the settlement.

This could explain his hyperbolic and rash declarations about the soil's barrenness. He formed these conclusions after only two months. Interestingly, Griffith did not look to return to England, which surely would have been safer for a free Black African but rather anticipated traveling to a region that had already proved it could make men rich but also could enslave them.

Despite Griffith's grim prognosis, after four months in Sierra Leone, the situation showed signs of improvement. For starters, fewer people died over the next two years, four or five in total. Griffith did not leave.[86] He and others began the hard work of cultivating the land and building a community around the medieval principle of frankpledge. They organized into tithing units and elected a hundreder to serve as chief magistrate or governor, Richard Weaver.[87] In terms of the communal policing inherent in frankpledge, the settlers pursued this course, at least in one case, with great zeal but to mixed results. Soon after becoming governor, Weaver fell sick. In his stead, James Reid assumed the post. During Reid's brief stint, someone robbed the community storehouse and stole sixty weapons along with other supplies. According to Weaver, the thief "made away with the chiefest part of the stores."[88] Because Reid, Weaver notes, "could give no account" of the stolen goods "but took the opportunity of running away by night," Weaver and others accused him of stealing and then selling the supplies.[89] In the form of restitution, they seized Reid's home and "all what little [he] had in the world and sold it, to pay for those things that was lost."[90] Both Weaver and Reid wrote letters to Sharp telling their sides of the story. A close reading of their letters reveals the extent to which the two men embraced but also challenged the policing tenet of frankpledge. Their letters and the indications of administrative strife contrast Sharp's utopic vision.

Weaver writes the following from Sierra Leone, dated April 23, 1788:

Honoured Sir,

I now inform you of our proceedings during the time of our arrival at Sierra Leone, which was on the 9th day of May 1787: and on the 14th day the land was paid for; and next day all the people went on shore to cut a passage to get on the hill, to display the English colours. Then the body of people called a meeting, on purpose to choose their officers, whereby they choosed me to be their chief in command.

During the time that I was in station, every thing was carried on quite regularly, until please God afflicted me with sickness, which was about three months and three weeks: then one John [*sic*] Reid was chosed in my stead, who made away with the chiefest part of the stores, and sold them; and even the body of the people missed the things, and called him to account for the same, when he could give no account of them at all, but took the opportunity of running away by night, and has been away ever since.

And now I acquaint you of the state of our people, and situation we are in. Several of the people have left the place, I may safely say the chief part of them; some a trading in vessels for slaves [*sic*]; other at factories, doing what they can to get provision for their support, for we are very much in distress here: and King Tom has taken upon himself to sell two of the people, and he says that he will sell more of them, whereby I think within my own breast that Government did not take the pains to send us here to be made slaves of. And, Sir, I now acquaint you that we came too late to plant any rice, or any thing else, for the heavy rains washes all out of the ground; and we must stay till next month, to plant a little rice. And, Sir, I inform you that I was the person that went on board the Vernon at first, with my wife and child, and there continued till we arrived at Sierra Leone.

Sir, I am your humble and obedient servant,

Richard Weaver[91]

Weaver opens the letter by explaining how the settlers very prudently handle business. They purchased land, and in a rite of possession, they planted an *English* flag atop a hill. If Weaver believed this an odd act given that Sierra Leone was to be an independent and free settlement, as Sharp had insisted on numerous occasions, he does not note it in the letter. Then, as a "body," which connotes political structure and social cohesion, they set about the business of establishing the community's leadership structure. Weaver emphasized his own competency by noting that while he was in charge, "every thing was carried on quite regularly." Presumably, affairs would have continued in that fashion if not for the Divine intervention that struck him ill and brought Reid to power. Weaver, it seems, uses the opening lines of his letter to reaffirm the settlers' commitment to Sharp's vision and to Britain. Perhaps the forming of the town under "English colours" was a reminder of the imperial kinship between Province of Freedom and Britain. That reminder morphs into a critique in the second half of the letter when Weaver points out the material deficits with which the settlers struggle. The writing turns a bit defensive, too, when Weaver explains why some settlers chose to abandon the colony, seeking whatever opportunities they can "to get provision for their support, for we are very much in distress here." Part of their distress is due to the kidnappings enacted by King Tom, an event that must have seemed like a nightmare made reality. It reflected the very same fears of those hundreds of Black Londoners who backed out of the trip (and those who went), afraid that it would lead to their reenslavement. So, when Weaver declares, "I think within my own breast that Government did not take the pains to send us here to be made slaves of," his words likely inflect anxiety regarding the intentions of metropole administrators.

Within the context of Weaver's conflict with Reid, his letter is intriguing for what it does not say. He provides scant detail about Reid's presumed crimes. In fact, he narrates the crimes in a sentence fragment, a dependent clause that identifies the man who succeeds him as governor. Here, the writing turns curt, and the narrative pace quickens, which suggests that Weaver consciously chose not to inform Sharp of the particulars. Perhaps he perceived them as minute or simply within the purview of his position as chief. Perhaps, though not likely, he believed the business with Reid a minor affair; after all, they had punished the perpetrator, averted crisis, and restored order—if it was ever threatened. Instead, he fills the white space of the page apprising Sharp of more pressing matters, like the kidnapped settlers and their efforts to sustain themselves in a new settlement where they were struggling to produce even a staple crop like rice. Also notable, Weaver's letter lacks intimacy or familiarity. He reminds Sharp of who he is at the end of the letter, suggesting his own obscurity. The fact that Sharp presumably did not know him emphasizes the degree of separation between Sharp (and other British personnel) and the power structure in Province of Freedom.

In September 1788, five months after Weaver wrote his letter, Reid sent his own letter to Sharp, one twice as long and more detailed. It reads:

Dear Friend,

We did not find our arrival at our new settlement according to our wishes; for we arrived in the rainy season and very sickly, so that our people died very fast, on account of our lying exposed to the weather, and no houses, only what tents we could make, and that was little or no help to us, for the rain was so heavy it beat the tents down. But now, thank God, we have got houses, such as the country will afford, which does middling well; and we that are in being [*sic*] try every experiment in regard of proving the land, to be sensible what it will produce, and find the more we cultivate the better the land seems to turn out, in regard of the country roots and herbs. But our English seeds do not thrive; none that we brought out with us, as we have tried them; but that is owing to the seeds being too old.

There is one thing that would be very helpful to us: if we had an agent or two out here with us, to carry on some sort of business in regard of trade, so that we could rely a little sometimes on them for a small assistance, until our crops were fit to dispose of, and then pay them. It would be of infinite service to all the poor settlers, as provisions are scarce to be got—no, not one mouthful sometimes—which obliges us to dispose of all our clothes, and other few necessaries that we have; though, God knows, they are not much, for we are almost naked of every thing.

I must now inform you of my misfortune that happened after Captain Thompson's departure from us, as I was left chief in command. Our people was served out muskets, every man as he was able to carry arms, and there was remaining about eighty-nine spare ones: them I had secured in our store-house as well as I could, though it was very poorly secured, so that I proposed having them brought up to my own house for better security; and when I came to muster the people to do this, I could get not one person to assist, neither would they, except one or two that lived in my house. Was obliged to do it; and, on examining the muskets, found there was only thirty-six remaining. There was sixty-three muskets stolen by our people, by whom I knew not. After that, Mr. Weaver and Mr. Johnson held with the people, and told them that I had made away with them myself, and got them under arms against me; and they rised on me, and seized my house, and took it from me, all what little I had in the world, and sold it, to pay for those things that was lost, all which I suppose you have heard of before this time. But when you receive this, you will be a better judge, and I hope you will take it into consideration.

After they broke me, they thought to have God's blessing, as they said. The first thing was a young lad found shot, lying in the woods, but never found who was the person that did it. The second was, they got in a little trouble with King Tom, and he catched two of them, and sold them on board a Frenchman bound for the West Indies. The third was, five of them went up to Bance Island, and broke open a factory belonging to one Captain Boys, and stole a number of things; but they were detected, and Captain Boys sold the whole five of them, etc. etc. . . .

I remain etc.

James Reid[92]

Reid apparently was more familiar with Sharp than was Weaver, as he addresses Sharp as "Dear Friend." Like Weaver, Reid begins his letter with an overview of the state of affairs, but his assessment is more optimistic. Although they struggled initially, by September, they were building homes and cultivating the land, finding that the harder they worked, "the better the land seems to turn out." He suggests here that whatever the people had—or did not have—was owing to their own work ethic. Reid represents the settlers as diligent, which is a crucial rhetorical point because it makes less presumptuous his request in the next paragraph for trading agents to work with the settlers rather than for them, so that "they could rely a little sometimes on [the agents] for a small assistance, until our crops were fit to dispose of." He presents a solution to the problem Weaver cites in his letter about the lack of resources that drove some settlers to abandon the town or commit crimes to get food and supplies. Reid exhibits a certain measure of confidence by presenting his idea to Sharp; he presents himself as one who has assessed the settlement's problems and has arrived at solutions that are reasonable and credible. He expected Sharp to take seriously his ideas and marshal the financial resources that were always in short supply.

Reid expected a similar level of consideration from Sharp in the second half of the letter when he endeavors to vindicate himself against Weaver's charges. We can make a couple of observations about Reid's rhetorical maneuvers. First, by virtue of turning to Sharp, Reid undermines—or attempts to—the communal-policing apparatus of frankpledge. He moves outside the governing structure to seek the arbitration of one who "will be a better judge." Second, he implies that the criminal behavior occurring in the colony was a kind of comeuppance, God enacting his wrath on the settlement in retribution for Reid's unfair treatment. Instead of "God's blessing," the town was vexed by the unsolved murder of a young boy and the sale of seven settlers into slavery. The town appeared on the verge of anarchy, hence Reid's appeal to Sharp. For his part, Sharp did not intervene. He understood his relationship to the colony as an advisory and supportive one, not dictatorial. Affirming the autonomy of the settlers, Sharp writes that "the Government of England permits the settlers to make their own laws (i.e., such as are not inconsistent with the Common Law of England), to hold their own courts, assemblies, folk-motes, etc. to choose their own chiefs and officers, and to keep up a free militia amongst themselves,—the settlement, on such conditions, must of necessity be perfectly free."[93]

Both Weaver's and Reid's letters reflect the same kinds of administrative concerns that characterize the early days of English colonies in seventeenth-century British America—erecting homes and civil and social structures like churches and schools, managing relations with neighboring indigenous communities, and finding ways to sustain themselves physically. There actually was some validity in Griffith's observations about the soil quality. Of all the things Weaver and Reid wrote in their letters, Sharp was most vexed by the news of settlers leaving the colony. An affront to his political vision, moral sensibility, and investment of time and money, he repeatedly vented his frustration in letters to his brothers, associates, and the settlers themselves. Writing to the colonists in September 1788, he notes with bemusement, "I could not have conceived that men who were well aware of the wickedness of slave-dealing and had themselves been sufferers (or at least many of them) under the galling yoke of bondage to slave-holders, some in the West Indies and others in America, should become so basely depraved as to yield themselves instruments to promote and extend the same detestable oppression over their brethren."[94] He urged the settlers to mete out strict punishments for any wayward settlers who sought readmission to the colony.

It is important to note here that, beyond updating Sharp, Weaver's and Reid's letters perform other rhetorical work. They engage with the numerous reports, mainly from ship captains and slave traders, that characterize the settlers at Province of Freedom as roguish and unruly. The fact that onlookers questioned and denigrated the character of the settlers was not unique. Their counterparts in British America also faced criticism from the metropole and from other colonies. The best example of this for the present context is perhaps Barbados, the Caribbean colony most often compared to Sierra Leone in terms of commercial viability and the slave trade. In the seventeenth century especially, Barbados acquired a reputation for immorality and lawlessness, due in large part to the rise of profitable sugar plantations on the island that made Barbados the richest of the British colonies. Visitors to the island determined that its white, planter inhabitants were awash with money and material comforts (including rum) to the detriment of moral and cultural concerns.[95] My point here is about the *type* of criticism directed at Province of Freedom. That criticism assumed a particularly racist hue. For example, Captain Thompson, after escorting the settlers to Sierra Leone, writes that the settlers are plagued by a "licentious spirit." They are lazy and stubborn, "which neither remonstrance, persuasion, or punishment have yet been able to subdue."[96] The Swedish author and advocate for African colonization C. B. Wadström writes about the first settlers in 1787, "Instead of that harmonious exertion which their critical situation demanded, laziness, turbulence and licentiousness of every kind so entirely pervaded this wretched crew, that scarcely a man of them could be prevailed on to work steadily, in building the hut that was to shelter him, or even to assist in landing the provisions by which he was to be supported."[97] In his litany of complaints, Griffith, too, determines that "neither can the people be brought to any rule or regulation, they are so very obstinate in their tempers."[98] Yet another observer blames the settlement's collapse in 1789 on the settlers' own impertinence, summarizing the failed two-year experiment thusly:

> The new colonists soon became extremely wretched; for instead of improving the advantages which the British government had pos-

sessed them of, and turning their thoughts towards agriculture and other useful arts, they sold the tools, stores, provisions, and even muskets that had been provided for them; nor were they ever, during their residence at this settlement, at the pains to raise a sufficient quantity of rice to subsist them for three months. In place of industry, their whole time and study was employed in purloining from one another, and holding Court for settling disputes.[99]

This assessment corresponds with many of the details in Weaver's and Reid's letters—the fact that the settlers traded goods intended to aid in farming, planted very little rice, and stole from each other. The observer notes, too, rather sardonically, the settlers' efforts to achieve order out of the chaos with a court system, an effort that, for the observer, produces the opposite outcome. Weaver and Reid both conceded to a certain measure of lawlessness and idleness in the town. It cannot be a coincidence, however, that many of the adjectives used to describe the settlers mirror the racialized descriptions of Black Africans well known in Renaissance England, particularly the emphasis on theft and laziness, stereotypes that still prevail today.[100] Observers predisposed to believe those racialized stereotypes brought that perspective to bear on their assessment of the settlers' behavior. As Wadström concedes, Black Africans "have continually suffered by misrepresentation. While our moral and philosophical writers have sacrificed them to system, and our travellers to prejudice, our merchants and planters, regarding them as mere beasts of burden, have devoted them to their avarice and cruelty."[101] Note that the observer in the passage above does not endeavor to explain why the settlers did not plant rice or why they stole. The passage works as cognitive shorthand for the presumed deficiencies of Black Africans. Weaver and Reid write against that perspective. They do so not by contradicting the accounts of white onlookers but by assigning a cause to the behavior, humanizing the settlers. The perceived absence of respectability among the settlers, then, does not illustrate an inherent barbarity or inhumanity but their struggle to survive.

A letter addressed to Sharp and sent on behalf of the settlers, dated September 3, 1788, articulates more explicitly what we can only infer about Weaver's and Reid's rhetorical aims. They begin the letter by challenging certain presumptions of ingratitude, incompetence, and indolence, asking Sharp not to "impute any of our former failings (if they are to be traced as

such) to the want of industry, gratitude, or a knowledge of our superior duties toward our good Christian friends." The "failings" to which the letter
refers are those issues that detractors already cited: slow progress in cultivating farmland, building homes, securing proper water sources, and so forth.
In each instance, the settlers explain (or excuse away) the slow progress. For
example, they have been hindered in their efforts to build up their water lots
"through our weakness in number of people."[102] This also complicates their
efforts to plant crops. They have been slow to build homes because they lack
the cement (comprised of limestone and oyster shells) for the construction.
Yet, they assure Sharp, "we are determined to follow your plans in building,
as soon as the weather will permit us, especially the three principal houses—
viz. church, court-house, and prison."[103] They prioritize structures—or at
least tell Sharp they do—that foster spiritual, intellectual, and civil policing.
In directly addressing the "aspersions" traveling into England about the settlement from observers like Captain Thompson, they tell Sharp that they are
"conscious of the many injuries done" to their reputation as a result of the
negative reports, and they give "Satan his due" as "he exerted himself more
than what we might have expected."[104] They accuse British agents on the
ground in Sierra Leone of trying to sabotage their settlement. Province of
Freedom is plagued by "enemies . . . such as those which have been choked
with bribes, so as to fall under a sacrifice of their own wretched avarice."[105]
It is not the Black settlers, then, who lack good character. Rather, the problem is that there are "diabolical spirts, under a false pretence [*sic*] of doing
us good, who have too truly been first the instigators of all our confusions,
and likewise of the many miseries which we have experienced since our
landing on this soil."[106] For sure, this letter aims to shift away from settlers
the responsibility—or the blame, depending on one's orientation—for their
early failures. Even if the reader is inclined to dismiss their response in this
letter as a litany of excuses, the point is that they actively take advantage of
their access to Sharp to construct their own image. They speak back using
the textual form most readily available to them—the letter—to engage in the
larger discourse about their settlement and their character.

In a sense, these Black settlers employ letter writing as a kind of performance, one designed to shift and control the narrative about their character.
This agentive act complicates Konstantin Dierks's notion of an "ideology
of agency." Dierks examines the manner in which letter writing functioned

as a covert power mechanism for white, middle-class American colonists on the eve of the Revolutionary War. In fact, he argues that the epistolary act contributed to the emergence of an American middle class as it encoded structures of white privilege and supremacy. Access to letter writing—the acquisition of literacy, the material objects necessary to write, communications infrastructures like printing shops and stationery stores—created a dividing line between the haves and have-nots that reified racialized class differences. What is more, according to Dierks, this shifting class structure also created a change in the cultural work of letters. Prior to this period, letters could be a source of power for the writer, who could exert some measure of control over the moral and ethical behaviors of others or set social agendas. By the end of the eighteenth century, Dierks argues, the rising white, middle class in America aligned letter writing less with power and more with agency, defined by Dierks as "one's own and of other people's individual or collective ability to take purposeful action and to have determinative effect in their *own* lives."[107] That is to say, this new class of people understood letters as a tool of introspection, a privilege employed by a white, middle class. Dierks reminds us of the crucial cultural and social work that letter writing can perform for a community. For the settlers in Sierra Leone, letter writing was still very much an act of power if also an act of agency. Through the letter form, they sought to influence public perception of their settlement and build communal cohesion by speaking in the letter with one voice. In this way, the tools of letter writing became accessible to all, giving the appearance of a democratizing effect that collapsed class and social differences in the settlement.

As a source of power, the town's letter seems to have had some effect. For instance, after receiving the letter from the Black settlers and those of Weaver and Reid, Sharp remarkably adopts their perspective of the settlement. Writing to his niece Anna Jemima in 1788, Sharp excuses the settlers' lack of productivity as the result of "the extream poverty of the Settlers, who had nothing to enable them to purchase any live Stock, without which it was impossible for them to obtain sufficient subsistence."[108] Likewise, in a letter addressed to members of Parliament in 1789, Sharp notes, "I am aware that the settlers will be roundly charged with being a set of mere robbers and banditti, dangerous to the existence of the neighbouring slave-factories;— for such was the language of a letter which I saw about twelve months ago, from an agent at one of the slave-factories to his employers; though the occasion itself, on which he wrote, proved that the settlers, as a body, had behaved with the utmost propriety."[109] Wadström adopts a similarly sympathetic viewpoint by insisting that what he determined was bad behavior displayed by Black settlers "must be understood with various exceptions and limitations; and that, the turbulence of some, and the unreasonableness and jealousy of many of them, are more or less to be looked for, in any body of men, who have been so unfavourably circumstanced."[110] He nuances his criticisms of those early Black settlers by differentiating between those who arrived in 1787 and those who arrived to form Freetown five years later. He notes that the negative character traits that he sees manifest in some Black Africans, like those in 1787, "are not incident to them as blacks, but as men. And who will say, that, if he had struggled through a like succession of vexations, hardships and disappointments, his character would not have been marked by the same prejudices and untoward dispositions, which belong to some of the present colonists of S. Leona."[111]

As news about the colony's state continued to trickle in to Sharp, he received the information with a mixture of optimism and doubt. In 1787 he fretted over his "poor little ill-thriven swarthy daughter, the unfortunate colony of Sierra Leone."[112] To one associate in October 1788, he writes about the defection of settlers, "I was apprehensive that a total desertion was probable, and that all the public and private expenses that had been bestowed on this undertaking were in danger of being lost, together with that beautiful tract of land, and the opportunity of forming in it a free settlement (as an asylum for the poor) on the most eligible spot in all Africa."[113] He pushed through his apprehensions and continued devising plans to aid the settlement. In the summer of 1788 he raised the funds to outfit a ship, a brig named the *Myro,* which sent the colonists much-needed supplies and more settlers to augment their numbers. With the ship, he also sent letters, one addressed to the new settlers aboard the *Myro* and one to the original settlers. Notably, his letter to the new settlers was a series of instructions for organizing themselves into tithing units—just as their predecessors had organized. He warns them that each man at least sixteen years old "should prepare" himself "with knowledge of military exercise, by a daily training one-third part of the able men at a time, during the voyage" so they will be prepared to serve in the settlement's militia. He explains to them, too, the mechanics of the "watch and ward" that is "an effectual check against the ill behavior of individuals."[114] The *Myro* was a staging ground for the new settlers to acclimate themselves to frankpledge. As further support, the supplies he sent along on the ship included more weapons to build up a militia and uniforms—coats, leather caps, and capes—for those serving in the watch and ward.

Perhaps the greatest challenge to Sharp's vision—and there were many, to be sure—did not come from the settlers themselves. Like their predecessors in Massachusetts Bay, Plymouth, and Jamestown, those at Province of Freedom struggled to establish and manage relations with their indigenous neighbors. Those struggles turned catastrophic in 1789, when the settlers involved themselves in a power struggle between the Temne headman King Jammy, King Tom's successor, and American and British slave traders at Bance Island (or Bunce Island). According to the account later submitted to the colony's Court of Directors in 1791, the conflict began when British and American enslavers kidnapped and sold into slavery four of the Temne people. In response, King Jammy kidnapped four American sailors, subsequently killing three of them. The fourth escaped to the slave factory at Bance Island. Not soon after, British sailors, led by a Captain Savage, burned a Temne town, which the sailors claim was accidental. None of this would have affected the settlers at Province of Freedom had they heeded these words from Sharp, penned in November 1789, about how to coexist with the political factions in the region: "What is done beyond your boundaries you cannot help or prevent, except the offenders belong to your community; neither must you interfere with others in the least, except by kind and friendly warnings of God's impending vengeance against oppressors; and this only when you have any fair opportunities of mentioning the subject, without giving personal offence."[115] Sharp's advice came a little too late as it seems that the settlers had already committed the act that would condemn them. Purportedly, they showed British sailors the way to King Jammy's town. Consequently, King Jammy issued the verdict that Province of Freedom would burn as a final act of retaliation. He gave the settlers three days to vacate the settlement and then carried out the attack. According to Sharp, "The Natives have entirely destroyed all the houses and buildings in the new settlement."[116] Settlers scattered throughout the region. Some sought refuge at the slave factory on Bance Island, and others relocated to nearby indigenous towns, thus ending the first experiment at Province of Freedom.

In the wake of the settlement's failure, one narrative that emerged about how and why Province of Freedom failed renders the settlers as victims, an intriguing portrayal given the numerous reports criticizing the settlers' character. Reports in 1792 and 1794 describe the settlement's collapse as the result of an "unhappy dispute" for which the settlers have "little or no blame."[117] In her 1794 narrative about her husband's role in building up the second iteration of the settlement in 1791, Anna Maria Falconbridge refers to those original settlers as "miserable refugees."[118] Equiano and Cugoano both condemn not the character of the settlers but that of those British agents sent to assist the settlers. Perhaps as a nod to Sharp, Equiano notes that the resettlement idea, "however unfortunate in the event, was humane and politic in its design, nor was its failure owing to government."[119] Both Equiano and Cugoano deem the failure inevitable because of, in Cugoano's words, "the adverse motives of those employed to be the conductors thereof."[120] He continues, "We think it will be more than what can be well expected, if we ever hear of any good in proportion to so great, well-designed, laudable and expensive charity," referring to the resettlement plan.[121]

Despite Cugoano's pessimism, Sharp remained hopeful and persistent. He spearheaded the reestablishment of the colony but without the same degree of idealism that had guided his actions in 1786. The biggest change was that the settlers lost the guise of autonomy, with all administrative decisions coming through the oversight of a trading company, initially called the St. George's Bay Association in 1790 but, a year later, renamed the Sierra Leone Company. In an act of serendipity, even before the town's demise, Sharp had already begun the groundwork for creating such a company based on Reid's suggestion that two agents be sent to the settlement to mediate trade. Apparently, Sharp did trust Reid's assessment. In fact, in a prospectus, *Free English Territory in Africa,* he credited the idea of establishing a trade company to Reid and the other settlers. He summarizes the content of Reid's letter, telling potential investors that "they [the settlers] earnestly required in their last letters, that some respectable Merchants or factors might be prevailed on to settle among them, in order to keep open a constant Communication with England by their Trade, which, they think, will be a means of relieving their wants."[122] Under the auspices of the newly incorporated Sierra Leone Company, settlers reestablished their colony as Granville Town but in a new location two miles east of the old. Importantly, this second iteration did not rely solely on frankpledge governance. The company, which was run by a thirteen-man court of directors, of which Sharp was a member though not the chairman, appointed its own agents and eventually a governor and council to oversee the colony—rather than allowing the colonists to govern themselves. In Christopher Fyfe's words, "A colony governed by absentees in England replaced the self-governing Province of Freedom."[123] Sharp's vision, then, gave way to the larger political and economic interests of the company. As I discuss in the next chapter, the Sierra Leone Company's administrative choices made even more pronounced the centrality of respectability ideals. Tenets of frankpledge formed alongside a mode of respectability more recognizable to us today, one that emphasizes the *kind* of people who populate the settlement more so than the kind of governance system that regulates it.

FIVE

"SEND ME OVER ONE WORTHY"

REIMAGINING RESPECTABILITY

IN

SIERRA LEONE

The Sierra Leone Company, willing to receive into their Colony—
such Free Blacks as are able to produce to their Agents, Lieutenant
Clarkson, of His Majesty's Navy, and Mr. Lawrence Hartshorne,
of Halifax, or either of them, satisfactory Testimonials of their characters, (more particularly as to Honesty, Sobriety, and Industry)
think it proper to notify, in explicit manner, upon what Terms they
will receive, at Sierra Leone, those who bring with them written
Certificates of Approbation from either of the said Agents, which
Certificates they are hereby respectively authorized to grant or withhold at Discretion.
    —Advertisement of the Sierra Leone Company, 1791

IN 1794 MEMBERS OF the Providence African Society in Rhode Island
had a plan. Begun in 1789 with the aim of supporting the movement of Black
Americans "back to Africa," the society sent a representative to Sierra
Leone, their secretary James Mackenzie. It was a scouting mission to ascertain the possibility of Rhode Island Blacks immigrating to what had become
by 1794 the colony of Freetown. Perhaps advertisements calling for free

Blacks who were honest, sober, and industrious, like the one quoted in the epigraph above, enticed the would-be immigrants. Mackenzie set sail in 1795. By that time British-backed settlement in Sierra Leone had passed through three phases—the first resulting in Province of Freedom (or Granville Town) in 1787; a second, in 1791, that produced a second settlement also named Granville Town but situated two miles away from the original site; and a third, in 1792, that created the settlement of Freetown, located on the site of the original Province of Freedom/Granville Town. It benefited from an influx of nearly 1,200 Black Africans, mostly Loyalists who had gone to Nova Scotia, Canada, after the Revolutionary War but found insufferable the material conditions and racial politics. Most of the surviving settlers from Sharp's 1787 settlement had drifted to Freetown to join the Nova Scotians by 1795. Gone was the self-governance of frankpledge; settlers still organized into tithing units but as a means of surveillance, not self-governance; they were now under the authority of a white, English governor, Zachary Macaulay, selected by the colony's Court of Directors, its governing board.

Macaulay accepted Mackenzie's proposal for resettling Rhode Island Blacks in Freetown. He agreed to accommodate twelve families, supplying each family with a town lot and ten acres of land across the peninsula on Bullom Shore for farming, and he assured Mackenzie that they would enjoy all the rights appertaining to British subjects. In exchange, he stipulated four conditions: First, as advertised in 1791, the head of each of those twelve families would need to submit a testimonial vouching for his upstanding moral character written by a clergyman or the president of the Abolition Society of Rhode Island. Second, the would-be settlers would need to agree to abide by the laws of the settlement and annually pay a one-shilling quitrent, a kind of land tax. Third, the settlers would be responsible for their own transportation to Sierra Leone. Fourth, if the settlers did not cultivate their ten-acre lots within two years, he would confiscate the lots. That last condition responded directly to what many critics of the day argued was a failing of those original settlers in 1787 who spent their time trading goods rather than farming the land. Presumably, Mackenzie and the members of the Providence African Society found the terms acceptable. They identified the twelve families and prepared for a departure that never came. They failed to produce recommendation letters. The heads of the twelve families sought letters from the same Rev. Samuel Hopkins who supported Black repatriation to Africa and dialogued with Phillis Wheatley about her serving as a missionary in West Africa. In 1784, Hopkins had sought funding for his own emigration plan. He refused to provide the letters for reasons not exactly known. So, the plan failed. That failure tells us a great deal about the centrality of respectability and its consequences for Sierra Leone colonization.[1]

The previous chapter developed along two lines of discussion: one about how Sharp understood respectability through frankpledge, the other about how Black settlers through letters engaged the respectability rhetoric of Sharp and others. In this chapter I extend the discussion by examining more closely the literary landscape that starts to emerge specifically in and about what became Freetown. The letter writing of figures like Richard Weaver and James Reid, discussed in the previous chapter, joins a wider body of texts written on behalf of Black settlers in the 1790s to control the narrative about Black settlement and respectability in the British colonial spaces of eighteenth-century Sierra Leone. Through life writing and letters, those early settlers maintained familial contacts, intervened in political and religious discourses, and contested the colony's power structure that in the 1790s often made them feel dispossessed and disenfranchised. What is more, a clearer picture emerges about how indigenous Black Africans intervened in the sociopolitical landscape. Through letters, we can see instances of one indigenous ruler taking advantage of respectability politics to improve his position within his own community and also on a global stage.

The central question in this chapter, then, is what can the literature tell us about how Black repatriates and natives in Sierra Leone engaged respectability and why? To address this question, I examine the textual production of three Black African figures who were actively involved in the sociopolitical life of Freetown between 1792 and 1800. I examine the autobiography of Methodist missionary and teacher Boston King; a letter written to British agents on behalf of King Naimbanna II, the supreme ruler of the Temne; and the letters and accounts representing the deeds of the Methodist evangelist Mary Perth. All of these figures in various ways embody and subvert the tenets of respectability that were so intimately tied to notions of liberty, justice, and upward mobility. Importantly, their manipulation of the rhetoric illustrates for us how that rhetoric circulated through the Atlantic, circumscribing the life experiences of Black Africans in the United States and West Africa alike. I begin the discussion with a brief overview of the development of Freetown in the wake of the 1789 destruction of Province of Freedom. Then, I discuss the texts of King, King Naimbanna II, and Perth, who all employed various strategies to manipulate respectability rhetoric—with the end goal of self-government.

FROM PROVINCE OF FREEDOM TO FREETOWN

The dissolution of Province of Freedom in 1789 had dire consequences for those Black settlers who had traveled from the United States and England with the hope of economic stability and autonomy. To salvage some part of his vision for a self-governing town of Black refugees, free from the vices of the slave trade, Sharp joined with other English philanthropists to create the St. George's Bay Association in 1790 and then the Sierra Leone Company (SLC) a year later. After marshaling the financial resources to found a new settlement, the SLC sent a British surgeon named Alexander Falconbridge to Sierra Leone in 1791 to renegotiate a land treaty with local Temne leaders and to gather up the scattered settlers, about sixty. Under Falconbridge's tumultuous leadership, the settlers founded a new Granville Town some two miles from the site of the original. The new settlement, importantly, reflected more clearly the structure of a colony, which is to say, the settlers did not govern themselves. Instead, the SLC managed Granville Town from afar, sending over a board-approved governor to oversee the town's daily affairs. That political structure created tension over the next decade for those Black settlers who had been lured to Sierra Leone, in part, by Sharp's promises of self-governance.

A year after the SLC established a new Granville Town, they supported the relocation to Sierra Leone of more than 1,100 Black Americans from Nova Scotia, Canada. Those Black Nova Scotians were mostly Loyalists who had immigrated to Nova Scotia rather than England after the Revolutionary War. In Nova Scotia they quickly settled into predominantly Black communities, the largest of them at Birchtown. The harsh weather, food scarcity, and racial discrimination compelled many of them to leave when presented with the opportunity, which came in 1791. In order to augment the numbers at Granville Town, the SLC sent to Nova Scotia the English naval lieutenant Jonathan Clarkson with the offer of free passage and land to those Black Nova Scotians willing to relocate. The SLC found favorable the Black Nova Scotians because they had a reputation for piety and strong moral character. Their communities, led mostly by self-taught evangelists, reflected strong religious identities tied mostly to newly founded Methodist and Baptist denominations.[2] This contrasted with those 1787 settlers, who, as discussed in chapter 4, onlookers described as lazy, roguish, and unruly. The new arrivals in 1792 formed their own settlement, which they named Freetown, on the site of the original Province of Freedom.[3] Freetown eventually incorporated those residents of Granville Town. The pious reputation of the Black Nova Scotians coincided with the SLC's heightened religious emphasis. As Suzanne Schwarz points out, the company "regarded missions as pivotal to the reform of African society," and those newly arriving Black Methodists from Nova Scotia "played an important role in the development of Sierra Leone as a site of pioneering missionary endeavour."[4] In addition to a governor, the Court of Directors also appointed a cleric to oversee spiritual matters, which meant managing the religious practices and energies of the Black settlers. Religion was a key strategy through which Black settlers in Sierra Leone, like their counterparts in the United States, mediated respectability discourses. This was the case, for example, with the Methodist preacher and missionary Boston King.

BOSTON KING'S "MEMOIRS" AND THE GREAT MORAL DILEMMA

Boston King, a former enslaved person and a Loyalist, converted to Methodism upon his immigration to Nova Scotia after the Revolutionary War. He was born on a South Carolina plantation near Charleston in 1760. When King was sixteen years old, the man who enslaved him apprenticed him to a carpenter, a harsh, abusive master. He ran away to Charleston, where he joined the British army, which had seized the city in 1780. For the army, he worked as an officer's servant, a courier, and sailor. At war's end, he evacuated from a port in New York to Nova Scotia with a number of his fellow Black Loyalists, including his wife, Violet. In Nova Scotia, he and Violet settled in Birchtown, and he worked as an itinerant preacher, fisherman, and carpenter. He opted to immigrate to Sierra Leone in 1792 with his family in order to missionize to indigenous Black Africans. In Freetown, King continued his evangelical work. He ministered to Freetown Blacks and taught them basic literacy; he also taught and missionized in the surrounding towns. In 1794, to enhance his missionizing efforts, he traveled to England and attended the Methodist-run Kingswood School in Bristol. He returned to Sierra Leone in 1796. Eventually, he left Freetown and traveled some one hundred miles inland to proselytize the Sherbro people. He died among the Sherbro in 1802.[5]

King published a brief account of his life, *Memoirs of the Life of Boston King,* in serial form between March and June 1798 in the *Methodist Magazine* in London. He represents the narrative as a humble endeavor, evoking the same humility topos that pervaded early Black American life writing.[6] He notes in the very first paragraph, "It is by no means an agreeable task to write an account" of his life.[7] He has done so at the request of "many respectable friends" but acknowledges his "inability for such an undertaking" (351). Also, like his predecessors, King likely crafted his narrative in community. Ryan Hanley has painstakingly mapped out the ways in which the narrative seems to have been heavily edited and maybe augmented by Thomas Coke, an early leader of the Methodist Church in England, and possibly by abolitionist William Wilberforce.[8] The nine-thousand-word narrative defies easy categorization as it is part slave narrative, part Methodist conversion narrative, part confessional, part religious apologia, part travelogue, and part historical narrative about the early settlements of Nova Scotia and Sierra Leone. However one chooses to label the text, it is remarkable in the present context because it reflects respectability rhetoric and does so mostly in the form of exhortations, a product of King's evangelical role in the Methodist church. These exhortations appear as lengthy soliloquies spoken by King and other characters or as short bursts of self-righteous proclamation. The emotive acts function as a cover of sorts, allowing King to indulge in behavior that otherwise would have been transgressive and disrespectful.

Religious exhortation provides an avenue through which King stretches the bounds of respectable behavior, rearticulating conceptions of obedience, submission, and humility. The narrative's preoccupation with these concepts manifests in King's emphasis on his early childhood and his yearning for freedom. He tells the reader that he first learned of God from a father who was "stolen away from Africa when he was young" and who "lived in the fear and love of God" (351). His father "lost no opportunity of hearing the Gospel, and never omitted praying with his family every night" (351). When he was twelve, he writes, God warned him in a dream about the evilness of "swearing and cursing" (352). He explains that "this dream made such an impression upon my mind, that I refrained from swearing and bad company" (352). The dream does not convert King; it confirms what he already knows and compels him to "acknowledge that there was a God" (352). Although he was exposed to Christianity at an early age, he does say that he struggled with his faith, not always knowing "how to serve God," an uncertainty reflected in his strivings toward freedom (352).

A movement from enslavement to liberty shapes King's narrative, as it does for most Black life writing of the late eighteenth and nineteenth centuries, including the autobiographies of the only other Black Nova Scotians who produced narratives about their life experiences, David George and John Marrant.[9] King's narrative, though, vacillates between his yearning for freedom and his fear that seeking out that freedom contradicts God's will. He muses at one point, "Sometimes I thought, if it was the will of God that I should be a slave, I was ready to resign myself to his will; but at other times I could not find the least desire to content myself in slavery" (355). "Memoirs" tacitly accepts slavery as a fact of life. He does not explicitly challenge the institution or dwell on the brutal acts of inhumane enslavers. Instead, he emphasizes racial reconciliation. He remarks at the end of his story, "I am now fully convinced, that many of the White People, instead of being enemies and oppressors of us poor Blacks, are our friends, and deliverers from slavery, as far as their ability and circumstances will admit" (366). Rather than attacking white enslavers in the antebellum South, King acknowledges common ground with those who have done all that "their ability and circumstances will admit" (366). He views as tolerable, for example, the treatment of enslaved people living in Baltimore, Philadelphia, and New York, where they "have as good victuals as many of the English; for they have meat once a day, and milk for breakfast and supper; and what is better than all, many of the masters send their slaves to school at night, that they may learn to read the Scriptures" (355). The narrative's muted critique of slavery is a product of King's efforts to appear respectable to his mostly Methodist readers. As Hanley argues, the editors of King's narrative, if not King himself, wanted to ensure that the narrative would not "stray into the category of 'radical' abolitionism" and threaten the political and religious order, as was already happening in places like Haiti.[10] Instead, Hanley maintains, Coke saw King's narrative as an opportunity to ensure his Methodist cohort and others that the Methodist Church "did not desire a break from the established church . . . and reaffirmed their reliability and the respectable nature of Methodism."[11] Despite fears about political radicalism, King's narrative does appear transgressive, manifesting in those moments when he and other Blacks exhort.

King embeds a series of exhortations into the text, moments in which he proclaims God's grace and mercy or cautions against immoral behavior. The exhortations appear as lengthy soliloquies, one-line censures directed at other characters or the summarized speech acts of those he converts after his own conversion. Respectability rhetoric pervades the exhortations. We see this first in how he describes his conversion, which does not occur instantaneously but over the course of a year. When finally he is convinced that God has given him a clean heart, he exclaims: "All my doubts and fears vanished away: I saw, but faith, heaven opened to my view; and Christ and his holy angels rejoicing over me. . . . I could truly say, I was now become a new creature. All tormenting and slavish fear, and all the guilt and weight of sin were done away." He spreads God's word to others. Referring to himself as an "exhorter among the people," he writes: "Soon after, I found a great concern for the salvation of others; and was constrained to visit my poor ungodly neighbours, and exhort them to fear the Lord, and seek him while he might be found. . . . I began to exhort both in families and prayer-meetings, and the Lord graciously afforded me his assisting presence" (359). For two years, King proselytizes communities in Nova Scotia before migrating to Sierra Leone and ministering to his "poor brethren in Africa," who he assumed "never heard the Name of God or of Christ (359).

The transgressive nature of King's exhortations is magnified in Nova Scotia. For example, to make ends meet, he works at one point on a fishing boat. The captain of the boat is, in King's words, "as horrible a swearer as I ever met with" (361). In addition to swearing, the captain "would stamp and rage at the men, when they did not please him." His behavior was so "ungodly" to King that his "soul was exceedingly grieved," and he "repented that [he] ever entered into his service" (361). King compares his circumstance to that of the biblical figure Lot, who he says experienced a similar vexation witnessing the "ungodly deeds of the people of Sodom" (361). He derives some comfort from the comparison—not to mention a great deal of spiritual authority—that emboldens him to confront the captain about his behavior. He tells the captain, "Dear sir, don't you know that the Lord hath declared, that he will not hold them guiltless who take his Name in vain? And that all profane swearers shall have their portion in the lake that burneth with fire and brimstone?" The captain, King tells us, "bore the reproof with patience and scarce ever gave me an unkind word." King notes, though, that his exhortation does not work miracles. Afterward, the captain nonetheless "persisted in his impiety, and the men, encouraged by his example, imitated him to the utmost of their ability" (361).

Disappointed that his words actually exacerbate the situation, he retreats to the woods, where he meditates and prays.[12] He thinks about his current predicament akin to Lot, Job, and the motif of the suffering servant of God. Then he concludes that his approach is all wrong. "I saw my folly in imagining that it was in my power to turn them from their evil ways," he says. "The Lord shewed me, that this was his prerogative" (361). He notes, "My duty consisted in entreating them, and bearing patiently their insults, as God for Christ's sake had borne with me. And he gave me a resolution to reprove in a right spirit, all that swore in my presence" (362). In other words, King has presumed a spirit of vanity in thinking that his exhortations alone can result in salvation.

King directs his lengthiest exhortation to indigenous Black Africans in Sierra Leone. He immigrates to Freetown with his wife in March 1792. Although his wife dies of malaria soon after their arrival, King pursues his spiritual dream of proselytizing "the poor benighted inhabitants" in the towns neighboring Freetown (359). However, he encounters two obstacles. One, his responsibilities in Freetown prevent him from preaching to the indigenous communities more than one day a week, on Sundays. He wants to preach more frequently. To solve this problem, he obtains permission from the governor to work on Bullom Shore, closer to those communities. Once there, he endeavors to start a school to teach literacy to indigenous children, which leads to the second obstacle. The parents of those children appear lukewarm about the school and King's instruction. Only four children attend. As a result, one Sunday after service, King tells his churchgoers:

> It is a good thing that God has made the White People, and that he has inclined their hearts to bring us into this country, to teach you his ways, and to tell you that he gave his Son to die for you; and if you will obey his commandments he will make you happy in this world,

and in that which is to come; where you will live with him in heaven; and all pain and wretchedness will be at an end; and you shall enjoy peace without interruption, joy without bitterness, and happiness to all eternity. The Almighty not only invites you to come unto him, but also points out the way whereby you may find his favour, viz. turn from your wicked ways, cease to do evil, and learn to do well. He now affords you a means which you never had before; he gives you his Word to be a light to your feet, and a lantern to your paths, and he likewise gives you an opportunity of having your children instructed in the Christian Religion. But if you neglect to send them, you must be answerable to God for it. (365)

King positions himself as the conduit through which God will fulfill all the benefits King says Black Africans can enjoy if they convert to Christianity. He normalizes Christian values and the idea of worldly prosperity, quintessential respectability rhetoric. Equally worth noting, the exhortation praises the generosity and missionary efforts of "White People." In a narrative about racial reconciliation, King endeavors here to assuage the animosity or suspicion Black Africans might harbor about this new British settlement; he also, again, appeals to white readers back in London worried about Black radicalism. King's words take on another level of significance when we remember that just a stone's throw away British and French slave forts are still actively dealing in the transatlantic slave trade. "The White People" to whom King refers, even using the definite article "the" to suggest there is only one kind of white people, are British agents and missionaries supporting Freetown, who "God has made." The use of that definite article effectively effaces slave-dealing whites and turns the attention of his congregants toward a population he wants to convince them is less threatening. King delivers the speech through the "disadvantage" of a translator, which apparently does not compromise its efficacy. As a result of the exhortation, the number of students in his school increases from four to twenty.[13]

Particularly intriguing about King's use of exhortations is that they allow him to cross social and cultural boundaries. Through exhortation, for example, he crosses a cultural divide to connect with his indigenous counterparts in a way he had been unable to previously, as evident by the increased enrollment afterward. He also exhorts to mixed-race audiences in Nova Scotia, and when he travels to England in 1794 to attend the Methodist Kingswood School, he says that he "formed a resolution never to attempt to preach" while he stayed in England. Earlier in the narrative, he admitted to a certain measure of self-consciousness when preaching in front of whites "because [he] had no learning, and [he] knew that they had" (365). However, at the urgings of his white benefactors, he found preaching in England "profitable to [his] own soul, to be exercised in inviting sinners to Christ" (366). While preaching in England, with his white counterparts as witness, he experiences a final conversion or awakening, this time racial: "While I was preaching at Snowsfields-Chapel, the Lord blessed me abundantly, and I found a more cordial love to the White People than I had ever experienced before" (366). Again, King refers to a single, homogeneous identity group, but this time he includes white enslavers in that group. "In the former part of my life," he writes, "I had suffered greatly from the cruelty and injustice of the Whites, which induced me to look upon them, in general, as our enemies: And even after the Lord had manifested his forgiving mercy to me, I still felt at times an uneasy distrust and shyness towards them" (366). So here King confesses his struggle with racial prejudice, his difficulties with encountering white people as anything other than enemies and oppressors. This moral flaw lingers even after his conversion. However, once he allows himself to exhort in England, he is delivered of that flaw. "The Lord removed all my prejudices," he proclaims, "for which I bless his holy Name" (366). The process of exhortation, specifically preaching in this case, liberates King and produces in his mind racial harmony. Beyond producing racial harmony, the exhortations challenge racial hierarchies that produce the kind of oppression alluded to above. With his exhortations, King defies social norms and embodies an elevated status not available to him in other circumstances. We see this dynamic when King admonishes his employer on the fishing boat. In everyday interactions, racial rules of engagement prohibit Blacks from asserting themselves to whites. The exhortations inoculate King from social ramifications. The boat captain simply listens "with patience," and they keep working.

The exhortations also disrupt gendered hierarchies. One illustration of this occurs through the example of a woman who converts as a result purportedly of King's missionary efforts. Once King decides to preach, he co-pastors a congregation in Preston. The congregation consists of thirty-four people, twenty-four of whom "professed faith in Christ" (362). King frets over the other ten. He serves the congregation for a year when one day he prays to God: "How long shall I be with this people before the work prosper among them! O Lord God! If thou hast called me to preach to my Black Brethren, answer me this day from heaven by converting one sinner, that I may know that thou hast sent me" (362). That very Sunday afternoon, during a meeting of the church's elders, or society, a woman interrupted the meeting. After asking permission to speak, she pronounces the following:

> This people is the people of GOD; and their GOD shall be my GOD.... Blessed be the Name of the Lord for ever, for I know he hath pardoned, my sins for the sake of his Son Jesus Christ. My mind has been so greatly distressed for these three weeks, that I could scarcely sleep; while I was under the preaching all my grief vanished away, and such light broke in upon my soul, that I was enabled to believe unto salvation. O praise the Lord with me, all ye that love his Name; for he hath done great things for my soul. (362–63)

King accepts the woman's profession of faith as evidence of his own ministerial power. After hearing her words, he says, "I blessed GOD for answering my petition, and was greatly encouraged to persevere in my labours" (363). The moment is equally telling because of what it suggests about the woman herself. She does not articulate her conversion experience during the actual church service but afterward, during a meeting of the church's leadership. King does not name the members of the society attending the meeting, but we might reasonably surmise that those members meeting in that space on that Sunday afternoon are overwhelmingly male. So, this woman interjects her presence, her voice into a male-dominated space. According to King, the woman "knocked at the door" and "desired to be admitted among us, that she might declare what the Lord had done for her soul" (362). She gains access to the space and speaks so convincingly about her experience that society members "were melted into tears of joy" (363). The exhortation mode allows her to break with social norms and elevate herself in a way deemed socially acceptable. In another setting her presence might have been ignored, her voice silenced; here she speaks through exhortation, and the power of the exhortation affects her listeners so that, as King tells us, she "immediately entered into connection with us, and many others in a few weeks after" (363). It was not unusual for Black women to garner respect and visibility in church settings when professing this kind of normalizing rhetoric. As Higginbotham notes about how respectability politics emerges in the late nineteenth century, the politics provided an avenue through which Black churchwomen amplified their voices in a religious public sphere. The woman in King's church found that voice a century earlier, as did figures like Jarena Lee, Nancy Prince, and Julia Foote in other corners of the early Black diaspora.

Not incidentally, King's own wife, Violet, also employed exhortations that challenged gendered boundaries. Violet was one of the first Black Loyalists to convert to Methodism in Nova Scotia, according to King: "The Lord . . . brought her out of the horrible pit, and set her soul at perfect liberty" (357). King does not provide any direct speech from Violet but alludes to her exhortation efforts in the wake of her conversion. He says, "The joy and happiness which she now experienced, were too great to be concealed, and she was enabled to testify of the goodness and loving-kindness of the Lord, with such liveliness and power, that many were convinced by her testimony, and sincerely sought the Lord" (357). Like the female convert at Preston, Violet testifies with authority. Violet, though, takes witnessing a step further. King says that she "exhorted and urged others to seek and enjoy the same blessing" (357). So, she is not content to simply speak about her conversion like the woman at Preston; she proselytizes, an authoritative activity customarily reserved for men in the settlement. Her male counterparts, though not King himself, found her behavior problematic as "she was not a little opposed by some of our Black brethren" (357). Despite the pushback, she continued to proselytize. Violet, then, pushes gendered boundaries by shepherding others through their own professions of faith, an act that implies the exercise of power, of authority. Her fellow (male) settlers judge her behavior as disrespectful. To mitigate that judgment and for the benefit of readers who also might interpret Violet's actions as impertinent, King insists that his wife endured the neighbors' censure "with the meekness and patience becoming a Christian" (357). He tells us, too, that when the white Methodist clergyman Freeborn Garrettson visits Birchtown, he hears of her public witnessing and "he encouraged her to hold fast her confidence, and cleave to the Lord with her whole heart" (357). King offers us the evangelist's words to do what exhortations alone cannot do for his wife—inoculate her from judgment, render her respectable even as she transgresses gendered norms.

King understands his behavior and the behavior of all those with whom he interacts through a moralizing code of conduct that is based on a Christian value system. Importantly, it is a system that pits the human desire for freedom against a mandate that one appear meek and submit to God's will. King works through that conflict by ultimately situating himself within the biblical motif of a suffering servant who must sit passively and wait upon deliverance from God. Not only does he self-police, but he also endeavors to regulate the behavior of others through the use of exhortations, assessing the moral health of Nova Scotians like his wife, indigenous Black Africans, and his employers in Birchtown. As a survivalist technique, respectability enables King to escape slavery and achieve some measure of religious authority that might not have materialized otherwise, hence its appeal.

KING NAIMBANNA II AND THE
RESPECTABILITY OF TRANSCULTURATION

When those first Black English settlers arrived to Sierra Leone in 1787, they entered into a space controlled by a king with global diplomatic experience. By the 1780s, the Sierra Leone peninsula was a cosmopolitan space, its cultural character having been shaped by various ethnic African groups, such as the Temne and Mandingo. Add to this some three centuries of contact with European traders from Portugal, Spain, France, and England. France and England had built slave forts there to control the transatlantic slave trade. The supreme ruler, or Obai, of the Koya Temne, King Naimbanna II managed this cultural milieu in 1787. Perhaps due to his experiences navigating multicultural and transatlantic encounters, Naimbanna adopted a relatively lenient stance toward the settlers coming to Sierra Leone. He brokered land treaties in 1788 and 1791, over the fears of his council and despite some confusion about the precise terms of the treaties. In general, he welcomed trade with the English as illustrated through letters. He encouraged missionaries to educate those in his kingdom. He, for example, sought out Abram Elliot Griffith, whose correspondence with Sharp was discussed in the previous chapter, to serve as his personal secretary and establish a school for the Temne. In addition, he had three sons and sent each of those sons abroad to study languages and religions. One he sent north to study Islam among the Mandingo; another he sent into France to study Catholicism.

He sent his eldest son, John Frederic, in 1791 to England to learn English and study Protestantism under the tutelage of Sharp and Henry Thornton. He did so with the expectation that those sons would bring that knowledge back home for the benefit of his people. By all accounts, King Naimbanna II's receptive disposition toward the settlers aided the development of Freetown.

Most intriguing about King Naimbanna's engagement with the development of Freetown is the manner in which he manages diplomatic relationships through letters. In a discussion about respectability politics, Naimbanna II is a crucial figure because he appropriates English forms of communication, through letter writing, employing particular modes of civility and respectability. He manipulates the letter form to influence English (and European by extension) policies and shore up his own authority in the Sierra Leone region. King Naimbanna writes letters to several British agents associated with Freetown, among them Sharp, Clarkson, and Thornton. The letters generally are brief missives about trade and other business or, once he sends his son to England, about John Frederic's progress and financial support. In what follows, I focus on a 1791 letter King Naimbanna sends to Sharp by way of Falconbridge, with whom King Naimbanna had just concluded a new land treaty that would allow for the formation of a second Granville Town and subsequently Freetown. The letter explicates the king's foreign relations policy toward the English. He voices his contempt for the slave trade and criticizes European treatment of African nations even as he assures Sharp that he remains committed to maintaining friendly ties with the English. He also tells Sharp about how the slave trade has devastated his family and ends the letter with a request that Sharp take care of his son. The letter appears later in the official report of the Sierra Leone Company. A close reading of the letter illuminates the king's rhetorical strategies. By choosing to engage in the assimilative act of letter writing, using English generic conventions, the king does not merely don a respectable posture to elevate his image and increase his esteem in the eyes of his British counterparts. His is, in fact, a political move to secure resources for his people and mitigate the threats of the slave trade. That is to say, he deploys the letter to cement political and social bonds with Sharp with the idea that it would translate politically into stability for his people and political influence for himself. Early in the letter he tells Sharp:

It has been told, that these people, the free settlers from England, would in time drive me by force of arms back in the country, and take my ports from me. I have received several accounts, from factories and captains of ships, against the settlement, which I took no notice of, as I conceived it was, in my opinion, spite or envy that they had against their living in this country; but have served the settlers in any little request they asked of me, and have endeavoured to keep peace between them and my people, and also among themselves, by settling a great many disquiets between them. It was pleasure to do it, as I thought they would become useful to us all in this country, by teaching us things we do not know; and common reason must tell, that the most ignorant people in the world would be glad to see their country made good, if they had idea how it might be done.[14]

King Naimbanna informs Sharp about the on-the-ground politics that threaten the British settlement. In referencing the ill-will of slave traders and ship captains toward the settlement, King Naimbanna confirms what settlers had told Sharp in their own letter in 1788, mentioned in the previous chapter. Here, the king represents himself as an able leader who employs a great deal of savvy to ferret out the motives, the "spite or envy," of slave traders and maintain a peace that is in the best interest of all involved. He signals to Sharp that he is not a man easily manipulated. He also exhibits a measure of humility when he affirms the benefit of having a British settlement in the area that could teach his people "things we do not know." It would be easy to dismiss this declaration from King Naimbanna as naïve mimicry of a white, European hegemonic perspective. After all, European discourses about settlement and colonization cast native inhabitants as uncivilized and propagated the idea that European nations could spread their knowledge and religion into all the "benighted" corners of the world. The king, however, is not indulging in that discourse. Rather, he universalizes the lack of knowledge of his people, formulating it as a general state shared by all. In seeking what the English have to offer—as he does with the Mandingos and the French when he sends his sons to live among them—he simply employs "common reason," or logic, as "the most ignorant people in the world," not specifically in Africa or America but anywhere, "would be glad to see their country made good, if they had idea how it might be done."

In the next part of the letter, King Naimbanna II discusses the slave trade, and the rhetoric turns more deliberative:

> And again, I must let you know, that, If there were no other rea-
> son for my wishing for the welfare of the settlement, I should do it,
> that there might be a stop put to the horrid depredations that are
> so often committed in this country by all nations that come here to
> trade. There are three distant relations of mine now in the West In-
> dies, who were carried away by one Captain Cox, captain of a Danish
> ship; their names as follows—Corpro, Banna, and Morbour. These
> were taken out of my river Sierra Leona. I know not how to get them
> back. I never hurt or deprived any person of their right or property, or
> withheld from them what is their due; so I only let you know of these
> lads, that there will be an account taken of them one day or another.[15]

The king reveals a vulnerability that belies the certainty and assertiveness that characterize the previous paragraph. He knows how to maintain peace, how to sooth the "disquiets" among settlers and his people. He understands the value of interacting with the settlers and the British as they bring new knowledge. The slave trade, though, is a monstrous mechanism that escapes his ability to fully comprehend its mechanics, much less dismantle it. So, he hopes that encouraging a British-backed settlement of former slaves "might" end "the horrid depredations that are so often committed in this country by all nations that come here to trade." He assures Sharp that they share the same mission in seeing the slave trade come to an end but acknowledges his own impotence in bringing that about. After telling Sharp about his kid-napped relatives, he concedes, "I know not how to get them back." He can-not reconcile the universal, karmic forces that took them away as he "never hurt or deprived any person of their right or property, or withheld from them what is their due." By what logic should his beloved relatives be taken from him? The kidnappings seem illogical to a man who has employed a great deal of logic to justify his policy of tolerance toward the British settlers. The king's lament reveals his ethos, his sense of fair play and the need for equilibrium. The warning he offers, then, "that there will be an account taken of" his kidnapped relatives "one day or another," is his effort to restore the balance. These are conclusions we make when we take at face value the king's words.

If we read these words against the grain, the king attempts to mobilize Sharp's resources to help him recover his relatives. All the extraneous detail he provides to Sharp implies his intent. He names the relatives. He tells Sharp from where they were taken and to where, presumably, they were taken. He names the slave trader and his nationality. If this were simply an anecdote that the king wished to share to illustrate that the trade has affected him personally, the details would be superfluous. We can, then, read against the grain his lament, "I know not how to get them back." Short of traveling to the West Indies himself, he has access to resources and people, like Sharp, who can help him. Through the letter form, King Naimbanna II extends his agentive capacities across the Atlantic. The very act of writing this letter (or, more precisely, dictating it) suggests that he does not sit back passively and simply bemoan the fate of his kinsmen. He addresses a figure in England who had a reputation for staunchly defending the freedom of Black Africans, even rescuing them from the cargo holds of slave ships and tracking them down in the West Indies. Might the king be aware of Sharp's reputation? This could explain why he writes this letter to Sharp instead of Thornton, who by 1791 was the chairman of the Sierra Leone Company and therefore its chief representative. From this perspective, King Naimbanna's insistence "that wrong will be made right" can be read as a veiled threat. He holds as leverage the settlement itself. This reading gains credence when we consider the next paragraph in the letter, where the king once again turns to the welfare of the settlers:

> As to the settlers, I could only wish that you will send me over one worthy of taking the care and command of the place; then you need not be afraid of their prospering in this country. Mr. Falconbridge, during this time out here, I approved much. I ever was partial to the people of Great Britain, for which cause I have put up with a great deal of insults from them more than I should from any other country.
>
> My son, I hope, you will take care of, and let him have his own way in nothing but what you think right yourself.[16]

King Naimbanna endeavors explicitly to influence the management of the settlement. The vulnerability of the previous section of the letter gives way to a voice that is assertive, sure. He does not tell Sharp specifically why he found lacking the settler leadership previously, which we should remember was based on Sharp's frankpledge mechanism. The Black settlers governed themselves. Here, King Naimbanna might be implying that the previous system had resulted in chaos, the "disquiets" he mentions in the opening of the letter. As a sanctifying gesture, he offers the name of a man, Falconbridge, he thinks would be a suitable leader. Notably, he does not name any of the Black settlers, not Weaver or Reid or Griffith. To reaffirm his commitment to the settlement, he speaks of England in exceptional terms, telling Sharp that he is "partial" to the country's people, implying that he will do his part to ensure they "prosper in this country." However, and this is the point to which the letter seems to build, he informs Sharp that because of his partiality, he has tolerated "a great deal of insults," more than "from any other country." He does not tell Sharp of specific insults. We are left to our own conjectures, but the point is that the king has accused the people of Great Britain of disrespecting him despite the preferential treatment he has extended to them, which is again a problem of equilibrium. The chastisement anticipates the king's final deliberative move, a request that Sharp look after his son, a request that is also an obligation in the wake of censure.

There is some evidence that the political maneuvering works. The king makes four requests of Sharp, the last one implied: (1) to deal with him in a manner respectful and just; (2) to send over a competent leader, maybe even Falconbridge, to manage the settlement; (3) to oversee his son's education; and (4) to assist him in recovering his kidnapped relatives. Sharp specifically addresses three of the four requests in his reply to King Naimbanna II, dated November 11, 1791. He acknowledges the king's "continued favour" toward the settlement. He confirms that he will take care of the king's son, an act he specifically articulates as an obligation warranted by the king's generous treatment toward the settlers: "Even if I had not before thought myself under great obligations to you for your kind and very friendly conduct toward the poor Black settlers at Sierra Leone . . . yet [John Frederic's] natural good disposition, modesty, behavior, and great diligence and application to learning, would alone be sufficient to ensure my esteem and regard for him."[17] Sharp's respect extends to the son. After discussing specific details about John Frederic's education and care in London, Sharp then informs King Naimbanna of his efforts to recover the king's kinsmen. Again, this was not a direct request by the king, but Sharp was able to read between the lines as it were. He informs the king that he has made some initial inquiries with the governor in charge of the Danish slave factory on the African coast. He makes no promises to King Naimbanna about his ability to recover the relatives. The point, though, is that the king's letter prompts him to the action. The only request Sharp does not acknowledge in his letter is about the colony's leadership. Ultimately, the court does not appoint Falconbridge as governor.

As a form of respectability, King Naimbanna's letter exemplifies his willingness to engage diplomatically with England using English forms of correspondence. Importantly, King Naimbanna is not "writing upwards" as were those discussed in the previous chapter. Unlike Weaver, Reid, and Griffith, the king writes from beyond the British Empire, seeking to shape its political contours from the outside. He wields his sociopolitical power to marshal the tools of writing—materials like paper, quill, penknives, sealing wax, and a knowledge of literacy—to reach across the Atlantic.[18] Although we do not know much about his level of "letteracy," to use Eve Tavor Bannet's term, he finds access to British networks of power by employing the literacy services of one of the Black settlers to work as his personal secretary and as a teacher for the community, Griffith.[19] Griffith was a protégée of Sharp and learned to read and write while living in England. In the previous chapter, I discussed Griffith's correspondence with Sharp after his initial arrival in Province of Freedom in 1787. In that letter he threatened to leave the settlement and seek out his fortune in the West Indies. Perhaps the king's offer of a job, and the status that job implied, enticed him to stay. Whatever the reason, he becomes a key mediatory tool in how King Naimbanna II presents himself to Britain as a moderate, savvy ruler. He emerges in the British imaginary as a man with "a peaceable disposition," who is "generally respected and obeyed," as articulated in a SLC report in 1791.[20] Although not a colonial British subject, King Naimbanna functions similarly to Srinivas Aravamudan's Tropicopolitan, as he "exists both as fictive construct of colonial tropology *and* actual resident of tropical space, object of representation *and* agent of resistance."[21] For sure, King Naimbanna does not merely imitate a *respectable* textual form, enacting transculturation, he subverts that form by using it to make demands of his British audience and assert his authority as an African king.[22]

MARY PERTH AND THE NEGOTIATION OF
SPIRITUAL AND POLITICAL SPACES

As noted elsewhere in this chapter and throughout the book, Black Africans did not write letters simply as a social practice; letters enabled them to
construct respectable selves within both private and public spheres.[23] The
example of Mary Perth amplifies that point. Born in 1740, Perth was enslaved in Norfolk, Virginia, in the years leading up to the Revolutionary
War. In Norfolk, she learned to read and converted to Methodism. In the
early 1770s, she became a Methodist exhorter, or preacher. With a newborn
baby strapped to her back, she would travel from her master's home some
ten miles at night to lead worship services for fellow Methodists. American
troops ransacked Norfolk in 1776. In the ensuing chaos, Perth made her way
to British-controlled New York, where she lived as a free woman, working
as a domestic for the British army. In 1783, after the war ended, she secured
certificates of freedom and passage for herself, her husband, and her children
to relocate to Nova Scotia. From there, she immigrated with her family to
Freetown. Soon after their arrival in Freetown, Perth's husband died. As a
widow, she provided for herself and children by converting her home into a
boardinghouse and goods store; she was one of several women in the colony
who owned property and businesses.[24] She also worked as a housekeeper for
Macaulay and as a caretaker for those children of indigenous Africans whom
Macaulay invited to live with him and attend school.

Much of what we know about Perth comes from a few brief references
in the journals of Macaulay and a letter written by the Presbyterian minister
Rev. John Clark (also spelled Clarke), who lived in Freetown for three years
beginning in 1796. Both men praised Perth's religious fervor and work ethic.
In this way, Perth's representation in the textual archive of colonial Sierra
Leone is mediated mostly through the pens of white, male observers. The
one exception is a letter that Perth dictates, writer unknown, to a "Dear
Friend" in 1796. That letter along with the account of Perth's virtue rendered vividly in Clark's letter, addressed to his father in Scotland, tell us a
great deal about what respectability looked like for a Black woman working,
teaching, and preaching in Sierra Leone at the end of the eighteenth century.
For Perth, respectability exceeded notions of domesticity and encompassed

also active participation in the commercial and political life of Freetown; she owned a business and voted in colonial elections. Like Phillis Wheatley, discussed in chapter 2, Perth blurred the divide between the public and private that defined the roles for women elsewhere in the British Empire in the eighteenth century. In the discussion that follows, I offer a close reading of Perth's letter to her friend and of her representation in Clark's letter to illuminate the manner in which this formerly enslaved Black woman endeavored to achieve respectability by navigating the sociopolitical spaces of Freetown.

Like King Niambanna II, Mary Perth secured access to the tools of letter writing and with that access sought to control a public image. On July 29, 1796, she wrote to an unnamed male friend living in Scotland:

Dear Friend,

NOT being able myself to write to you, I have entreated a friend of yours and mine, to put down on paper what my soul has to reply to your blessed letter.

I thank you a thousand times for spending a thought on so poor and underserving a creature as I am: but I especially thank your God and my God, for having put it into your heart to send me, from a far country, such comfortable and refreshing words. I can say, I never received a letter which did me so much good. It has brought me on my knees with an overflowing heart many a time. O, how good is my God! he knows I desire to love him, he knows I love you too, for the love you show to my poor soul. I see that verily the love of God constrained you to send me that letter; as I read it I felt my soul as it were, stretching on wings toward Immanuel's better land, may the blessing of the Lord come upon you. My desire was to see your face in the flesh; yet; though I shall never have that desire accomplished, I shall see you hereafter, and shall acknowledge you as one who helped me on my way. What am I, O Lord, that thou shouldest be thus mindful of me that am poor and ignorant, miserable, blind and naked as I am, thou shouldest thus hedge me in with mercies to keep me from straying from thee.

I often have a longing to see that good land where you live; I think if it is full of such men as my dear friend, and such as have come with him, it must be nearer Zion than any place I have yet been in.[25] May the Lord bless you and make you a blessing, and may you have the consolation of his spirit to cheer you and do you good till you enter into his joy.

I am your unworthy servant in the Lord, and obliged and affectionate friend,

Mary Perth.
Free-town, July 29th, 1796[26]

Like Wheatley in her letters to Tanner, here Perth maintains the bonds of friendship through a rhetoric of Christian virtue, reflected in terms of humility, piety, gratitude, and proper sentiment. Not incidentally, Perth begins her missive by acknowledging her own inadequacy to write a letter that properly reflects the sentiment of her "soul." She is vague about the source of that inadequacy; maybe she could read but not write or she was a novice writer, or perhaps she lacked the material objects necessary to write. Black authors, even some of those who could read and write in the latter half of the eighteenth century, sometimes employed amanuenses. The point here is that Perth embodies a humble posture by conceding her inability to convey without assistance the depths of her affection and gratitude for her friend. That opening display of humility foreshadows a general self-consciousness that permeates the letter. As a reflexive gesture, she refers to herself as an "undeserving creature," a "poor soul," and an "unworthy servant in the Lord." In supplication, she addresses Christ, "O Lord, that thou shouldest be thus mindful of me that am poor and ignorant, miserable, blind and naked as I am, thou shouldest thus hedge me in with mercies to keep me from straying from thee." She rehearses familiar religious rhetoric, exhibiting a spiritual introspection that would have been recognizable to any Christian who might stumble upon her letter.

Presumably, Perth understood the letter's contents would express not just a strong attachment to a long-distance friendship but also say something of her character. As a form of cultural capital, the letter affords Perth an elevated position of esteem among her friends—both the recipient of the letter and the amanuensis—and among a larger Christian community. The letter appears in 1802 in a religious volume titled *Surprising Accounts of the Revival of Religion in the United States of America, in Different Parts of the World, and among Different Denominations of Christians with a Number of Interesting Occurrences of Divine Providence.* Edited and published by the Philadelphia printer William W. Woodward, the volume highlights the correspondence of Christian clergy and converts to prove the efficacy of revivalism in the United States and beyond. The letters, the editor insists, illustrate God's "Infinite Power and Majesty."[27] Because her letter reflects what the publisher and his readers perceive as proper Christian virtue, Perth represents in the volume the evangelical spirit of Black Africans who in all parts of the world "are turning their faces Zion-ward."[28] In a spiritual context, Perth's literary effort renders her a representative figure.

Within the sociopolitical context of Sierra Leone, however, Perth's letter writing is more anomalous. Most of her Black counterparts in the colony and King Niambanna II take advantage of the democratizing effects of letter writing to petition directly the colonial power structure. They advocate openly for more political agency and access to material resources—like paper to write more letters.[29] Women wrote letters to secure better domestic conditions. One letter writer, Rose Morral, for example, wrote to Clarkson in 1792 seeking a divorce as she found "no peace with her husband."[30] Another, also writing to Clarkson, begged for "Som Sope" to "wash my family Clos."[31] Perth's letter, notably, does not reference domestic matters, and her audience extends beyond the local leadership. She endeavors to construct a virtuous image even as she attempts to maintain affectionate bonds of friendship.

That Perth sought to control her image and understood the politics of public perception is reflected even more strongly in the letter the Presbyterian minister John Clark wrote to his father. Clark arrived in Sierra Leone in March 1796, just as Macaulay assumed the post as governor. In the 1790s, the Sierra Leone experiment assumed a much more religious and missionary zeal behind the energies of Macaulay and the Court of Directors' chairman Thornton. Macaulay was, as Cassandra Pybus articulates it, "a stern moralist."[32] Both Macaulay and Thornton joined Sharp as part of the Clapham Sect, a London-based group of evangelical Anglicans who advocated for social and moral reform in England, including the abolition of the slave trade. In Freetown, then, Clark oversaw the moral welfare of the settlers. The Black settlers were a devout hodgepodge of Baptists, Methodists, and a splinter Methodist sect referred to as the Countess of Huntingdon's Connexion.[33]

Some dozen Black preachers, many of them self-taught before leaving Nova Scotia, led congregations within the denominations. The settlers expressed themselves and exercised some measure of agency through worship. Church services consisted of animated sermonizing, singing, and other forms of ecstatic exhortation. Macaulay, in his journal, noted with consternation the Black churches' wild "extravagances" and "violent spirit" and hoped "that some sober-minded and authorized" preacher would come to the colony and "introduce more discipline and regularity . . . and correct the extravagant ebullitions of their spirit."[34] With Clark's arrival, Macaulay hoped to reign in the excesses by swaying settlers to what he deemed the doctrinally sound and morally upright practices of the Anglican Church. In other words, Clark was to create a more respectable religious infrastructure for the colony. Initially, the settlers welcomed Clark; he was for them simply another option for religious instruction. One preacher even changed the time of his church services so that his congregants could also attend Clark's. Settlers, the Methodists in particular, turned hostile toward Clark when rumors began that Macaulay intended to close the Black churches and force settlers to attend Clark's church. Such a move, as Christopher Fyfe points out, would have been an affront to one of the few forms of autonomy the settlers could claim by establishing their own churches.[35] In July 1796 some 130 settlers, unnamed, penned an angry letter informing Macaulay and Clark that they would ignore any law that threatened their "religious rights." "We consider ourselves a perfect church," they insisted, "having no need of the assistance of any worldly power to appoint or perform religious ceremonies for us."[36] Amid this tension Clark writes his letter about Perth, who, despite being a practicing Methodist, managed to endear herself to Clark and the colonial leadership.

Clark's letter appeared in the *Evangelical Magazine,* a monthly periodical published in London that promoted the missionary work of evangelical Protestants. Clark's letter appealed to the magazine's readership because it helped to illustrate the successful conversion efforts of the church's agents in the far corners (and beyond) of the British realm. Clark's own rhetorical aim was much more personal, as illustrated in the letter's opening. "I need not say," he begins the letter to his father, "I long to hear from you; this you will take for granted, when that I inform you, that I have received no letter from Scotland since that I left England. I hope you are well, because I sincerely wish you may be so."[37] He arrived in Sierra Leone four months earlier, on March 19. The opening hints at separation anxiety, and he intends the letter to maintain (or restore) familial contact, a bridge over geographical and sentimental distances. After expressing well wishes in the letter, Clark then attempts to fill the communicative void by ventriloquizing his father's voice. "What success has, or is there likely to attend the preaching of the Gospel amongst your people?" he imagines his father asking. Clark's answer: "Blessed be God! . . . There are a few here who have tasted that God is good, to whom he is indeed precious. . . . There is one old woman about seventy years of age . . . the like of whom I never talked with; she is more like one come down out of heaven to earth, than like one who is only preparing for glory" (461). He proceeds to describe in some detail Perth's biography and religious fervor, which dominates the space of the approximately 1,800-word letter.

He details her proselytizing activities while enslaved, the way she traveled at night, with baby in tow, some twenty miles round trip to preach in the Virginia woods. Not having received any formal training, he writes, she "has been made to sit as at the feet of Jesus, and has had his Spirit for her only teacher" (461). He refers to her as a "militant saint" and as "an aged disciple," a reference not just to her age but also to the length of time she has been "a follower of Christ." Clark describes in hyperbolic terms Perth's pious nature. He likens her to an angel before whom he is prone to "blush" (461). Her proselytization is so mesmerizing, Clark tells his father, that hours pass by like minutes in her presence. "It is so pleasant," he says, "to hear her talk with a child-like simplicity, yet with a celestial sublimity, about divine things" (461). Here, Clark subtly reminds his father that Perth is largely a self-taught preacher ("child-like simplicity"), and he portrays her spiritual acumen as innate and otherworldly. He tells his father, "Often do I wish you were a December night in her company. . . . the morning would become ere you was aware" (461–62). Importantly, Perth's spiritual fervor is not a result of anything Clark has done. She is not one of *his* converts. She arrives in Freetown already an experienced evangelical; Clark mostly spectates and marvels.[38] Nevertheless, he describes her piety to validate his own evangelical efforts and impress his father. Perth's example proves the missionizing potential of Freetown.

Beyond Clark's own rhetorical aims, however, the letter suggests Mary Perth had her own ambitions in Freetown. Like King, she experiences a socioeconomic elevation as a result of her religious piety. Indeed, Clark calls her an angel, "one come down out of heaven to earth" (461). One can only imagine the kind of moral uprightness with which Perth engaged her community to garner that kind of reputation. She becomes, Clark writes, "the best assistant I have here, next to my Bible" (461). These descriptions of Perth's behavior, her pious comportment, and the resulting improvement in her financial and social standing in Freetown, suggest that Perth understood the value in presenting herself as respectable. She actively constructs her personal narrative, as Clark writes in his letter, by relating to Clark details of her life before coming to Freetown. It is by Perth's own account, for example, that Clark learns about her conversion and nighttime travels through the Virginia wilderness. She relates to him backstory about her marriage and her husband's subsequent death. The details she provides—and equally important those details she does not provide—act as a filter shaping Clark's final product.[39] She provides enough biographical data to convince Clark to "write a short account of her life" at some later date (463). Clark's letter is a collaborative process, as is the general nature of writing. Perth's agency emerges alongside Clark's rhetorical ambitions. What is more, she possessed a particular savvy in negotiating the religious tensions of Freetown. As a devout Methodist, she managed to ingratiate herself to the colony's Presbyterian pastor and Anglican governor when so many of her Methodist counterparts provoked anger and anxiety. She emerged as a community leader, living in the household of the governor, owning her own business. She became a woman of means in the settlement and used her resources to move fluidly between the private and public realms of Freetown society. Respectability manifested in her domestic duties as a housekeeper and widow and in her religious duties as a spiritual leader for Freetown.

Boston King, King Naimbanna II, and Mary Perth modify their behaviors in ways that improve—or promise to improve—their material circumstances. For their efforts, each emerges as a model of good character, respectability. The texts of these three figures help us to understand how respectability transforms from a structure of external surveillance, controlled by a medieval-style system of frankpledge, into an internal, self-policing mechanism very much akin to what we understand of respectability politics today. Of particular note is that the rhetoric of respectability circulated through the Atlantic, circumscribing cultural formations in the United States, Canada, and West Africa alike. As individual examples, King, King

Naimbanna II, and Perth seem to bear out the potential of respectability politics. Each rises to a position of prominence—or maintains that position, in the case of the king—by manipulating discourses centered on character and respect. Their examples, though, illuminate for us the manner in which respectability politics can be insidious in its allure as it requires it adherents to labor incessantly in self-doubt and uncertainty. Although this kind of politics promises social elevation, it requires compromises that fundamentally undermine one's subjectivity. One might wonder, for example, how does King's wife, Violet, embody meekness and patience but also speak of her spiritual experiences with a "liveliness and power" that is authentic to her? King's "Memoirs" leads us to question whether it is possible to conform to a mainstream code of conduct even as one subverts the racial and gendered boundaries of that mainstream. We could ask, too, what does one lose when adhering to respectability politics? King Naimbanna must weigh his strategy of transculturation against the premature death of his son, who died aboard a ship in 1793 while returning to his Temne community, unable ultimately to convert whatever knowledge he had gathered on behalf of his father's people while living in England. What can be the value of a social elevation that comes with a demand for self-effacement, as reflected in Perth's letter to her friend? She takes advantage of the friendly letter but only through the introspection of humility. She enjoys a position of esteem in Sierra Leone precisely because she performs a mode of Christian virtue that the colony chaplain and governor found acceptable—and only for as long as they did so. It should be noted that just as Perth thrived by the tenets of respectability, she remained vulnerable to those tenets. In 1798, when Macaulay suspected Perth was overcharging customers at her store, he accused her of being vainglorious and greedy. He also complained that she neglected the African children in her care. For a time, he removed her from her post in his home, a move that weakened her influence in Freetown.[40]

Respectability politics is capricious; it is a tally of wins and losses, gains and setbacks. It does not, cannot, inoculate one from the traumas of enslavement, settler colonialism, and racism, structures with which Black Africans have had to contend since the advent of the transatlantic slave trade.

NOTES

PREFACE AND ACKNOWLEDGMENTS

1. Terming it a "politics of the hoodie," Osagie K. Obasogie and Zachary New-man understand respectability politics as a form of victim-blaming: "Responsibility for the violent encounters—or at least a missed opportunity to mitigate the possibility for harm—lies with the victims' dress and behavior, which serves as a warning for all other similarly colored individuals that the best, if not only, way to avoid such outcomes is to comport oneself in a respectable manner" (Obasogie and Newman, "Black Lives Matter and Respectability Politics in Local News Accounts of Officer-Involved Civilian Deaths: An Early Empirical Assessment," *Wisconsin Law Review* [2016]: 543). For more on the politics of Martin's hoodie, see Richard Thompson Ford, "Sagging and Subordination," chapter 12 in *Dress Codes: How the Laws of Fashion Made History,* 196–220 (New York: Simon and Schuster, 2021). See also Lin-ton Weeks, "Tragedy Gives the Hoodie a Whole New Meaning," National Public Radio, March 24, 2012, www.npr.org/2012/03/24/149245834/tragedy-gives-the -hoodie-a-whole-new-meaning.

2. Floyd's past was scrutinized, as Martin's was, with news outlets reporting on Floyd's criminal record and reported drug use.

3. One former detective admitted to providing misleading information in order to secure the warrant that enabled police to raid Taylor's home. Although local authorities declined to pursue charges against the officers who killed Taylor, the Justice Department did pursue federal charges (Richard A. Oppel Jr., Derrick Bryson Taylor, and Nicholas Bogel-Burroughs, "What to Know about Breonna Taylor's Death," *New York Times,* August 23, 2022, www.nytimes.com/article/breonna -taylor-police.html).

4. This call for peaceful protest, of course, was not unique to the Floyd protests. For example, after a grand jury voted not to indict the police officer who shot and killed Michael Brown in Ferguson, Missouri, in 2014, then-president Barack Obama released a statement urging "anyone who protests . . . to do so peacefully." He then quoted these words from Brown's grieving father: "Hurting others or destroying property is not the answer. No matter what the grand jury decides, I do not want my son's death to be in vain. I want it to lead to incredible change, positive change,

change that makes the St. Louis region better for everyone." After quoting Brown's father, Obama added: "Michael Brown's parents have lost more than anyone. We should be honoring their wishes." Here, Obama leverages the grief of Brown's parents to police Black rage (Obama, "Remarks by the President after Announcement of the Decision by the Grand Jury in Ferguson, Missouri," press release, The White House, November 24, 2014, https://obamawhitehouse.archives.gov/realitycheck/the-press-office/2014/11/24/remarks-president-after-announcement-decision-grand-jury-ferguson-missou).

5. This effort to valorize Black rage as righteous when it is expressed through peaceful means culminated in a study released in the fall of 2020 that concluded the vast majority of racial justice protests in the country have been peaceful (Harmett Kaur, "About 93% of Racial Justice Protests in the US Have Been peaceful, a New Report Finds," CNN, September 4, 2020, www.cnn.com/2020/09/04/us/blm-protests-peaceful-report-trnd/index.html).

6. MSNBC reporter Joshua Johnson interrogates protest as an inherently peaceful act (Johnson, "What Is a Peaceful Protest?," MSNBC, September 12, 2020, www.msnbc.com/msnbc/watch/what-is-a-peaceful-protest-91626053566).

7. Bryan Armen Graham, "Donald Trump Blasts NFL Anthem Protesters: 'Get That Son of a Bitch off the Field,'" *The Guardian,* September 23, 2017, www.theguardian.com/sport/2017/sep/22/donald-trump-nfl-national-anthem-protests.

8. Audrey Conklin and Andrew Murray, "Herschel Walker on Olympic Protests: 'If People Don't Like the Rules, Why Are You Here?,'" Fox News, July 23, 2021, www.foxnews.com/sports/herschel-walker-olympics-protests-american-flag.

9. Martin Luther King Jr., "Letter from a Birmingham Jail," ed. Ali B. Ali-Dinar, African Studies Center: University of Pennsylvania, www.africa.upenn.edu/Articles_Gen/Letter_Birmingham.html.

10. I owe a debt of gratitude to my colleague Casarae Lavada Abdul-Ghani, with whom I engaged in a number of discussions about riots and revolts during the Black Arts Movement, which shaped my own thinking about the nature of protests and respectability politics. I appreciate her willingness to engage in dialogue and prompt me to deeper questions and observations. For more on the cultural work of protests and riots in the latter half of the twentieth century, see Abdul-Ghani, *Start a Riot! Civil Unrest in Black Arts Movement Drama, Fiction, and Poetry* (Jackson: University Press of Mississippi, 2022).

INTRODUCTION

1. For more on Obama's deployment of respectability politics, see Julie Bosman, "Obama Takes on Absent Black Fathers in Speech," *New York Times,* June 16, 2008, www.nytimes.com/2008/06/16/world/americas/16iht-fathers.1.13733505.html.

2. Henderson notes that Obama deemphasized respectability politics as his presidency evolved over eight years (Henderson, "'Black Respectability' Politics Are Increasingly Absent from Obama's Rhetoric," *Washington Post,* December 3, 2014,

www.washingtonpost.com/news/the-fix/wp/2014/12/03/black-respectability
-politics-are-increasingly-absent-from-obamas-rhetoric/).

3. Tiffany M. Nyachae and Esther O. Ohito, "No Disrespect: A Womanist
Critique of Respectability Discourses and Extracurricular Programming for Black
Girls," *Urban Education* (2019): 9.

4. Evelyn Brooks Higginbotham, *Righteous Discontent: The Women's Movement in the
Black Baptist Church, 1880–1920* (Cambridge, MA: Harvard University Press, 1993), 187.

5. Ibid.

6. Willard Gatewood, *Aristocrats of Color: The Black Elite, 1880–1920,* 2nd ed.
(Fayetteville: University of Arkansas Press, 2000), 356.

7. Frederick C. Harris, "The Rise of Respectability Politics," *Dissent,* Winter
2014, www.dissentmagazine.org/article/the-rise-of-respectability-politics. See also
Harris's *The Price of the Ticket: Barack Obama and the Rise and Decline of Black Politics*
(Oxford: Oxford University Press, 2012).

8. Harris, "The Rise of Respectability Politics."

9. Victoria Wolcott, *Remaking Respectability: African American Women in Interwar Detroit* (Chapel Hill: University of North Carolina Press, 2001), 5.

10. Brittney C. Cooper, *Beyond Respectability: The Intellectual Thought of Race
Women* (Champaign: University of Illinois Press, 2017), 19.

11. Wolcott, *Remaking Respectability,* 5.

12. For more on discourses of racial uplift in the nineteenth century, see Carla
Peterson, *"Doers of the Word": African-American Women Speakers and Writers in the
North (1830–1880)* (New York: Oxford University Press, 1995); and Joycelyn Moody,
*Sentimental Confessions: Spiritual Narratives of Nineteenth-Century African American
Women* (Athens: University of Georgia Press, 2003).

13. "Isabel de Olvera Arrives in New Mexico," in *African American Women
Confront the West, 1600–2000,* ed. Quintard Taylor and Shirley Ann Wilson Moore
(Norman: University of Oklahoma Press, 2003), 31.

14. For more about the experiences specifically of Black women in colonial New
Spain, see Dedra S. McDonald, "To Be Black and Female in the Spanish Southwest:
Toward a History of African Women on New Spain's Far Northern Frontier," in
African American Women Confront the West, 1600–2000, ed. Quintard Taylor and
Shirley Ann Wilson Moore, 32–52 (Norman: University of Oklahoma Press, 2003).

15. Steve J. Stern, *The Secret History of Gender: Women, Men, and Power in Late
Colonial Mexico* (Chapel Hill: University of North Carolina Press, 1995), 99–103.

16. McDonald, "To Be Black and Female in the Spanish Southwest," 45.

17. See Smith, "Respectability Politics and Early African American Literature,"
in *African American Literature in Transition, 1750–2015,* vol. 1 (Cambridge: Cambridge University Press, 2022): 204–7.

18. See Josselyn, *An Account of Two Voyages to New-England: Made during the Years
1638, 1663* (Boston: William Veazie, 1865), http://galenet.galegroup.com/servlet
/Sabin?af=RN&ae=CY103135201&srchtp=a&ste=14/.

19. Ibid., 26.

20. Cassander L. Smith, "Africans in Early America," chap. 7 in *A Companion to American Literature,* vol. 1: *Origins to 1820,* ed. Theresa Strouth Gaul (Hoboken, NJ: Wiley-Blackwell, 2020), 105–20, https://doi.org/10.1002/9781119056157.ch7.

21. Wendy Anne Warren, *New England Bound: Slavery and Colonization in Early America* (New York: Norton, 2016), 194.

22. Jennifer Morgan, *Laboring Women: Reproduction and Gender in New World Slavery* (Philadelphia: University of Pennsylvania Press, 2004), 14.

23. Cooper, *Beyond Respectability,* 5.

24. Ibid.

25. The interactions between the two Black women speaks to the complications of respectability politics and the intersection of race and class. What of the plight of the Black maid? Was she, too, raped? Did she comply with expectations of sexual labor? What motivated her to preserve a hierarchical relationship with another enslaved woman? What was the power dynamic?

26. See also April Langley, *The Black Aesthetic Unbound: Theorizing the Dilemma of Eighteenth-Century African American Literature* (Columbus: Ohio State University Press, 2008); and Cedrick May, *Evangelism and Resistance in the Black Atlantic, 1760–1835* (Athens: University of Georgia Press, 2008).

27. A couple of notable exceptions are Christopher Fyfe, ed., *Our Children Free and Happy: Letters from Black Settlers in Africa in the 1790s* (Edinburgh: University of Edinburgh Press, 1991), which is a compilation of letters composed by early Freetown (Sierra Leone) settlers; and Christopher Hager, *Word by Word: Emancipation and the Act of Writing* (Cambridge, MA: Harvard University Press, 2013), a study of the letter-writing efforts of post-Emancipation African Americans, which is a bit later than the period under review in this book.

28. Although I don't discuss his letters in this book, the Black abolitionist and merchant Ignatius Sancho perhaps is the most prominent example of a Black African letter-writing tradition in this period. His letters were compiled and published posthumously in 1782. Other examples of Black Africans penning letters include Ayuba Suleiman Diallo, who was kidnapped from his home in present-day Senegal and sold into slavery on a Maryland plantation in 1731. A devout Muslim who could read and write in Arabic, Diallo composed a letter to his father shortly after his enslavement. That letter never reached his father but did reach powerful abolitionists in England who, two years later, orchestrated his freedom. Also, there is the example of a group of enslaved mixed-race families on a Virginia plantation who marshaled their writing resources to pen a letter to a British Anglican bishop to petition for their freedom in 1723 (Thomas N. Ingersoll, "Releese Us out of This Cruell Bondegg: An Appeal from Virginia in 1723," *William and Mary Quarterly* 51.4 [October 1994]). The literacy efforts of Diallo and those mixed-race families on a Virginia plantation predate 1760, what we typically point to as the origins of African American literature.

29. Mary A. Favret, *Romantic Correspondence: Women, Politics and the Fiction of Letters* (Cambridge: Cambridge University Press, 2005), 9.

30. Eve Tavor Bannet, *Empire of Letters: Letter Manuals and Transatlantic Correspondence, 1688–1820* (Cambridge: Cambridge University Press, 2005), ix.

31. Ibid., x.

32. Ibid.

33. Ibid., xvi.

34. See again Hager's *Word by Word,* for more about the extraordinary efforts of nineteenth-century African Americans to learn how to write and compose letters.

35. I discuss Griffith in more detail in chapters 4 and 5.

36. Konstantin Dierks, *In My Power: Letter Writing and Communication in Early America* (Philadelphia: University of Pennsylvania Press, 2011), 238.

37. See Sarah Pearsall, *Atlantic Families: Lives and Letters in the Later Eighteenth Century* (Oxford: Oxford University Press, 2008); and Susan Clair Imbarrato, Sarah Gray Cary from *Boston to Grenada: Shifting Fortunes of an American Family, 1764–1826* (Baltimore, MD: Johns Hopkins University Press, 2018).

38. Martyn Lyons, "Writing Upwards: How the Weak Wrote to the Powerful," *Journal of Social History* 49.2 (2015): 317.

39. Jürgen Habermas, *The Structural Transformation of the Public Sphere: An Inquiry into a Category of Bourgeois Society*, trans. Thomas Burger (Cambridge, MA: MIT Press, 1991), 36.

40. Ibid.

41. Ibid., 48.

42. See, for examples, Alan J. Rice, *Radical Narratives of the Black Atlantic* (New York: Continuum, 2003); Louise Chude-Sokei, "The Black Atlantic Paradigm: Paul Gilroy and the Fractured Landscape of 'Race,'" *American Quarterly* 48.4 (1996): 740–45; Norval (Nadi) Edwards, "'And Some Routes Not Taken': A Caribcentric Reading of *The Black Atlantic*," *Found Object* 4 (1994): 27–35; Walter Goebel and Saskia Schabio, eds., *Beyond the Black Atlantic: Relocating Modernization and Technology* (London: Routledge, 2006); and Lucy Evans, "*The Black Atlantic:* Exploring Gilroy's Legacy," *Atlantic Studies* 6.2 (2009): 255–68, https://doi.org/10.1080/14788810902981308.

43. Manning Marable, "Black Studies and the Racial Mountain," *Souls* 23 (Summer 2000): 17–36.

44. Ibid., 18.

45. Aisha Durham, Brittney Cooper, and Susana M. Morris, "The Stage Hip-Hop Feminism Built: A New Directions Essay," *Signs* 38.3 (Spring 2013): 724.

46. E. Frances White, *Dark Continent of Our Bodies: Black Feminism and the Politics of Respectability* (Philadelphia: Temple University Press, 2001), 35.

47. Durham, Cooper, and Morris, "The Stage Hip-Hop Feminism Built," 724–25.

48. Hedwig Lee and Margaret Takako Hicken, "Death by a Thousand Cuts: The Health Implications of Black Respectability Politics," *Souls* 18.2–4 (2016): 6.

49. Ta-Nehisi Coates, "Charles Barkley and the Plague of 'Unintelligent' Blacks: A History of Respectability Politics, from the Postbellum Period to Today," *Atlantic,*

October 28, 2014, www.theatlantic.com/politics/archive/2014/10/charles-barkley
-and-the-plague-of-unintelligent-blacks/382022/.

50. See Brando Simeo Starkey, "Respectability Politics: How a Flawed Conversation Sabotages Black Lives," The Undefeated (now Andscape), December 12,
2016, https://theundefeated.com/features/respectability-politics-how-a-flawed
-conversation-sabotages-black-lives/.

51. See, for example, Erin M. Kerrison, Jennifer Cobbina, and Kimberly Bender,
"'Your Pants Won't Save You': Why Black Youth Challenge Race-Based Police
Surveillance and the Demands of Black Respectability Politics," *Race and Justice*
8.1 (2018): 7–26.

52. For sure, there are many who critique Beyoncé in light of respectability politics. For example, Alicia Wallace deems exploitative Beyoncé's music and perfor-
mances, especially her *Lemonade* album. She argues that Beyoncé's song "Formation," despite references to her daughter's Afro and the Black Power movement,
actually perpetuates respectability politics with lines like, "You just might be a black
Bill Gates in the making / Always stay gracious, best revenge is your paper," that
call "on black people to remain within the confines of 'good behavior,' work toward
a comfortable financial position, and accept it as recompense" (Wallace, "A Critical
View of Beyoncé's 'Formation,'" *Black Camera* 9.1 [Fall 2017]: 194). Since 2012, the
Black feminist hip-hop scholars who comprise the Crunk Feminist Collective have
offered some of the most nuanced discussions about respectability and Beyoncé on
their blog (see, for example, "Crunktastic" [Brittney Cooper], "On bell, Beyoncé,
and Bullshit," May 20, 2014, www.crunkfeministcollective.com/2014/05/20/on-bell
-beyonce-and-bullshit/; "Crunktastic," "Disrespectability Politics: On Jay-Z's Bitch,
Beyoncé's 'Fly' Ass, and Black Girl Blue," January 19, 2012, www.crunkfeminist
collective.com/2012/01/19/disrespectability-politics-on-jay-zs-bitch-beyonces
-fly-ass-and-black-girl-blue/; Rboylorn [Robin Boylorn], "Pleasure Principles: 5
Lessons about Sex from Beyoncé," March 24, 2014, www.crunkfeministcollective
.com/2014/03/24/pleasure-principles-5-lessons-about-sex-from-beyonce/; Re-
gina N. Bradley [guest blogger], "I Been on [Ratchet]: Conceptualizing a Sonic
Ratchet Aesthetic in Beyoncé's 'Bow Down,'" March 20, 2013, www.crunkfeminist
collective.com/2013/03/20/i-been-on-ratchet-conceptualizing-a-sonic-ratchet
-aesthetic-in-beyonces-bow-down/). See also the essays in their *Crunk Feminist
Collection,* ed. Brittney C. Cooper, Susana M. Morris, and Robin M. Boylorn (New
York: Feminist Press at CUNY, 2017).

53. Kiana Fitzgerald, "Beyoncé Releases New Song 'Black Parade' in the
Final Hours of Juneteenth," National Public Radio, June 20, 2020, www.npr.org
/2020/06/20/881215617/beyonce-releases-new-song-black-parade-in-the-final
-hours-of-juneteenth.

54. Myles E. Johnson, "Beyoncé and the End of Respectability Politics," *New
York Times,* April 16, 2018, www.nytimes.com/2018/04/16/opinion/beyonce
-coachella-blackness.html.

55. Steve D. Mobley Jr. and Jennfier M. Johnson, "'No Pumps Allowed': The

'Problem' with Gender Expression and the Morehouse College 'Appropriate Attire Policy,'" *Journal of Homosexuality* 66.7 (2019): 875. For more on this hidden curriculum, see also Nadrea Njoku, Malika Butler, and Cameron C. Beatty, "Reimagining the Historically Black College and University (HBCU) Environment: Exposing Race and Secrets and the Binding Chains of Respectability and Othermothering," *International Journal of Qualitative Studies in Education* 30.8 (2017): 783–99.

56. Mobley and Johnson, "No Pumps Allowed," 874.

57. OED online, s.v. "respect, n. (and int.)," www.oed.com/view/Entry/163779.

58. See Lori Latrice Martin, *Black Community Uplift and the Myth of the American Dream* (Lanham, MD: Lexington, 2018).

ONE

"NO ROGUE, NO RASCAL, NO THIEF"
Respectability and "Adam Negro's Tryal"

1. Though it is beyond the scope of this project, Native Americans were targets of a similar rhetoric. In the seventeenth century, New England Puritans established praying towns where newly converted Natives lived in community. The laws governing those towns emphasized Christian virtue and European standards of style and conduct. For more on the assimilationist aims of praying towns, see Jean M. O'Brien, *Dispossession by Degrees: Indian Land and Identity in Natick, Massachusetts, 1650–1790* (Lincoln: University of Nebraska Press, 2003).

2. John Saffin, *A Brief and Candid Answer to a Late Printed Sheet Entitled, The Selling of Joseph* (Boston, 1701), 3. Subsequent citations from this source appear parenthetically in the chapter text.

3. The pamphlet's complete title reads, "A Brief and Candid Answer to a Late Printed Sheet, Entitled, The Selling of Joseph Whereunto is annexed, A True and Particular Narrative by way of Vindication of the Author's Dealing with and Prosecution of his Negro Servant, for his vile and exorbitant Behaviour towards his Master, and his Tenant Thomas Shepard; which hath been wrongfully Represented to their Prejudice and Defamation."

4. In 1893 Abner Goodell organized into a narrative the court proceedings of Adam and Saffin's legal battle (Goodell, "John Saffin and His Slave Adam," *Publications of the Colonial Society of Massachusetts* 1 [1895]: 85–112).

5. See David Kazanjian, "'To See the Issue of These His Exorbitant Practices': A Response to 'The Dispossessed Eighteenth Century,'" in "The Dispossessed," special issue, Eighteenth Century 55.2/3 (Summer/Fall 2014): 280.

6. Ibid.

7. Ibid.

8. Goodell, "John Saffin and His Slave Adam," 139.

9. Elisabeth Ceppi, *Invisible Masters: Gender, Race, and the Economy of Service in Early New England* (Hanover, NH: Dartmouth University Press, 2018), 105.

10. Ibid.

11. See Warren M. Billings, "Bound Labor: Slavery," chap. 6 in *The Old Dominion in the Seventeenth Century: A Documentary History of Virginia, 1606–1689* (Chapel Hill: University of North Carolina Press, 1975), 127.

12. *Records and Files of the Quarterly Courts of Essex County,* vol. 4, Harriet S. Tapley, transcriber, 219, http://salem.lib.virginia.edu/Essex/vol4/index/essvol4H.html.

13. Ceppi, *Invisible Masters,* 105.

14. Albert J. Von Frank, "John Saffin: Slavery and Racism in Colonial Massachusetts," *Early American Literature* 29.3 (1994): 262.

15. Saffin, *John Saffin, His Book, 1665–1708: A Collection of Various Matters of Divinity Law and State Affairs Epitomized Both in Verse and Prose* (New York: Harbor, 1928), 153–54.

16. Beyond being a merchant and jurist, Saffin was a noted poet in early America.

17. Von Frank, "John Saffin," 263.

18. Samuel Sewall, *Diary of Samuel Sewall, 1674–1729,* vol. 2 (Boston: Massachusetts Historical Society, 1879), 16, www.google.com/books/edition/Diary_of_Samuel _Sewall/hbsTAAAAYAAJ?hl=en&gbpv=1&bsq=selling%20of%20joseph.

19. Ibid.

20. Cotton Mather, *The Negro Christianized: An Essay to Excite and Assist the Good Work, the Instruction of Negro-Servants in Christianity* (Boston: Printed by B. Green, 1706), retrieved from http://name.umdl.umich.edu/N01059.0001.001. The essay was not exactly an antislavery tract. Like many Puritans, Mather accepted the idea that Divine order was predicated on masters and servants. He pens "Negro Christianized" to implore his fellow Puritans to act as "good" masters by overseeing the conversion of their enslaved Black servants. For more on Mather's understanding of masters and slaves, see Ceppi, *Invisible Masters,* chap. 4.

21. Society of Negroes and Cotton Mather, *Rules for the Society of Negroes. 1693* (Boston: Bartholomew Green[?], 1714[?]), https://quod.lib.umich.edu/e/evansdemo /R08350.0001.001/1:1?rgn=div1;view=fulltext.

22. Ibid., unpaginated.

23. Ibid.

24. It was not uncommon for rules to contain elements unique to the racialized, sociopolitical status of the members of a community. Like this all-Black society, Natives who lived in Indian praying towns were governed by rules that negated their particular cultural practices. In one of the first of those established towns, converted Natives devised a set of rules, influenced heavily by Puritan notions of civility, as preached by John Eliot, a Puritan minister and chief proponent of praying towns. Those rules included: "Every young man if not anothers servant, and if unmarried, he shall be compelled to set up a Wigwam and plant for himselfe, and not live shifting up and downe to other Wigwams; If any woman shall goe with naked breasts they shall pay two shillings sixpence; If any shall kill their lice betweene their teeth, they shall pay five shillings" (John Wilson et al., *The Day Breaking If Not the Sun Rising of the Gospel with the Indians in New England* [1648; reissued for J. Sabin, 1865], 28).

25. Wendy Anne Warren, *New England Bound: Slavery and Colonization in Early America* (New York: Norton, 2016), 194.

26. Ibid.

27. Adam was not the only enslaved Black person who sought Sewall's intervention. One year earlier, an enslaved man named Sebastian asked Sewall to help him marry an enslaved woman belonging to a different enslaver. In his diary, Sewall mentions that Sebastian's enslaver came to his house asking him to "promote" the marriage (Sewall, *Diary of Samuel Sewall,* vol. 5 [Boston: Massachusetts Historical Society, 1878], 29).

28. Goodell, "John Saffin and His Slave Adam," 105.

29. Ibid.

30. Ibid., 140.

31. Sewall also references Jethro's deeds in his diary (Sewall, *Diary,* 14, www.google.com/books/edition/Diary_of_Samuel_Sewall/sfYSAwAAQBAJ?hl=en&gbpv=0).

32. *Records of the Colony of New Plymouth, in New England,* vol. 5, ed. Nathaniel Bradstreet and David Pulsifer (Boston, 1855), Internet Archive, August 2008, https://archive.org/details/recordsofcolony005newp/page/230/mode/2up.

33. Providing an explanation with more nuance, Elisabeth Ceppi and Von Frank both argue that Saffin was motivated by a change in the transatlantic slave trade. Before the turn of the eighteenth century, the slave trade, largely monopolized by the Royal African Company (RAC), was minimally profitable to Massachusetts colonists. Once the RAC lost its monopoly in 1698, slavery suddenly became a more lucrative venture for settler colonists (Ceppi, *Invisible Masters,* 95; Von Frank, "John Saffin," 257–58). See also Lawrence Towner, "The Sewall-Saffin Dialogue on Slavery," *William and Mary Quarterly* 21.1 (January 1964): 40–52.

34. Contrary to what some historians have argued, Sewall does not write *The Selling of Joseph* as a public critique of Saffin's conduct toward Adam. For a more detailed discussion of the sociopolitical context surrounding Sewall's pamphlet, see chapter 7 of Warren's *New England Bound.* See also David Brion Davis, *The Problem of Slavery in Western Culture* (Oxford: Oxford University Press, 1966); and Mark A. Peterson, "The Selling of Joseph: Bostonians, Anti-Slavery, and the Protestant International, 1689–1733," *Massachusetts Historical Review* 4 (2002): 1–22.

35. Mason I. Lowance, ed., *A House Divided* (Princeton, NJ: Princeton University Press, 2003), 2.

36. Sewall, *Diary,* 18.

37. Ibid., 17.

38. Ibid., 18.

39. Ibid.

40. Ibid.

41. Ibid.

42. Ibid., 17. This matter of economic development, according to James J. Allegro, not religion and morality, was a primary driving force for an antislavery sentiment

that emerged in colonial Massachusetts in the early eighteenth century (Allegro, "'Increasing and Strengthening the Country': Law, Politics, and the Antislavery Movement in Early-Eighteenth-Century Massachusetts Bay," *New England Quarterly* 75.1 [March 2002]: 5–23).

43. Sewall, *Diary*, 17.

44. Warren, *New England Bound*, 197.

45. Lowance offers a crucial observation here that Sewall's pamphlet not only presents an argument against slavery, but it also embarks on a discussion "concerning full racial equality, that would be debated throughout the nineteenth century" (Lowance, *A House Divided*, 10).

46. For a detailed discussion about how early Puritans, like Saffin, reconciled economic and religious imperatives to justify Black African enslavement, see Ceppi, *Invisible Masters;* and Warren, *New England Bound.*

47. The source of Massachusetts colonists' anxiety regarding the presence of Black Africans was a growing fear of slave revolts. As Winthrop Jordan argues: "Fear of Negro slave rebellion . . . was ever-present. . . . In many areas it was a gnawing, gut-wringing fear" (Jordan, *White over Black: American Attitudes toward the Negro, 1550–1812* [New York: Norton, 1977], 110–11). Because Black Africans were thought of as unusually prone to savagery and brutality, the fear of a slave revolt was the fear of indiscriminate, furious violence. The Black population remained relatively small in Massachusetts, but it more than doubled during the first half of the eighteenth century. Saffin, then, could have been stoking paranoia that Black Africans would someday outnumber and overpower the white population, as it had already done in locations in the Caribbean, like Barbados. Barbados itself had experienced its share of slave revolt attempts, with aborted plots occurring in 1649, 1674, and 1692. For more on the population of Blacks in colonial Massachusetts, see Warren, *New England Bound.* See also Leon Higginbotham, *In the Matter of Color: Race and the American Legal Process: The Colonial Period* (New York: Oxford University Press, 1978); and William Piersen, *Black Yankees: The Development of an Afro-American Subculture in Eighteenth-Century New England* (Amherst: University of Massachusetts Press, 1988). For more on slave revolts and fear in the early Americas, see Jason T. Sharples, *The World That Fear Made: Slave Revolts and Conspiracy Scares in Early America* (Philadelphia: University of Pennsylvania Press, 2020).

48. Moore reprints Saffin's pamphlet, sans appended narrative, in the appendix of his book (George H. Moore, *Notes on the History of Slavery in Massachusetts* [New York: D. Appleton, 1866], 251–56).

49. Goodell speculates that Moore might have omitted the appendix because there appeared to be missing pages. Whether or not pages were missing from the appendix, Goodell argues, it was complete enough for the reader to gain a clear sense of Saffin's intent in writing it. He includes the appendix in his essay "John Saffin and His Slave Adam." In the essay, Goodell compiles and explains the court transcripts, appeals, and other documents Adam and Saffin filed in their three-year battle. He includes Saffin's appended narrative to illustrate the similarities and differences be-

tween Saffin's account of the legal battle and the actual court documents. Goodell does not include the main text of Saffin's pamphlet.

50. For several examples, see Lawrence Towner, "The Sewall-Saffin Dialogue on Slavery," *William and Mary Quarterly* 21.1 (January 1964): 40–52; Allegro, "Increasing and Strengthening the Country"; Larry Tise, *Proslavery: A History of the Defense of Slavery in America, 1701–1840* (Athens: University of Georgia Press, 1987); and John Wood Sweet, *Bodies Politic: Negotiating Race in the American North, 1730–1830* (Baltimore, MD: Johns Hopkins University Press, 2003). Anthologies include excerpts from the pamphlet but not the appendix. See, for example, *The Heath Anthology of American Literature*, 5th ed., vol. A: *Colonial Period to 1800*, ed. Paul Lauter (New York: Houghton Mifflin, 2006), 552; Carla Mulford, ed., *Early American Writings* (New York: Oxford University Press, 2002), 652–54; and Myra Jehlen and Michael Warner, eds., *The English Literatures of the Americas 1500–1800* (New York: Routledge, 1997), 821–24. Wendy Anne Warren's discussion in *New England Bound* provides a rare exception to this trend.

51. In this way, I agree with David Kazanjian's assessment of Sewall's and Saffin's pamphlets, that they "obscure the case of Adam and, indeed, Adam himself beneath their abstract legalese and formal logic." This remains the case so long as one does not account for the appendix to *A Brief and Candid Answer* (Kazanjian, "To See the Issue of These His Exorbitant Practices," 280).

52. A first trial had been scheduled for May but then postponed until the September date. According to Goodell, there was confusion about the proper jurisdiction and perhaps the validity of certain depositions for which witnesses were absent (Abner C. Goodell, "John Saffin and His Slave Adam," *Publications of the Colonial Society of Massachusetts* 1 [1895]: 90).

53. Sewall writes in his diary on September 11, 1701: "Mr. Saffin tampered with Mr. Kent, the foreman, at Capt. Reynold's, which he denied at Osburn's. Conived at his tenant Smith's being on the jury, in the case between himself and Adam [a negro], about his freedom" (Sewall, *Diary*, 41).

54. Dominik Nagl, "The Governmentality of Slavery in Colonial Boston, 1690–1760," *Amerikastudien/American Studies* 58.1 (2013): 9.

55. Nagl describes this form of slave management as one in which enslavers control the enslaved through a combination of incentives, such as religious instruction, designed to elicit "the voluntary internalization of norms, rules, and patterns of deferential behavior" on the part of the enslaved. This seemingly benign approach combines with physical force when necessary (22).

56. Von Frank, "John Saffin," 254.

57. Goodell justifies reprinting only the appendix: "I have reason to believe, and I think it will presently appear, that it is substantially complete" ("John Saffin and His Slave Adam," 87). Goodell makes this determination based on the fact that Saffin's appended narrative cuts off with the relation of a deposition given in October 1701. A corroboration between that appended narrative and court transcripts shows that no significant legal event occurred between that October 1701 deposition and the

time, shortly after, that the pamphlet went to press. If there is missing text, Goodell postulates, it is immaterial. Based on what has survived of the appendix, we get a clear understanding of how Saffin attempts to spin significant legal events to justify his actions toward his slave Adam.

58. Sewall, *Diary,* 445.

59. For more on the significance of Sewall's apology, see Richard Francis, *Judge Sewall's Apology: The Salem Witch Trials and the Forming of an American Conscience* (New York: HarperCollins, 2005).

60. For a more detailed discussion of the lives of enslaved people in early New England, see Sweet, *Bodies Politic.* See also Oscar Reiss, *Blacks in Colonial America* (Jefferson, NC: McFarland, 1997); and William Piersen, *Black Yankees: The Development of an Afro-American Sub-Culture in Eighteenth-Century New England* (Amherst: University of Massachusetts Press, 1988).

61. Nagl, "The Governmentality of Slavery in Colonial Boston," 12.

62. Saffin also criticized Shepard's decision to grant Adam a small tract of land on which Adam could grow crops for profit. This exercise of freedom, from Saffin's perspective, fed Adam's insolence.

63. Douglass's fight with Covey also begins with Douglass attempting to avoid the confrontation. He fights back only once it becomes clear that there is no escape. Adam does not enjoy the luxury of narrating his own moment. But we do have a record of his actions. The fight did not subdue him and perhaps served a function similar to Douglass, reviving his desires to be free.

64. Frederick Douglass, *Narrative of the Life of Frederick Douglass* (Boston: Anti-Slavery Office, 1845), 72, retrieved from https://docsouth.unc.edu/neh/douglass/douglass.html.

65. Goodell, "John Saffin and His Slave Adam," 96.

66. Von Frank, "John Saffin," 265.

67. *Acts and Resolves, Public and Private, Province of the Massachusetts Bay: To Which are Prefixed the Charters of the Province,* vol. 1: *1692–1714* (Boston: Wright and Potter, Printers to the State, 1869), 578–79 and 606–7. For more on how laws restricted Black African liberties, see Warren, *New England Bound,* 201.

TWO

"THOSE WHO SEEM'D TO RESPECT ME"

Phillis Wheatley at the Border of Respectability

1. Increasingly, scholars refer to Wheatley as Phillis Wheatley Peters, incorporating her married last name. They note that, once she married, Wheatley signed her poetry and letters as Phillis Peters, so the addition of Peters recognizes her agency in taking control of her name and identity. At the time of writing this book, I have not decided whether the name change speaks to her control and agency or merely illustrates marriage conventions of the time. Perhaps a little of both? How much meaning might we ascribe to either name, Wheatley or Peters? Both stand in for

what we cannot know about the conditions of Wheatley's birth and early childhood. In this chapter, I refer to her married name only on first reference and in parentheses to recognize this ongoing conversation. I subsequently refer to her as Wheatley because the moments I point to as most informative in shaping her respectability strategies occur before she married. For more on this matter of naming, see Honorée Fanonne Jeffers, *The Age of Phillis* (Middletown, CT: Wesleyan University Press, 2020); Zachary Hutchins, "Provocation: 'Add New Glory to Her Name': Phillis Wheatley Peters," *Early American Literature* 56.3 (Spring 2021): 663–67; and Tara Bynum, Brigitte Fielder, and Cassander Smith, "Dear Sister: Phillis Wheatley's Futures," *Early American Literature* 57.3 (Winter 2022): 663–79.

2. Though the evidence is circumstantial, scholars commonly accept that this ad, which appeared in the *Boston Post-Boy & Advertiser,* references Wheatley. See, for example, Vincent Carretta, *Biography of a Genius in Bondage* (Athens: University of Georgia Press, 2011); and Jennifer Thorn, "Phillis Wheatley's Ghosts: The Racial Melancholy of New England Protestants," *Eighteenth Century* 50.1 (Spring 2009): 73–99.

3. Advertisement, *Boston Post-Boy & Advertiser,* August 3, 1761, p. 3, America's Historical Newspapers, https://infoweb-newsbank-com.libdata.lib.ua.edu/apps/readex /doc?p=EANX&t=pubname%3A1089C7C672FD2D48%21Boston%2BPost -Boy&sort=YMD_date%3AA&fld-base-0=alltext&val-base-0=%22Likely %20negroes%22&fld-nav-0=YMD_date&val-nav-0=&docref=image/v2%3 A1089C7C672FD2D48%40EANX-1089CE6DC051E8C0%402364467–1089 CE6E02912290%402–1089CE6ECC94BBD0%40Advertisement&firsthit=yes.

4. Phillis Wheatley, *The Writings of Phillis Wheatley,* ed. Vincent Carretta (Oxford: Oxford University Press, 2019), 125. Please note my use of Carretta's edited collection of Wheatley's poems and letters as the primary source for quoting Wheatley's work. Subsequent citations from this source appear parenthetically in the chapter text.

5. I use the term "acculturation" here in the very basic sense that Wheatley adopts the practices and attitudes of a British colonial mainstream culture. Later in the chapter, I discuss her strategies of cultural adaptation more complexly as a form of assimilation.

6. The Wheatleys granted her freedom three months before Susannah's death.

7. For a concise discussion on this point, see Antonio T. Bly, "'Pretends He Can Read': Runaways and Literacy in Colonial America, 1730–1776," *Early American Studies* 6.2 (Fall 2008): 261–94. Bly argues about Wheatley, "In context, Wheatley was clearly not the phoenix of her race, as Henry Louis Gates Jr. and other literary scholars have claimed. . . . [S]he was one of many literate blacks. Put another way, the African-born poet personified the African American literary tradition," but there was also an "African American literacy tradition" that we can map through close readings of runaway slave ads (269).

8. For a concise discussion of the nature of this social network, see Tara Bynum, "Reading and Building a Nation; or, Everyday Living (while Black) in Early America," in *African American Literature in Transition, 1750–1800,* vol. 1, 181–203 (Cambridge: Cambridge University Press, 2022).

9. In *Black Looks: Race and Representation,* hooks discusses what many view as radical and impossible, Black desirability. She argues for Black self-love as an anti-racist response to whiteness and white supremacy: "Collectively, black people and our allies in struggle are empowered when we practice self-love as a revolutionary intervention that undermines practices of domination. Loving blackness as political resistance transforms our ways of looking and being, and thus creates the conditions necessary for us to move against the forces of domination and death and reclaim black life" (hooks, *Black Looks: Race and Representation* [Boston: South End Press, 1992], 20). My thinking about Wheatley and Blackness in this way is informed by the work of Michelle Hite and Deanna Koretsky, who discuss the application of hooks's theory to the teaching of Wheatley in predominantly Black classrooms at Spelman College (Michelle S. Hite and Deanna P. Koretsky. "Loving Blackness across Arts and Sciences," *Early American Literature* 57.3 [2022]: 827–34, doi:10.1353/eal.2022.0073).

10. Will Harris, "Phillis Wheatley, Diaspora Subjectivity, and the African American Canon," *MELUS* 33.3 "Multicultural and Multilingual Aesthetics of Resistance" (Fall 2008): 36.

11. Perhaps it goes without saying that Crevecoeur's construction focuses on those of European nationalities and ethnicities (Crevecoeur, *Letters from an American Farmer* [N.p., Applewood, 2007], 55, www.google.com/books/edition/Letters_from_an_American_Farmer/a7e92ie1h68C?hl=en&gbpv=0).

12. Victor Nee and Richard D. Alba, *Remaking the American Mainstream: Assimilation and Contemporary Immigration* (Cambridge, MA: Harvard University Press, 2009), 13, https://www.google.com/books/edition/Remaking_the_American_Mainstream/qfTiUv4mv_sC?hl=en&gbpv=0.

13. See Catherine Ramírez, "Assimilation," in *Keywords for Latino/a Studies,* ed. Deborah R. Vargas, Nancy Raquel Mirabal, and Lawrence La Fountain-Stokes, 14–18 (New York: New York University Press, 2017), 18.

14. Lori Latrice Martin, *Black Community Uplift and the Myth of the American Dream* (Lanham, MD: Lexington, 2018), 17.

15. Evelyn Brooks Higginbotham, *Righteous Discontent: The Women's Movement in the Black Baptist Church, 1880–1920* (Cambridge, MA: Harvard University Press, 1993), 216.

16. Ibid., 217.

17. Ibid., 218.

18. Ibid.

19. See Higginbotham, *Righteous Discontent;* Victoria W. Wolcott, *Remaking Respectability: African American Women in Interwar Detroit* (Chapel Hill: University of North Carolina Press, 2001); and Brittney Cooper, *Beyond Respectability: The Intellectual Thought of Race Women* (Champaign: University of Illinois Press, 2017).

20. For a summary of the critical tradition, see Henry Louis Gates Jr., *The Trials of Phillis Wheatley: America's First Black Poet and Her Encounters with the Founding Fathers* (New York: Basic Civitas, 2003).

21. This impulse was particularly strong in the 1980s and 1990s. See, for example, Sondra O'Neale, "A Slave's Subtle War: Phillis Wheatley's Use of Biblical Myth and Symbol," *Early American Literature* 21.2 (Fall 1986): 144–65; Cynthia J. Smith, "'To Maecenas': Phillis Wheatley's Invocation of an Idealized Reader," *Black American Literature Forum* 23.3 (1989): 579–92; James A. Levernier, "Style as Protest in the Poetry of Phillis Wheatley," *Style* 27.2 (Summer 1993): 172–93; Paula Bennett, "Phillis Wheatley's Vocation and the Paradox of the 'Afric Muse,'" *PMLA* 113.1 (January 1998): 64–76; Hilene Flanzbaum, "Unprecedented Liberties: Re-Reading Phillis Wheatley," in "Poetry and Poetics," special issue, *MELUS* 18.3 (Autumn 1993): 71–81; and Marsha Watson, "A Classic Case: Phillis Wheatley and Her Poetry," *Early American Literature* 31.2 (1996): 104. More recent examples include John C. Shields, *Phillis Wheatley's Poetics of Liberation: Backgrounds and Contexts* (Knoxville: University of Tennessee Press, 2008); Mary Catherine Loving, "Uncovering Subversion in Phillis Wheatley's Signature Poem: 'On Being Brought from Africa to America,'" *Journal of African American Studies* 20.1 (March 2016): 67–74; Will Harris, "Phillis Wheatley, Diaspora Subjectivity, and the African American Canon," in "Multicultural and Multilingual Aesthetics of Resistance," special issue, *MELUS* 33.3 (Fall 2008): 27–43; and Antonio T. Bly, "'By Her Unveil'd Each Horrid Crime Appears': Authorship, Text, and Subtext in Phillis Wheatley's Variants Poems," *Textual Cultures* 9.1 (Winter 2014): 112–41.

22. Samantha Pinto, *Infamous Bodies: Early Black Women's Celebrity and the Afterlives of Rights* (Durham, NC: Duke University Press, 2020), 39.

23. Perhaps the best example of Wheatley's wordplay is her poem "An Answer to the Rebus, by the Author of These Poems," which responds to the poem "A Rebus, by I.B."

24. For example, in addition to her letter to Thornton, see also the letter she pens to the Mohegan and Presbyterian minister Samson Occom in 1774, in which she proclaims boldly that freedom is an inherent desire for all Black Africans (*Writings of Phillis Wheatley*, ed. Carretta, 119).

25. I apply this term, which more often describes cultural perceptions and stereotypes targeted at Asian American communities, to Wheatley to suggest that her contemporaries viewed her as similarly exemplary.

26. See, for example, Henry Louis Gates Jr., "Introduction: Writing 'Race' and the Difference It Makes," in "'Race,' Writing, and Difference," special issue, *Critical Inquiry* 12.1 (Autumn 1985): 1–20; and Roxann Wheeler, *The Complexion of Race: Categories of Difference in Eighteenth-Century British Culture* (Philadelphia: University of Pennsylvania Press, 2000). See also Emmanuel Chukwudie Eze, introduction to *Race and the Enlightenment: A Reader* (Cambridge, MA.: Blackwell, 1997); and Balkun, "To 'Pursue th' Unbodied Mind.'"

27. For examples of this perspective, see David Hume, "Of National Character," in *Race and the Enlightenment*, ed. Eze; and Immanuel Kant, "On National Characteristics, So Far as They Depend upon the Distinct Feeling of the Beautiful and Sublime," ibid.

28. Thomas Jefferson, *Notes on the State of Virginia with Related Documents,* ed. David Waldstreicher (New York: Palgrave, 2002), 180.

29. Jefferson, *Notes,* 177–78.

30. For a concise discussion of this assumption, see Gates, "Introduction: Writing 'Race' and the Difference It Makes."

31. Eric Slauter, "Neoclassical Culture in a Society with Slaves: Race and Rights in the Age of Wheatley," *Early American Studies* 2.1 (Spring 2004): 83.

32. For more on how African Americans intervened in the politics and discourses of the American Revolution, in addition to Slauter, see Betsy Erkkila, "Phillis Wheatley and the Black American Revolution," in *A Mixed Race: Ethnicity in early America,* ed. Frank Shuffleton, 225–40 (New York: Oxford University Press, 1993); and David Waldstreicher, "Ancients, Moderns, and Africans," *Journal of the Early Republic* 37.4 (Winter 2017): 701–33. See also Vincent Carretta, introduction to *Unchained Voices: An Anthology of Black Authors in the English-Speaking World of the Eighteenth Century,* ed. Carretta (Lexington: University Press of Kentucky, 1996), 1–14.

33. "Slave Petitions for Freedom," in *The Radical Reader: A Documentary History of the American Radical Tradition,* ed. Timothy Patrick McCarthy and John Campbell McMillian (New York: New Press, 2003), 26.

34. Jupiter Hammon, "An Address to the Negroes in the State of New York (1787)," in *The Collected Works of Jupiter Hammon*, ed. Cedrick May, 65–78 (Knoxville: University of Tennessee Press, 2017).

35. Ibid., 72.

36. Ibid.

37. Ibid., 73.

38. May argues that Hammon's politics are more radical, certainly more nuanced, than this one speech might suggest (May, introduction to *The Collected Works of Jupiter Hammon* [Knoxville: University of Tennessee Press, 2017], xxi–xxxviii).

39. Gates, "Introduction: Writing 'Race' and the Difference It Makes," 9. In his introduction, Gates articulates the politics of authorship for Black Africans: "Text created author; and black authors, it was hoped, would create, or re-create, the image of the race in European discourse. The very face of their race was contingent upon the recording of the black *voice*" (11).

40. Katherine Clay Bassard, *Spiritual Interrogations: Culture, Gender, and Community in Early African American Women's Writing* (Princeton, NJ: Princeton University Press, 1999), 21.

41. Frances Smith Foster, *Written by Herself: Literary Production by African American Women, 1746–1892* (Bloomington: Indiana University Press, 1993), 19.

42. Ibid., 2.

43. Carla L. Peterson, *"Doers of the Word": African-American Women Speakers and Writers in the North (1830–1880)* (New Brunswick, NJ: Rutgers University Press, 1998), 3.

44. Hortense J. Spillers, "Mama's Baby, Papa's Maybe: An American Grammar Book," in "Culture and Countermemory: The 'American' Connection," special issue, *Diacritics* 17.2 (Summer 1987): 64–81.

45. Ibid., 67.

46. Ibid.

47. See Alexander Weheliye, *Habeas Viscus: Racializing Assemblages, Biopolitics, and Black Feminist Theories of the Human* (Durham, NC: Duke University Press, 2014); and Charles W. Mills, *The Racial Contract* (1997; Ithaca, NY: Cornell University Press, 2014), Kindle.

48. Frantz Fanon, *Black Skin, White Masks*, trans. Charles Lam Markmann (New York: Grove, 1967), 189.

49. Ibid.

50. Ibid., 11.

51. Spillers, "Mama's Baby," 67.

52. Ibid., 80.

53. Peterson, "*Doers of the Word*," 7.

54. A "community sphere," according to Peterson, "functioned as an intermediate sphere situated somewhere between the domestic/private and the public." This sphere, she argues, "can be viewed as 'public' as it is located outside the 'home' and remains preoccupied with the welfare of the general population, but it is also 'domestic' in that it represents an extension of the values of 'home' into the community; and it is 'private' insofar as it is able to remain hidden, abstracted from the gaze of the dominant culture. For nineteenth-century African Americans, this sphere was vital to the preservation of both the bodily integrity and the psychic security of families and individuals" (ibid., 16).

55. "Intersectionality" is a theoretical framework that accounts for the ways in which multiple identity positions intersect to shape a person's life experiences. Crenshaw arrived at this articulation after noticing that "Black women are sometimes excluded from feminist theory and antiracist policy discourse because both are predicated on a discrete set of experiences that often does not accurately reflect the interaction of race and gender. These problems of exclusion cannot be solved simply by including Black women within an already established analytical structure. Because the intersectional experience is greater than the sum of racism and sexism, any analysis that does not take intersectionality into account cannot sufficiently address the particular manner in which Black women are subordinated" (Kimberlé Crenshaw, "Demarginalizing the Intersection of Race and Sex: A Black Feminist Critique of Antidiscrimination Doctrine, Feminist Theory and Antiracist Politics," *University of Chicago Legal Forum* 1.8 [1989]:140).

56. Pinto, *Infamous Bodies*, 26.

57. Ibid., 8.

58. Ibid., 31–32.

59. Ibid., 40.

60. Balkun speculates that Wheatley's ability to conceive of identity in such flexible terms "may have been one she was forced to develop in order to overcome perceptions about her own limitations as an African (Balkun, "To 'Pursue th' Unbodied Mind': Phillis Wheatley and the Raced Body in Early America," in *New Essays*

on Phillis Wheatley, ed. John C. Shields and Eric D. Lamore, 371–96 [Knoxville: University of Tennessee Press, 2011], 377).

61. For an extensive treatment of this question, see Eric Slauter, "Looking for Scipio Moorhead: An 'African Painter' in Revolutionary America," in *Slave Portraiture in the Atlantic World,* ed. Agnes Lugo-Ortiz and Angela Rosenthal, 89–118 (Cambridge: Cambridge University Press, 2013).

62. See, for example, Samantha Pinto, "Fantasies of Freedom: Phillis Wheatley and the 'Deathless Fame' of Black Feminist Thought," in her *Infamous Bodies;* and Walt Nott, "From 'Uncultivated Barbarian' to 'Poetical Genius': The Public Presence of Phillis Wheatley," in "Poetry and Poetics," special issue, *MELUS* 18.3 (Autumn 1993): 21–32.

63. See, for example, Astrid Franke, "Phillis Wheatley, Melancholy Muse," *New England Quarterly* 77.2 (June 2004): 224–51; Betsy Erkkila, "Phillis Wheatley and the Black American Revolution," in *A Mixed Race: Ethnicity in Early America,* ed. Frank Shuffleton (New York: Oxford University Press, 1993), 225–40; and Honoree Jeffers, "Looking for Miss Phillis," in *The Age of Phillis* (Middlebury, CT: Wesleyan University Press, 2020), 186. In several poems and a critical essay at the end of her book of poems, Jeffers makes a case that Wheatley dons a nose ring, an adornment particular to the Senegambia region that scholars speculate was Wheatley's birthplace.

64. See Joanna Brooks, "Our Phillis, Ourselves," *American Literature* 82.1 (March 2010): 1–28; and Eric Slauter, "Neoclassical Culture in a Society with Slaves: Race and Rights in the Age of Wheatley," *Early American Studies* 2.1 (Spring 2004): 81–122.

65. For more on how Wheatley indirectly alludes to her own grief through the elegies and that of her parents, besides Brooks, see Bassard, *Spiritual Interrogations;* and April Langley, *The Black Aesthetic Unbound: Theorizing the Dilemma of Eighteenth-Century African American Literature* (Columbus: Ohio State University Press, 2008).

66. See Franke, "Melancholy Muse," 234.

67. See Brooks, "Our Phillis, Ourselves"; Bassard, *Spiritual Interrogations;* and Langley, *The Black Aesthetic Unbound.* See also Gordon E. Thompson, "Methodism and the Consolation of Heavenly Bliss in Phillis Wheatley's Funeral Elegies," *CLA Journal* 48.1 (September 2004): 34–50; and Antonio T. Bly, "On Death's Domain Intent I Fix My Eyes," *Early American Literature* 53.2 (2018): 317–41.

68. In his study of Wheatley's use of a neoclassical style, David Waldstreicher notes that Wheatley posed a unique problem for white American Revolutionists. She evoked the classics in her poetry (or ancients) in order to challenge the idea of progression and modernity that the Revolution promised by pointing to the nation's practice of a brand of enslavement that suggested regression rather than progression into a modern era. Waldstreicher argues: "It isn't just that she proved Africans could write poetry, that they were capable, so race as justification for slavery was a lie. It's that she showed that modern, American slavery was worse than the ancient kind precisely insofar as it did not celebrate or even free individuals like Wheatley. She raised the distinct possibility that history was going backwards, not forwards, in America" (Waldstreicher, "Ancients, Moderns, and Africans," 727).

69. Franke, "Melancholy Muse," 243.

70. Frances Smith Foster, *Written by Herself: Literary Production by African American Women, 1746–1892* (Bloomington: Indiana University Press, 1993), 33. She employs that neoclassical style, as James A. Levernier points out, to create "a subversive persona that speaks on multiple levels" (Levernier, "Style as Protest in the Poetry of Phillis Wheatley," *Style* 27.2 [Summer 1993]: 175).

71. Mary Catherine Loving, "Uncovering Subversion in Phillis Wheatley's Signature Poem: 'On Being Brought from African to America,'" *Journal of African American Studies* 20.1 (March 2016): 70.

72. Foster, *Written by Herself,* 39.

73. Franke, "Melancholy Muse," 243.

74. L. Lamar Wilson, "Birthing America's Kweer," *South: A Scholarly Journal* 51.1 (Fall 2018): 28.

75. Helen Burke, for example, argues that Wheatley "derides her talents in relation to" Homer, Virgil, and Terence through her reference to a 'grov'ling mind' (34). Her "self-deprecation," Burke argues, is a convention of the day (Burke, "The Rhetoric and Politics of Marginality: The Subject of Phillis Wheatley," *Tulsa Studies in Women's Literature* 10.1 [1991]: 34).

76. My perspective here echoes Cynthia J. Smith, who argues that the reference to a "grov'ling mind" is a "statement of frustration at the limits imposed [on Wheatley] by time and place, by race and status" and, I would add, by gender (586). The poem is a struggle for credibility. Smith further notes: "The difficulty involved in reading a poem like 'To Maecenas' is that knowing of Wheatley's circumstances as a slave, the reader is too ready to read the poem as slavish praise heaped upon a benefactor. Such a reader accepts unquestioningly the premise that someone in Wheatley's position would have feelings of inadequacy; and, of course, such a reader would hear the notes of dependency, servility, and flattery more loudly than the strains of anger, frustration, and bold self-assertion—all equally in evidence" in the poem (Smith, "'To Maecenas': Phillis Wheatley's Invocation of an Idealized Reader," *Black American Literature Forum* 23.3 [1989]: 590).

77. Burke, "The Rhetoric and Politics of Marginality," 34.

78. Watson, "A Classic Case: Phillis Wheatley and Her Poetry," 119.

79. Paula Bennett, "Phillis Wheatley's Vocation and the Paradox of the 'Afric Muse,'" *PMLA* 113.1 (January 1998): 68.

80. Wilson, "Birthing America's Kweer," 28.

81. Brooks, "Our Phillis, Ourselves"; Jennifer Thorn, "Phillis Wheatley's Ghosts"; and Lucia Hodgson, "Infant Muse: Phillis Wheatley and the Revolutionary Rhetoric of Childhood," *Early American Literature* 49.3 (2014): 663–82.

82. Hodgson, "Infant Muse," 663.

83. Ibid., 667.

84. "Sass," a term often used to describe the behavior of young Black girls that is deemed impertinent, Antonio T. Bly understands in relation to Wheatley's poetic aesthetics as "an expression of agency that on the surface appears either deferential or in keeping with the social etiquette of the day" (Bly, "On Death's Domain," 319).

85. Bly, "By Her Unveil'd Each Horrid Crime Appears," 132.

86. As Adélékè Adéèkó reminds us, this is an example of Wheatley's inventive language: "Wheatley's African . . . is an invention of a Christian speaking to a community of other Christians." Carretta uses the term "fortunate fall" to describe the attitudes of some early Black Africans who viewed their enslavement as a kind of spiritual deliverance (Adélékè Adéèkó, "Writing African under the Shadow of Slavery: Quaque, Wheatley, and Crowther," *Research in African Literatures* 40.4 [Winter 2009)]: 15; Carretta, introduction to *Unchained Voices,* 2–3).

87. David Waldstreicher argues, "Wheatley's invocations of Africa are decidedly double-edged. They use presumptions of African pagan backwardness to challenge easy notions of progress" and, I would add, of virtue (Waldstreicher, "Ancients, Moderns, and Africans," 722).

88. Adéèkó, "Writing African under the Shadow of Slavery," 18.

89. This paradox of enslavement as deliverance—or a "fortunate fall," as Vincent Carretta terms it—was common in early American literature (Carretta, introduction to *Unchained Voices,* 2–3).

90. Rafia Zafar, *We Wear the Mask: African Americans Write American Literature, 1760–1870* (New York: Columbia University Press, 1997), 19.

91. Ibid.

92. Ibid.

93. Tara Bynum, "Phillis Wheatley on Friendship," *Legacy* 31.1 (2014): 43.

94. Bassard, *Spiritual Interrogations,* 23.

95. For quick context on Quaque's missionary efforts, see Adéèkó, "Writing African under the Shadow of Slavery. See also G. J. Barker-Benfield, *Phillis Wheatley Chooses Freedom: History, Poetry, and the Ideals of the American Revolution* (New York: New York University Press, 2018).

96. Watson, "A Classic Case: Phillis Wheatley and Her Poetry," 104.

97. Hilene Flanzbaum, "Unprecedented Liberties: Re-Reading Phillis Wheatley," in "Poetry and Poetics," special issue, *MELUS* 18.3 (Autumn 1993): 72. For a more quantitative discussion of the critical reception of Wheatley's poetry, see Mukhtar Ali Isani, "The Contemporaneous Reception of Phillis Wheatley: Newspaper and Magazine Notices during the Years of Fame, 1765–1774," *Journal of Negro History* 85.4 (Autumn 2000): 260–73.

98. Thomas Clarkson, *An essay on the slavery and commerce of the human species, particularly the African, translated from a Latin dissertation, which was honoured with the first prize in the University of Cambridge, for the year 1785, with additions* (London, 1785), 112, in Early English Books Online Text Creation Partnership, http://name.umdl .umich.edu/N15396.0001.001.

99. Ibid., 113.

100. Benjamin Rush, *An Address to the Inhabitants of the British Settlements in America, upon Slave-Keeping* (New York: Hodge and Shober, 1773), 4, Early American Imprints, https://infoweb-newsbank-com.libdata.lib.ua.edu/iw-search/we /Evans/?p_product=EAIX&p_theme=eai&p_nbid=M4AE4CLGMTYyMDA2

NDY10C410TMyNDU6MToxNDoxMzAuMTYwLjIoLjExNw&p_action
=doc&p_queryname=page3&f_qdnum=1&f_qnext=&f_qrnum=1&f_qname=1
&f_qprev=&p_docref=v2:0F2B1FCB879B099B@EAIX-0F30189B77F2113
8@12992-@1–0F90419C97CB6E40&f_mode=printCitation.

101. Brooks, "Our Phillis, Ourselves," 10. After noting that Wheatley was "deeply connected within white women's coteries of manuscript circulation in New England and Philadelphia" (9), Brooks argues that the influence of white women is most pronounced in Wheatley's elegies, which enabled her to "achieved her early reputation . . . by transacting in feelings of grief and loss among white women" (11). She, according to Brooks, performed "the emotional labor of condolence and sympathy for [white women]. [White women's] participation in this transactional, sentimental culture of mourning enabled them to indulge feelings of self-consciousness, self-regard, and willful passivity imbricated with their increasingly privileged merchant-class status. It also allowed white women to evade taking responsibility for their economic privilege—which capitalized on the unfreedom of enslaved men and women like Wheatley—and ultimately to evade their responsibility to the poet herself" (8).

102. Wendy Raphael Roberts, "'Slavery' and 'To Mrs. Eliot on the Death of Her Child': Two New Manuscript Poems Connected to Phillis Wheatley by the Bostonian Poet Ruth Barrell Andrews," *Early American Literature* 51.3 (2016): 665–81. Roberts uncovers manuscript poems penned by Andrews to argue that "the discovery of a contemporaneous, white female manuscript poet who engaged Wheatley in verse and boldly attempted to define the political meaning of her 'comprehensive poems' expands the possibilities for understanding Wheatley's relationships with local poets" (674).

103. Carretta, *Biography of a Genius in Bondage,* 91.

104. Margaretta Matilda Odell, *Memoir and Poems of Phillis Wheatley, A Native African and a Slave* (Boston: Geo. W. Light, 1834), 29, Documenting the American South, https://docsouth.unc.edu/neh/wheatley/wheatley.html.

105. Ibid., 9.

106. Ibid., 11.

107. Ibid., 12.

108. Carretta, Biography of a *Genius in Bondage,* 175–76.

109. Sancho, *Letters of the Late Ignatius Sancho, An African. In Two Volumes. To Which Are Prefixed, Memoirs of His Life,* vol. 1 (London: J. Nichols, 1782), 175, Documenting the American South, https://docsouth.unc.edu/neh/sancho1/sancho1.html.

110. Hammon, "An Address to Miss Phillis Wheatly [*sic*], Ethiopian Poetess, in Boston, who came from Africa at eight years of age, and soon became acquainted with the gospel of Jesus Christ," in *The Completed Works of Jupiter Hammon: Poems and Essays,* ed. Cedrick May (Knoxville: University of Tennessee Press, 2017), 11.

111. Ibid., 12.

112. Ibid.

113. Ibid., 11.

114. The presumed deficiencies of Black women, in fact, as Martha Saxton points out, became a negative reference point by which the femininity of white women was defined (see Martha Saxton, *Being Good: Women's Moral Values in Early America* [New York: Hill and Wang, 2003]).

115. Harriet Jacobs, *Incidents in the Life of a Slave Girl, Written by Herself* (Boston, 1861), 86, https://docsouth.unc.edu/fpn/jacobs/jacobs.html.

116. See, for example, "A Short Account of the Life of Elizabeth Colson" (1727), "The Confession of Flora Negro" (1748), and the trial transcripts of Candy and Mary Black from the Salem Witch Trials (1692), all in *The Earliest African American Literatures: A Critical Reader,* ed. Zachary Hutchins and Cassander L. Smith (Chapel Hill: University of North Carolina Press, 2021).

117. Thorn makes the crucial point that most studies of enslaved Black women, sexuality, and reproduction limit their scope to the South and the Caribbean, which is "routinely taken as metonyms of 'slavery' as a whole," which flattens the discussion about enslaved Black women and reproduction in early America (Thorn, "Phillis Wheatley's Ghosts," 77). Here, Thorn echoes the criticisms of others, like Bassard, who argues similarly: "historians, concerned with 'representativeness[,]' have situated the majority of studies of American slavery in the nineteenth-century U.S. South. Thus the plantation system has been treated as 'normative' of pre-Emancipation black experience, an assumption, with serious consequences for theories of African American subjectivity and discourse" (Bassard, *Spiritual Interrogations,* 11).

118. Thorn, "Phillis Wheatley's Ghosts," 78.

119. Ibid.

120. For more on the dual forms of labor that Black enslaved women were expected to perform on southern and Caribbean plantations, see Jennifer L. Morgan, *Laboring Women: Reproduction and Gender in New World Slavery* (Philadelphia: University of Pennsylvania Press, 2004).

121. Several scholars have argued for other factors that enabled Wheatley's entrance into the public sphere. See, for example, Thorn, who posits that "Wheatley's poetry writing and her transatlantic celebration as eighteenth-century icon of African humanity depended fundamentally, if covertly, upon her being non-reproductive and physically unthreatening: in this sense, 'like a child'" (Thorn, "Phillis Wheatley's Ghosts," 80).

122. Walt Nott, "From 'Uncultivated Barbarian' to 'Poetical Genius': The Public Presence of Phillis Wheatley," in "Poetry and Poetics," special issue, *MELUS* 18.3 (Autumn 1993): 21.

123. Ibid., 23.

124. Ibid.

125. Phillip M. Richards, "Phillis Wheatley, Americanization, the Sublime, and the Romance of America," *Style* 27.2 (Summer 1993): 202.

126. In his study of Wheatley's maternal and exegetical influence on an African American poetic tradition, L. Lamar Wilson also recognizes the cultural work

Wheatley performs for white audiences: "As African American writers have often done before white witnesses, Wheatley frames herself not only as an interlocutor for black slaves in America but also for white Americans fashioning a national identity separate from their British (and otherwise European)" (Wilson, "Birthing America's Kweer," *South: A Scholarly Journal* 51.1 [Fall 2018)]: 29).

127. Kirstin Wilcox, "The Body into Print: Marketing Phillis Wheatley," *American Literature* 71.1 (March 1999): 9.

128. Ibid., 7.

129. Ibid., 19.

130. It might be more useful to consider Wheatley operating within Peterson's "community sphere." This point echoes conversations happening in gender and women's studies about the drawbacks of framing early American public and private spaces in terms of gender, especially before the nineteenth century. For a concise discussion of early Americanists' investment in this gendered concept of public and private spaces and its problematic framework, see Terri L. Snyder, "Refiguring Women in Early American History," *William and Mary Quarterly* 69.3 (July 2012): 421–50. See also Kathleen M. Brown, "Beyond the Great Debates: Gender and Race in Early America," *Reviews in American History* 26.1 (March 1998): 96–123.

131. This is true, as well, of Lucy Terry Prince (see Frances Smith Foster, "Sometimes by Simile, a Victory's Won: Lucy Terry Prince and Phillis Wheatley" in *Written by Herself: Literary Production by African American Women, 1746–1892*, 23–42 [Bloomington: Indiana University Press, 1993]).

132. The archival work of Cornelia H. Dayton also suggests that the Peterses had at least one child, maybe more, who died as an infant (Dayton, "Lost Years Recovered: John Peters and Phillis Wheatley Peters in Middleton," *New England Quarterly* 94.3 [September 2021]: 309–51).

133. Odell's memoir is the primary source for this critical (mis)perception of Peters.

134. Carretta, *Biography of a Genius in Bondage;* Jeffers, *Age of Phillis;* Dayton, "Lost Years Recovered."

135. Dayton, "Lost Years Recovered," 328.

136. Ibid., 331.

137. Quoted in Dayton, "Lost Years Recovered," 314.

138. Hilene Flanzbaum, "Unprecedented Liberties: Re-Reading Phillis Wheatley," in "Poetry and Poetics," special issue, *MELUS* 18.3 (Autumn 1993): 79.

THREE
(SOME) BLACK LIVES MATTER
Olaudah Equiano and the ~~Social~~ Racial Contract

1. I should note here the debate about Equiano's origins, based largely on the archival work of Vincent Carretta. In his biography of Equiano, Carretta argues that Equiano likely was younger than eleven when he was kidnapped and that he might have been born in South Carolina rather than West Africa. Regarding Equi-

ano's birthplace, Carretta bases his conjectures on a baptism record and ship log. Although questions about Equiano's birthplace circulated even during his own lifetime, Carretta's findings in the 1990s gave those questions new significance. Since then, scholars have grappled with the inconsistencies. At issue here is not so much whether Equiano made up facts or lied about his birthplace. If he did, he would not be the first autobiographer to get creative with the biographical details. As Paul Lovejoy notes, the narrative is "subject to the same criticisms of selectivity and self-interested distortion that characterize the genre of autobiography." The larger issue is one about archival evidence and how we assess it. In this case, it seems that two archival documents, neither written by Equiano himself and both with rhetorical aims of their own—Cathy Davidson parses out those rhetorical aims quite beautifully—have been accepted largely at face value. It is not clear on what grounds those documents are more credible versions of Equiano's early life than his own account. For more on the veracity of Equiano's account, see Lovejoy, "Autobiography and Memory: Gustavus Vassa, alias Olaudah Equiano, the African," *Slavery and Abolition* 27.3 (2007): 318; Carretta, "Olaudah Equiano or Gustavus Vassa? New Light on an Eighteenth-Century Question of Identity," *Slavery and Abolition* 20.3 (1999): 96–105; and Davidson, "Olaudah Equiano, Written by Himself," in "The Early American Novel," special issue, *NOVEL: A Forum on Fiction* 1.2 (Fall 2006–Spring 2007): 18–51. See also Alexander X. Byrd, "Eboe, Country, Nation, and Gustavus Vassa's *Interesting Narrative*," *William and Mary Quarterly* 63.1 (January 2006): 123–48.

2. I discuss in more detail this resettlement plan in chapters 4 and 5 of this book.

3. Rafia Zafar, "It Is Natural to Believe in Great Men," in *We Wear the Mask: African Americans Write American Literature, 1760–1870*, 89–116 (New York: Columbia University Press, 1997), 90.

4. It is not incidental that Equiano begins his narrative by acknowledging, "I believe there are few events in my life, which have not happened to many . . . but when I compare my lot with that of most of my countrymen, I regard myself as a particular favorite of Heaven" (Equiano, *The Interesting Narrative of the life of Olaudah Equiano, or Gustavus Vassa, The African Written by Himself*, ed. Werner Sollors [New York: Norton, 2001], 19). Subsequent citations from this source appear parenthetically in the chapter text.

5. Charles W. Mills, *The Racial Contract* (1997; Ithaca, NY: Cornell University Press, 2014), Kindle.

6. My formulation here is another way of articulating Philip Gould's argument about eighteenth-century antislavery writing. Gould argues that early antislavery literature represented the slave trade as especially barbaric, revealing a cultural anxiety about what a capitalist society should look like. That anxiety was expressed through a discourse of manners in which sentiment was linked to capitalism. The barbaric designation of the slave trade, furthermore, offered a point of reference, Gould maintains, for what was considered good commerce versus bad commerce. The slave trade was especially egregious because its barbarity created an apparent contradiction. It, according to Gould, "challenged the compatibility of commercial society—slave-

trading society—with enlightened civilization" (Gould, *Barbaric Traffic: Commerce and Antislavery in the Eighteenth-Century Atlantic World* [Cambridge, MA: Harvard University Press, 2003], 4).

7. Mills, *The Racial Contract*, location 155.

8. Ibid., location 868.

9. See Arna Bontemps, *Great Slave Narratives* (Boston: Beacon, 1969); and Paul Edward, *The Life of Olaudah Equiano or Gustavus Vassa, the African* (London: Dawsons, 1969). See also Henry Louis Gates Jr., *The Classic Slave Narratives* (New York: Penguin, 1987); and Vincent Carretta, *The Interesting Narrative and Other Writings* (New York: Penguin, 1995); both works are central texts for the canonization of Equiano's narrative, which is now required reading in many college classrooms.

10. See, for example, Ronald Paul, "'I Whitened My Face, That They Might Not Know Me': Race and Identity in Olaudah Equiano's Slave Narrative," *Journal of Black Studies* 39.6 (July 2009): 848–64; Monica Weis, "Olaudah Equiano at Sea: Adrift in White Culture," in "Literature of the Sea," special issue, *CEA Critic* 63.1 (Fall 2000): 21–26; and Peter Jaros, "Good Names: Olaudah Equiano or Gustavus Vassa," *Eighteenth Century* 54.1 (Spring 2013): 1–24. Many of the critics whose works are cited in the next several notes position themselves across multiple threads of discussion, rendering a complex, rich, overall conversation about Equiano's cultural and historical contributions.

11. Susan M. Marren, "Between Slavery and Freedom: The Transgressive Self in Olaudah Equiano's Autobiography," *PMLA* 108.1 (January 1993): 94–105.

12. See, for example, Houston A. Baker Jr., *Blues, Ideology, and Afro-American Literature: A Vernacular Theory* (Chicago: University of Chicago Press, 1984); and Ross J. Pudaloff, "No Change without Purchase: Olaudah Equiano and the Economies of Self and Market," *Early American Literature* 40.3 (2005): 499–527, which argues that "exchange" is the "privileged" trope in Equiano's narrative (504). See also Elizabeth Jane Wall Hinds, "The Spirit of Trade: Olaudah Equiano's Conversion, Legalism, and the Merchant's Life," *African American Review* 32.4 (Winter 1998): 635–47. Hinds argues that Equiano embodies multiple selves, expressing at varying times an enslaved self, a merchant, a juridical subject and a convert. See also Andrew Kopec, "Collective Commerce and the Problem of Autobiography in Olaudah Equiano's 'Narrative,'" *Eighteenth Century* 54.4 (Winter 2013): 461–78; Joseph Fichtelberg, "Word between Worlds: The Economy of Equiano's *Narrative*," in "Eighteenth-Century American Cultural Studies," special issue, *American Literary History* 5.3 (Autumn 1993): 459–80; and David Kazanjian, "Racial Capitalism: Mercantile Exchanges and Mercantilists Enclosures," in *The Colonizing Trick: National Culture and Imperial Citizenship in Early America*, 35–88 (Minneapolis: University of Minnesota Press, 2003).

13. Hinds, "The Spirit of Trade," 635.

14. Baker, *Blues, Ideology, and Afro-American Literature*, 32.

15. Ibid., 37.

16. See, for example, Rebecka Rutledge Fisher, "The Poetics of Belonging in the Age of Enlightenment: Spiritual Metaphors of Being in Olaudah Equiano's 'Inter-

esting Narrative,'" in "Forming Nations, Reforming Empires: Atlantic Polities in the Long Eighteenth Century," special issue, *Early American Studies* 11.1 (Winter 2013): 72–97. Fisher argues that Equiano negotiates the political divide between empire and nation-state to develop a sense of national belonging through his religious conversion. He articulates that sense of belonging through the use of ontotheological metaphors. Similarly, Srinivas Aravamudan argues that Equiano undertakes a process of "nationalization" in which he speaks a nationalist discourse in order to resist sociopolitical erasure. For Aravamudan, religion, evangelism specifically, "becomes a bridge between personal loss and a new public identity" (Aravamudan, *Tropicopolitans: Colonialism and Agency, 1688–1804* [Durham, NC: Duke University Press, 1999], 241). See also Adam Potkay, "Olaudah Equiano and the Art of Spiritual Autobiography," *Eighteenth-Century Studies* 27.4 (1994): 677–92; Valerie Smith, "Form and Ideology in Three Slave Narratives," in *Self-Discovery and Authority in Afro-American Narrative,* 9–43 (Cambridge, MA: Harvard University Press, 1987); Willie James Jennings, "Equiano's Words," in *The Christian Imagination,* 169–203 (New Haven, CT: Yale University Press, 2010); Eileen Razzari Elrod, "Moses and the Egyptian: Religious Authority in Olaudah Equiano's Interesting Narrative," *African American Review* 35.3 (Autumn 2001): 409–25; Samantha Manchester Earley, "Writing from the Center or the Margins? Olaudah Equiano's Writing Life Reassessed," *African Studies Review* 46.3 (December 2003): 1–16; Joanna Brooks, "Soul Matters," *PMLA* 128.4 (October 2013): 947–52; and Sylvester A. Johnson, "Colonialism, Biblical World-Making, and Temporalities in Olaudah Equiano's Interesting Narrative," *Church History* 77.4 (December 2008): 1003–24.

17. See, for example, Geraldine Murphy, "Olaudah Equiano, Accidental Tourist," in African-American Culture in the Eighteenth-Century," special issue, *Eighteenth-Century Studies* 27.4 (Summer 1994): 551–68; and Frank Kelleter, "Ethnic Self-Dramatization and Technologies of Travel in 'The Interesting Narrative of the Life of Olaudah Equiano, or Gustavus Vassa, the African, Written by Himself,'" *Early American Literature* 39.1 (2004): 67–84.

18. V. Smith, "Form and Ideology in Three Slave Narratives," 20. Marion Rust notes a similar narrative rupture in Equiano's text resulting from his tendency to adhere to an "imperialist ethics" that he "both benefit[s] from and despise[s]," producing a "precarious self-articulation as both African and European" (Rust, "The Subaltern as Imperialist," in *Passing and the Fictions of Identity,* ed. Donald E. Pease and Elaine K. Ginsberg, 21–36 [Durham, NC: Duke University Press, 1996], 24). For other perspectives on voice in Equiano's narrative, see Henry Louis Gates Jr., *The Signifying Monkey: A Theory of African American Literary Criticism* (Oxford: Oxford University Press, 1988); and Tanya Caldwell, "'Talking Too Much English': Languages of Economy and Politics in Equiano's 'The Interesting Narrative,'" *Early American Literature* 34.3 (1999): 263–82. Resisting readings of Equiano as an African or hybrid figure, Caldwell emphasizes instead the extent to which Equiano adopts a wholly British voice that reflects the political and social sensibilities of eighteenth-century British culture in order to mute racial difference and advocate for his social

and political inclusion. See also Wilfred D. Samuels, "Disguised Voice in *The Interesting Narrative of Olaudah Equiano, or Gustavus Vassa, the African*," *Black American Literature Forum* 19.2 (Summer 1985): 64–69, who argues that Equiano is a trickster figure employing varying voices to condemn white inhumanity.

19. For example, in addition to Fisher and Jennings, see Íde Corley, "The Subject of Abolitionist Rhetoric: Freedom and Trauma in 'The Life of Olaudah Equiano,'" *Modern Language Studies* 32.2 (Autumn 2002): 139–56; George E. Boulukos, "Olaudah Equiano and the Eighteenth-Century Debate on Africa," *Eighteenth-Century Studies* 40.2 (Winter 2007): 241–55; Werner Sollors, "Olaudah Equiano, an Enlightenment Cosmopolitan in the Age of Slavery," in *African American Writing* (Philadelphia: Temple University Press, 2016), 15–37; and Robin Sabino and Jennifer Hall, "The Path Not Taken: Cultural Identity in the Interesting Life of Olaudah Equiano," in "African American Literature," special issue, *MELUS* 24.1 (Spring 1999): 5–19.

20. See Davidson, "Olaudah Equiano, Written by Himself"; and V. Smith, "Form and Ideology in Three Slave Narratives." Davidson argues, "In its ranging and unpredictable hybridity, in its urgency, in its embrace of trauma and uncertainty as a central trope, and in its high moral purpose coupled with a capacious refusal to adhere to a stable form, *The Interesting Narrative* resembles the post-Revolutionary American novel" (22).

21. Zafar, *We Wear the Mask*, 92.

22. Vincent Carretta, *Equiano the African: Biography of a Self-Made Man* (New York: Penguin, 2005), 303. Specifically, Carretta argues that the narrative is, among other things, "spiritual autobiography, captivity narrative, travel book, adventure tale, slave narrative, rags-to-riches saga, economic treatise, apologia, testimony, and possibly even historical fiction."

23. John Bugg, "Equiano's Trifles," *ELH* 80.4 (Winter 2013): 1045–66. Bugg maintains: "The trifles break new ground. We see Equiano experimenting with the new modes of expression to sketch ideas, complaints, and paradoxes not easily accommodated by conventional abolitionist discourse. The trifles absorb the vexed thoughts and emotions that arise from Equiano's telling of his life story, including anger, revenge, suspicions of the value of freedom, and meditations on the prospect of a black community in Britain" (1050).

24. Ramesh Mallipeddi, "Filiation to Affiliation: Kinship and Sentiment in Equiano's Interesting Narrative," *ELH* 81.3 (Fall 2014): 923–54.

25. Hinds, "The Spirit of Trade," 637; Gates, *The Signifying Monkey*, 152; Murphy, "Accidental Tourist," 553.

26. Because Equiano spent so little time in the United States—about two years total, according to William L. Andrews—Andrews asserts that Equiano more properly should be considered an "Anglo-African writer," not "one of the early voices of the Afro-American autobiographical tradition" (Andrews, *To Tell a Free Story: The First Century of Afro-American Autobiography, 1760–1865* [Champaign: University of Illinois Press, 1988], 57). For alternative perspectives, see Frances Smith Foster,

Witnessing Slavery: The Development of Ante-bellum Slave Narratives (Madison: University of Wisconsin Press, 1994); and Gates, *The Signifying Monkey.*

27. For example, see again those early studies of Bontemps, *Great Slave Narratives*; Edwards, *The Life of Olaudah Equiano;* Gates, *The Classic Slave Narratives*; and Vincent Carretta, *The Interesting Narrative.* See also Foster, *Witnessing Slavery;* Caldwell, "Talking Too Much English," in which Caldwell nuances the reading of Equiano's text as autobiography; and Kopec, "Collective Commerce." Kopec considers Equiano's narrative within the novelistic tradition rather than autobiography or memoir because, he argues, Equiano depends upon the strategy of typification, central to the early novel, to advocate for the potential of West African commerce.

28. Davidson, "Olaudah Equiano," 19.

29. Vincent Carretta's archival work in the 1990s and the subsequent publication of his authoritative biography of Equiano in 2005 have done the most to advance this aspect of Equiano scholarship. Davidson and Lovejoy, along with several others, contest the impulse by many scholars to question the veracity and significance of Equiano's narrative in light of Carretta's archival findings. In addition to Davidson and Lovejoy's work, see Jaros, who offers the caveat that "reducing the problem of Equiano/Vassa's identity to the problem of his nativity risks imposing a coherence on him that is at odds with his own self-presentation" (Jaros, "Good Names," 2). See also Yael Ben-Zvi's "Equiano's Nativity: Negative Birthright, Indigenous Ethic, and Universal Human Rights," *Early American Literature* 48.2 (2013): 399–423, in which she argues that Equiano's nativity matters less than the narrative's investment in advocating for universal human rights, rights that extend to those born into an enslaved status. See also Alexander X. Byrd, "Eboe, Country, Nation, and Gustavus Vassa's *Interesting Narrative,*" *William and Mary Quarterly* 63.1 (2006): 123–48.

30. For example, see Kopec, "Collective Commerce"; Paul, "I Whitened My Face"; and Kelleter, "Ethnic Self-Dramatization and Technologies of Travel."

31. Paul, "I Whitened My Face," 863.

32. Kopec, "Collective Commerce," 474.

33. Hinds, "The Spirit of Trade," 640.

34. Zafar, *We Wear the Mask,* 95.

35. When the British abolition movement emerged in earnest in the latter eighteenth century, abolitionist mostly did not advocate for universal emancipation. In pamphlets, newspapers, letters, on the floor of Parliament, in narratives like Equiano's, they saw as a first and more practical priority the end of the slave trade with the idea that if the pipeline were eliminated, the institution itself would die in time. For a concise discussion of the early aims of the British abolition movement, see Carretta, "Turning against the Slave Trade," in *Equiano the African,* 236–69. For a more detailed discussion of the history of British abolitionism, see Thomas Clarkson, *The History of the Rise, Progress, and Accomplishment of the Abolition of the African Slave-Trade by the British Parliament* (London, 1808).

36. Caldwell, "Talking Too Much English," 265; Marren, "Between Slavery and Freedom," 101. As an alternative, the process of assimilation that Marren and Cald-

well note as central to Equiano's narrative, Aravamudan calls "colonial mimicry." In his formulation of Equiano as a "tropicopolitan," Aravamudan argues that Equiano "speaks the discourse of nationality and collectivity in the manner of the later eighteenth century" in order to resist the British colonizing project whereby tropes of otherness work to silence and erase colonial subjects (Aravamudan, *Tropicopolitans,* 21–22).

37. Keith Sandiford, *Measuring the Moment: Strategies of Protest in Eighteenth-Century Afro-English Writing* (London: Susquehanna University Press, 1988), 128.

38. Jaros, "Good Names," 9.

39. Ibid., 3.

40. Ibid., 17.

41. Lisa Lowe, *The Intimacies of Four Continents* (Durham, NC: Duke University Press, 2015), 1.

42. Ibid., 3.

43. Ibid., 47.

44. Ibid., 17.

45. Ibid., 62.

46. Ibid., 70.

47. For more on slavery conditions in the West Indies, see Randy M. Browne, *Surviving Slavery in the British Caribbean* (Philadelphia: University of Pennsylvania Press, 2017); Russell R. Menard, *Sweet Negotiations: Sugar, Slavery, and Plantation Agriculture in Early Barbados* (Charlottesville: University of Virginia Press, 2006); and Richard S. Dunn (1972), *Sugar and Slaves: The Rise of the Planter Class in the English West Indies, 1624–1713* (Chapel Hill: University of North Carolina Press, 2012).

48. Carretta argues that Equiano likely was younger than eleven when kidnapped and enslaved (Carretta, *Equiano the African,* 17).

49. Mallipeddi, "Filiation to Affiliation," 925.

50. Samuels, "Disguised Voice," 69.

51. See Igor Kopytoff and Suzanne Miers's introduction to *Slavery in Africa: Historical and Anthropological Perspectives,* ed. Miers and Kopytoff (Madison: University of Wisconsin Press, 1979). For a more recent take on this, see Willie James Jennings, "Equiano's Words," in *The Christian Imagination,* 169–203 (New Haven, CT: Yale University Press, 2010). Like Kopytoff and Miers, Jennings notes a fundamental difference between African and American slavery. In African societies, Jennings argues, "the idea of production primarily for exchange rather than communal use was destructively alien. Therefore by manipulating a barter system that was intensely bound to use-value, each agreement, each sale suggested to African peoples engaged in trade the possibility of long-term obligatory relations. However, this communal metaphysic was being slowly eroded by an unbelievably virulent form of contractual individualism underwritten by sheer violence and European technological mastery." He refers to this violence as "the tragedy of trade's chaos" (172).

52. See Lisa Lindsay, "Slavery, Absorption, and Gender: Frederick Cooper and the Power of Comparison," *History in Africa* 47 (2020), 67, 72, https://doi.org/10.1017/hia.2019.22; Frederick Cooper, "The Problem of Slavery in Af-

rican Studies," *Journal of African History* 20.1 (1979): 103–25, doi:10.1017/S0021853700016741; Paul Lovejoy, *Slavery in the Global Diaspora of Africa* (Milton Park, Oxfordshire, UK: Taylor and Francis, 2019); Paul Lovejoy, *Slavery, Commerce and Production in the Sokoto Caliphate of West Africa* (Trenton, NJ: Africa World Press, 2005); and Mohammed Bashir Salau, *Plantation Slavery in the Sokoto Caliphate: A Historical and Comparative Study* (Rochester, NY: University of Rochester Press, 2018), www.google.com/books/edition/Plantation_Slavery_in_the_Sokoto_Calipha /s6V8DwAAQBAJ?hl=en&gbpv=0.

53. Mills, *The Racial Contract*, 913.

54. Jennings, "Equiano's Words," 184.

55. Ben-Zvi, "Equiano's Nativity," 400.

56. For Hobbes, the Right of Nature refers to a perfect state of freedom in which "each person hath, to use his own power, as he will himself, for the preservation of his own nature; that is to say, of his own life; and consequently, of doing anything, which in his own judgement, and reason, he shall conceive to be the aptest means thereunto." Understanding man in his natural state as mostly hedonistic, Hobbes argues, like Locke a little later, that people enter into social contracts, agreeing to relinquish some degree of liberty to protect themselves from the hedonistic impulses of others (Thomas Hobbes, *Leviathan* [1651], in *The Selected Political Writings of John Locke*, ed. Paul E. Sigmund [New York: Norton, 2005], 243–44).

57. When an individual is forced to act violently against another in order to preserve his freedom, according to Locke, the parties exist in a state of war. Locke argues, "he who attempts to get another man into his absolute power does thereby put himself into a state of war with him; it being to be understood as a declaration of a design upon his life." In that case, Locke concludes, an individual so oppressed is bound by nature to resist (Locke, "The Second Treatise of Government" [1689], in *The Selected Political Writings of John Locke,* 24). Similarly, Hobbes argues that the state of war is inherent, by virtue of individuals living in a state of nature whereby "every one [is] against every one" (Hobbes, *Leviathan,* 246).

58. Kelleter, "Ethnic Self-Dramatization and Technologies of Travel," 74.

59. Jaros, "Good Names," 9.

60. Hinds, "The Spirit of Free Trade," 643.

61. Carretta, *Equiano, the African,* 170.

62. Rust, "The Subaltern as Imperialist," 24.

63. Pudaloff, "No Change without Purchase," 507.

64. Ibid., 501.

65. Ibid., 502.

66. Ibid., 508.

67. Ibid., 501.

68. Fichtelberg, "Word between Worlds," 474.

69. Eileen Razzari Elrod, "Moses and the Egyptian: Religious Authority in Olaudah Equiano's *Interesting Narrative,*" *African American Review* 35.3 (Autumn 2001): 410.

70. Fichtelberg, "Word between Worlds," 471.

71. According to Samantha Manchester Earley, Equiano does express some remorse about his work on Irving's plantation. "It is clear," she argues, "that he also resisted further participation in the oppression of his own countrymen, for, as we discover later, he interprets the misdeeds and mishaps that befell him after he left that Musquito Shore plantation as God's punishment" (Earley, "Writing from the Center or the Margins?," 8). It is the case that Equiano endured a number of cruelties after leaving the plantation, including being strung up by the waist onboard a ship. He does not, though, directly link those sufferings to divine punishment for his participation in the slave trade. Rather, those experiences, I would argue, further illustrate the cruelty of white enslavers and islanders.

72. Marren, "Between Slavery and Freedom," 100.

73. Mallipeddi, "Filiation to Affiliation," 925.

74. Perhaps Equiano refers here to the fact that slavery was de facto illegal in England; there was no specific law explicitly banning the practice—nor a law permitting it. The landmark Mansfield ruling in the Somerset case did not occur until a decade later, which protected Black Africans from being forcibly removed from England and enslaved. For more, see Carretta, *Equiano, the African,* 202–7.

75. Equiano evokes mostly common law and the idea that slavery was a status reserved for non-Christians; a prevailing narrative among slavery apologists was that the practice targeted those of *heathen* nations, not other Christians. Based on this rationale, many opponents of slavery and those enslaved themselves, naturally assumed that conversion to Christianity would make them free. That idea was challenged in British society, most notably perhaps in the 1729 Yorke-Talbot slavery opinion, in which two legal administrators for the Crown declared that baptism did not automatically manumit an enslaved person.

76. Jennings, "Equiano's Words," 182.

77. For more on the link among language, race, and respectability, see Robin R. Means Coleman and Jack L. Daniel, "Mediating Ebonics," *Journal of Black Studies* 31.1 (September 2000): 74–95.

78. This is not the only time that Equiano is called out for speaking "too well." When two white men accost him in Savannah and threaten to claim him as their fugitive property, Equiano says: "I told them to be still and keep off; for I had seen those kind of tricks played upon other free blacks, and they must not think to serve me so. At this they paused a little, and one said to the other—it will not do; and the other answered that I talked too good English" (121).

79. Hinds, "The Spirit of Trade," 641.

80. Ibid.

81. Pudaloff, "No Change without Purchase," 517.

82. Lowe, *Intimacies of Four Continents,* 61.

83. Pudaloff, "No Change without Purchase," 516.

84. Ibid.

85. Kelleter, "Ethnic Self-Dramatization and Technologies of Travel," 78.

86. Importantly for Jaros, respectability rhetoric comes to an ironic crisis point in this moment. Equiano's "value as a commodity," he argues, "supplements his reputation for integrity as he petitions for self-possession in the face of a dishonorably broken promise." The language of integrity that runs throughout the narrative and that is reflected here in King's hesitancy to honor his promise, according to Jaros, illustrates Equiano's understanding of the importance of character as integral to personhood (Jaros, "Good Names," 9).

87. Baker, *Blues, Ideology, and Afro-American Literature,* 35.

88. Ibid., 36.

89. Elizabeth Maddock Dillon, "A Sea of Texts: The Atlantic World, Spatial Mapping, and Equiano's *Narrative,*" in *Religion, Space, and the Atlantic World,* 25–54 (Columbia: University of South Carolina Press, 2017), 29.

90. Ibid., 30.

91. Lowe, *Intimacies of Four Continents,* 61.

92. Jaros, "Good Names," 12.

93. Philip Gould argues that moments like these juxtapose "the virtue of Equiano's commercial identity with the barbarity of the African slave trade." The focus on his own suffering, Gould notes, enables Equiano to render himself the victim of barbaric commercial practices rather than an agent perpetuating such practices when he, for example, participates in the buying, selling, transporting, and overseeing of enslaved people (Gould, *Barbaric Traffic,* 133).

94. Kelleter, "Ethnic Self-Dramatization and Technologies of Travel," 78.

FOUR

"MY POOR LITTLE ILL-THRIVEN SWARTHY DAUGHTER"
Granville Sharp and the Respectability of
Deportation to Province of Freedom

1. It should be noted that in this context, the term "Black Poor" was an ambiguous racial marker. Originally, the label applied to seamen of color, or lascars (mostly Black African and South Asian), with the Royal Navy who found themselves unemployed and destitute after the war. The steady influx of African American Loyalists in the 1780s meant the term increasingly applied to people of sub-Saharan African descent. By 1786, Mary Beth Norton estimates, some 1,200 Black Africans lived in London, most of them destitute (Norton, "The Fate of Some Black Loyalists of the American Revolution," *Journal of Negro History* 58.4 [October 1973]: 406).

2. Samuel Sewall, *Diary of Samuel Sewall, 1674–1729,* vol. 2 (Boston: Massachusetts Historical Society, 1879), 18, www.google.com/books/edition/Diary_of_Samuel _Sewall/hbsTAAAAYAAJ?hl=en&gbpv=1&bsq=selling%20of%20joseph.

3. I discuss the efforts of this society in more detail in chapter 5.

4. Sharp refers to himself as a "friend to blacks" in a letter addressed to Sierra Leone settlers in 1790. In that letter, he recapitulates his résumé as a racial ally in order to generate goodwill not just among the settlers but also among the indigenous

leaders in the neighboring kingdoms (see Prince Hoare, *Memoirs of Granville Sharp, Esq. Composed from His Own Manuscripts, and Other Authentic Documents in the Possession of His Family and of the African Institution* [London, 1820], 359, in Slavery and Anti-Slavery, https://www.google.com/books/edition/_/_LIEAAAAYAAJ ?hl=en&sa=X&ved=2ahUKEwj_8sih7tP8AhVjSDABHSEHBjwQre8FegQI AxAv).

5. Michael J. Turner, "The Limits of Abolition: Government, Saints, and the 'African Question' c. 1780–1820," *English Historical Review* 112.446 (April 1997): 320.

6. Founded in 1786, the Committee for the Relief of the Black Poor was a privately run charity that solicited donations to provide financial aid and other resources—like medical care—to those lascars who became unemployed and indigent after the war. As more and more African American loyalists flooded the city, they became the primary target of the committee's philanthropic efforts.

7. For a concise discussion of British efforts to penetrate the interior of sub-Saharan Africa, see Emma Christopher, "A 'Disgrace to the Very Colour': Perceptions of Blackness and Whiteness in the Founding of Sierra Leone and Botany Bay," *Journal of Colonialism and Colonial History* 9.3 (Winter 2008), Project MUSE, https://doi.org/10.1353/cch.0.0025.

8. For more on the commercial aims of abolitionists, see Suzanna Schwarz, "'A Just and Honourable Commerce': Abolitionist Experimentation in Sierra Leone in the Late Eighteenth and Early Nineteenth Centuries," *African Economic History* 45.1 (2017): 1–45, https://doi.org/10.1353/aeh.2017.0000.

9. For more on how the Sierra Leone settlement challenged conceptions of British Empire, see Isaac Land and Andrew M. Schocket, "New Approaches to the Founding of the Sierra Leone Colony, 1786–1808," *Journal of Colonialism and Colonial History* 9.3 (Winter 2008), *Project MUSE,* https://doi.org/10.1353/cch.0.0021.

10. Isaac Land, "On the Foundings of Sierra Leone, 1787–1808," in *BRANCH: Britain, Representation and Nineteenth-Century History,* ed. Dino Franco Felluga, Extension of Romanticism and Victorianism on the Net, https://branchcollective.org /?ps_articles=isaac-land-on-the-foundings-of-sierra-leone-1787-1808.

11. See Richard Eden, "The Discription of the Two Viages Made Owt of England into Guinea" (1555), in *The Decades of the Newe Worlde or West India,* in *The First Three English Books on America,* ed. Edward Arber (Westminster: A. Constable, 1895), 373–88, www.google.com/books/edition/The_First_Three_English_Books_on_America /aRwzAQAAMAAJ?hl=en&gbpv=0.

12. In one of the more often quoted passages from Eden's description of West Africa, he insists that Black Africans are "a people of beastly lyuynge, without a god, lawe, religion, or common welth, and so scorched and vexed with the heate of the soonee, that in many places they curse it when it ryseth" (Eden, "The Discription of the Two Viages," 384). Scholars have used this passage to illustrate early English attitudes toward Black Africans and racial difference.

13. Ibid., 386.

14. Ibid., 387.

15. Ibid.

16. Ibid. It should be noted here that Eden does not initiate a new discourse about African wealth. He echoes the descriptions of travel writing predecessors, in particular Leo Africanus and John Mandeville (Africanus, *A Geographical Historie of Africa*, trans. John Pory [London, 1600]; Mandeville, *Here Begynneth a Lytell Treatyse . . . [and] Speketh of the Wayes of the Holy Londe Towarde Jherusalem, of Marueyles of Ynde of other Dyuerse Cou[n]trees* [1499]).

17. William Towerson, "The First Voyage Made by Master William Towrson Marchant of London, to the Coast of Guinea, with Two Ships, in the Yeere 1555," in *Principal Navigations, Voiages, and Discoveries of the English Nation,* by Richard Hakluyt (London, 1599), 26, https://quod.lib.umich.edu/e/eebo/A02495.0001.001 /1:77.2?rgn=div2;view=fulltext.

18. Ibid.

19. Ibid.

20. Ibid., 27.

21. Lok had prior experience in West Africa, having captained that voyage to West Africa in 1554.

22. See Towerson, "William Towerson's Second Voyage to Guinea, 1556–7," in *Europeans in West Africa: 1450–1560,* vol. 2, ed. John William Blake, 360–429 (London: Hakluyt Society, 1942), 406.

23. The Portuguese were the first Europeans to establish consistent trade with West Africa, having established a trade fort there as early as 1482. They claimed a monopoly on the region and protected that claim with martial force.

24. For more on the political landscape of Sierra Leone prior to 1787, including interactions of nations indigenous to the region, see Christopher Fyfe, introduction to *A History of Sierra Leone* (Oxford: Oxford University Press, 1962), 1–12.

25. Eden, "The Discription of the Two Viages," 376.

26. Ibid., 387.

27. Towerson, "The Third and Last Voyage of M. William Towrson to the Coast of Guinie and the Castle de Mina, in the Yeere 1577," in *Principal Navigations,* 51. Over the next two centuries, English travelers took those fears about climate and the body with them to the Americas, mainly the Caribbean. For more about English anxieties regarding tropical climates in the Americas, see Karen Ordahl Kupperman, "Fear of Hot Climates in the Anglo-American Colonial Experience," *William and Mary Quarterly,* 3rd ser., 41.2 (April 1984): 213–40.

28. For a concise discussion about how these fears circumscribed British colonization plans in West Africa in the eighteenth century, see Christopher, "A 'Disgrace to the Very Colour.'"

29. Fothergill, himself a botanist, encouraged Smeathman's efforts, helping to fund his trip. For more on Fothergill's involvement and that of other Quakers, see Stephen J. Braidwood, "Founding Fathers," in *Black Poor and White Philanthropists: London's Blacks and the Foundation of the Sierra Leone Settlement, 1787–1791,* 5–62 (Liverpool: Liverpool University Press, 1994).

30. Henry Smeathman, "Plan of a Settlement to be Made Near Sierra Leone on the Grain Coast of Africa [. . .]" (London: Sold by T. Stockdale in Piccadilly, G. Kearsley in Fleet St. and J. Sewell in Cornhill, 1786), A2, Center for Research Libraries, https://dds-crl-edu.libdata.lib.ua.edu/crldelivery/410.

31. Ibid., 4.

32. Ibid., 8–9.

33. Ibid., 6.

34. Ibid.

35. Ibid., 9.

36. Ibid., 7–8.

37. Ibid., 9.

38. Smeathman, "Substance of Two Letters Addressed to Dr. Knowles, of London, on the Productions and Colonization of Africa, by Dr. Henry Smeathman," in C. B. Wadström, *An essay on colonization, particularly applied to the western coast of Africa, with some free thoughts on cultivation and commerce also brief descriptions of the colonies already formed, or attempted, in Africa, including those of Sierra Leona and Bulama*, vol. 2 (London, 1794), 197–207, 198. Slavery and Anti-Slavery, http://find.galegroup.com.libdata.lib.ua.edu/sas/infomark.do?&source=gale&prodId=SAS&userGroupName=tusc49521&tabID=T001&docPage=article&callisto ContentSet=GKEL&searchType=AdvancedSearchForm&docId=U3604 090106&type=multipage&contentSet=ECCO&version=1.0&relevancePageBatch=U104090104&docLevel=FASCIMILE.

39. Fyfe argues that Smeathman had the more nefarious motive of tricking the Black poor back into slavery. According to Fyfe, Smeathman wanted labor for a "large-scale cotton-growing" investment he shared with two London merchants (Fyfe, *A History of Sierra Leone*, 15). For more on Smeathman's personal motives, see Ellen Gibson Wilson, *The Loyal Blacks* (New York: G. P. Putnam's Sons, 1976); John Peterson, *Province of Freedom: A History of Sierra Leone 1787–1870* (Evanston, IL: Northwestern University Press, 1969); and Braidwood, *Black Poor and White Philanthropists*.

40. Fyfe, A *History of Sierra Leone*, 141.

41. Christopher, "A 'Disgrace to the Very Colour,'"

42. Anthony Benezet, *Some Historical Account of Guinea* (Philadelphia, 1771), 1, Slavery and Anti-Slavery, http://find.galegroup.com.libdata.lib.ua.edu/sas/infomark.do?&source=gale&prodId=SAS&userGroupName=tusc49521&tabID=T001&searchType=&docId=U104034622&type=multipage&contentSet=ECCO&version=1.0&relevancePageBatch=&docLevel=FASCIMILE.

43. Ikuko Asaka, *Tropical Freedom: Climate, Settler Colonialism, and Black Exclusion in the Age of Emancipation* (Durham, NC: Duke University Press, 2017), 10.

44. See Fyfe, *A History of Sierra Leone*, 16. For more on the settlers' preference for Sierra Leone over Nova Scotia and the Bahamas, see also Norton, "The Fate of Some Black Loyalists." In his comprehensive study of that first colonization effort between 1786 and 1791, Braidwood argues that the Black settlers themselves were far

more agentive and vocal in the shaping of the colonization project that most studies acknowledge (Braidwood, *Black Poor and White Philanthropists*).

45. John Matthews, *A voyage to the River Sierra-Leone on the coast of Africa: containing an account of the trade and productions of the country, and of the civil and religious customs and manners of the people: in a series of letters to a friend in England* (London, 1788), 52, Slavery and Anti-Slavery, http://find.galegroup.com.libdata .lib.ua.edu/sas/infomark.do?&source=gale&prodId=SAS&userGroupName=tusc 49521&tabID=T001&searchType=&docId=GF100256313&type=multipage&con tentSet=ECCO&version=1.0&relevancePageBatch=GF100256313&docLevel =FASCIMILE.

46. Ibid., 39.

47. Ibid., 21.

48. Ibid., 63.

49. Ibid., 174.

50. Equiano, *Interesting Narrative*, 177. Equiano and Sharp, while well-meaning, did not account for the possibility that multiple kinds of trade could coexist. As Adiele E. Afigbo points out, a legitimate trade in material goods did develop in the interior of Africa but did so as a "twin brother of the 'illegitimate trade' in slaves; indeed, the two developed sort of as Siamese twins." Enslaved labor made possible the cultivation and transport of legitimate goods in the African interior and along the coast. Afigbo notes that enslaved people and material goods were "carried on along the same routes, and . . . were displayed and sold in the same markets. As the slaves for sale were marched up and down the region, they also carried items of legitimate trade" (Afigbo, "Africa and the Abolition of the Slave Trade," in "Abolishing the Slave Trades: Ironies and Reverberations," special issue, *William and Mary Quarterly*, 3rd ser., 66.4 (October 2009): 709.

51. Land, "On the Founding of Sierra Leone."

52. This system of law and order, as Sharp notes, harkens back to the biblical policing system Moses employed when organizing the Israelites upon their exodus from Egypt, explained in Exodus 18:13–26.

53. Granville Sharp, *A Short Sketch of Temporary Regulations (Until Better Shall Be Proposed) for the Intended Settlement of the Grain Coast of Africa, near Sierra Leona* (London, 1786), 1, Eighteenth Century Collections Online, http://find.galegroup.com .libdata.lib.ua.edu/ecco/infomark.do?&source=gale&prodId=ECCO&userGroup Name=tusc49521&tabID=T001&docId=CW104147684&type=multipage &contentSet=ECCOArticles&version=1.0&docLevel=FASCIMILE.

54. Ibid., 3–4. Importantly, Sharp acknowledges some measure of cultural commensurability.

55. For more information about frankpledge in medieval England, see William Alfred Morris, *The Frankpledge System* (London: Longmans, Green, 1910); and Phillip R. Schofield, "The Late Medieval View of Frankpledge and the Tithing System: An Essex Case Study," in *Medieval Society and the Manor Court*, ed. Zvi Razi and Richard Smith, 408–49 (Oxford: Clarendon, 1996).

56. Sharp, *A Short Sketch*, 2.

57. Ibid., 83.

58. Ibid., 1–2.

59. Sharp, *An account of the Constitutional English polity of Congregational Courts: and More Particularly of the Great Annual Court of the People, Called the View of Frankpledge* [. . .], 2nd ed. (London, 1786), 252, Eighteenth Century Collections Online, http://find.galegroup.com.libdata.lib.ua.edu/ecco/infomark.do?&source=gale& prodId=ECCO&userGroupName=tusc49521&tabID=T001&docId=CW 125108488&type=multipage&contentSet=ECCOArticles&version=1.0&docLevel =FASCIMILE.

60. Ibid., 255

61. "Two letters from Granville Sharp to Jacques-Pierre Brissot de Warville," Schomburg Center for Research in Black Culture, Manuscripts, Archives and Rare Books Division, New York Public Library, New York Public Library Digital Collections, https://digitalcollections.nypl.org/items/d3f91c50-b33e-0133-4a17 –00505686d14e.

62. Granville Sharp to John Coakley Lettsom, October 13, 1788, mss CN 147, Box 1 (22), Zachary Macaulay Papers, 1793–1888, Huntington Library, San Marino, CA.

63. Sharp, *Congregational Courts*, 19.

64. Ibid., 5.

65. For a more extended discussion, see Granville Sharp, *A General Plan for Laying Out Towns and Townships, on the New-acquired Lands in the East Indies, America, or Elsewhere: In Order to Promote* [. . .] (London, 1794), Sabin Americana, Gale, http://galenet.galegroup.com.libdata.lib.ua.edu/servlet/Sabin?af=RN&ae =CY101950940&srchtp=a&ste=14.

66. Smeathman was talking and writing about his plan as early as 1783 (Smeathman, "Substance of Two Letters," 197–207).

67. Sharp, *Congregational Courts*, 279.

68. Sharp, *A Short Sketch*, 21.

69. Ibid., 22.

70. Peterson, *Province of Freedom: A History of Sierra Leone 1787–1870* (Evanston, IL: Northwestern University Press, 1969), 21.

71. Prince Hoare, *Memoirs of Granville Sharp*, 374.

72. In November 1781, the British slave ship *Zong* was headed toward Jamaica. Running low on drinkable water—due to poor navigation and planning that extended the travel days—the crew threw overboard more than 130 captured Black Africans. In doing so, they sought to collect the insurance money for the loss of "cargo." The insurance company refused to pay, arguing that the loss of cargo was due to negligence on the part of the enslavers. The court sided with the insurance company. Equiano sought Sharp's help to have the men tried for the murders of those Black Africans. Despite Sharp's intervention, the men escaped prosecution.

73. Olaudah Equiano, *The Interesting Narrative*, ed. Brycchan Carey (Oxford: Oxford University Press, 2018), 187.

74. Hoare, *Memoirs of Granville Sharp,* 313. Among those boarding the ships for Sierra Leone were nearly 112 whites, which included administrators, craftsmen with families, a pastor, and up to 70 white women described alternatively as prostitutes and wives of Black settlers (Norton, "Black Loyalists of the Revolution," 416; Christopher Fyfe, *A History of Sierra Leone* [Oxford: Oxford University Press, 1962], 19).

75. Hoare, *Memoirs of Granville Sharp,* 260.

76. For more on how these two colonizing plans unfolded in tandem, see Christopher, "A 'Disgrace to the Very Colour.'"

77. Ottobah Cugoano, *Thoughts and Sentiments on the Evil and Wicked Traffic of the Slavery: and Commerce of the Human Species, Humbly Submitted to the Inhabitants of Great-Britain* (London, 1787), 142, https://quod.lib.umich.edu/e/eccodemo /K046227.0001.001/1:5?rgn=div1;view=fulltext.

78. "G.S. to Dr. Lettsom, MD," in *Memoirs of Granville Sharp,* 316.

79. Equiano, *Interesting Narrative,* 188.

80. See, for example, Anna Maria Falconbridge, *Two Voyages to Sierra Leone during the Years 1791–2–3: In a Series of Letters* (London, 1794), 66; and the report of the Sierra Leone Company, *Substance of the Report of the Court of Directors of the Sierra Leone Company to the General Court, Held at London on Wednesday the 19th of October, 1791* (London, 1792), 3, Slavery and Anti-Slavery, http://find.galegroup.com.libdata.lib.ua.edu/sas/infomark.do?&source=gale&prodId=SAS&userGroupName =tusc49521&tabID=T001&docPage=article&callistoContentSet=GKEL&search Type=BasicSearchForm&docId=U3602373006&type=multipage&contentSet =ECCO&version=1.0&relevancePageBatch=U102373003&docLevel=FASCIMILE. For historical perspective on the nature of the women, see Wilson, *The Loyal Blacks,* 151–52; and Fyfe, *A History of Sierra Leone,* 17.

81. During his stay on the Banana Islands a decade earlier, Smeathman married one of King Tom's daughters; she died shortly after. Also of note is that the land treaty would become a major source of tension between the Temne and English. The tension stemmed from two issues: First, King Tom was a subordinate of the regent King Naimbanna II, seated in the town of Robanna. King Tom did not have the authority to negotiate a land deal with the English. Second, even after King Naimbanna II took over negotiations with the English a year later, there was some confusion on both sides about the nature of the agreement. The Temne understood the deal to be a rental agreement of sorts granting English colonists the right of usage in exchange for periodical tributes. The English sought a land purchase, a one-time payment. The misunderstanding plagued relations between the colony and the Temne for almost a decade (see Fyfe, *A History of Sierra Leone,* chap. 1).

82. That and this, according to Sharp: "the greatest blame of all is to be charged on the intemperance of the people themselves; for the most of them (both Whites and Blacks) became so besotted during the voyage, that they were totally unfit for business when they landed, and could hardly be prevailed on to assist in erecting their own huts. Besides, the distempers occasioned by their intemperance carried off a large proportion of them before they reached the coast" (Hoare, *Memoirs of Granville Sharpe,* 84).

83. Sierra Leone Company, *Substance of the Report,* 5.

84. Griffith had worked as a servant in London and was a protégé of Sharp, who funded his education.

85. "Elliot to Mr. Granville Sharp," in Hoare, *Memoirs of Granville Sharp,* 320–21.

86. Eventually he becomes a secretary, scribe, and confidante for King Naimbanna.

87. Weaver was a Black Loyalist from Philadelphia.

88. "Mr. Weaver, Chief Magistrate in the Colony of Sierra Leone, to Granville Sharp, Esq.," in Hoare, *Memoirs of Granville Sharp,* 321.

89. Ibid.

90. "Mr. James Reid, Chief in Command in the New Colony of Sierra Leone, to Granville Sharp, Esq.," in Hoare, *Memoirs of Granville Sharp,* 323.

91. "Mr. Weaver, Chief Magistrate in the Colony of Sierra Leone, to Granville Sharp, Esq.," in Hoare, *Memoirs of Granville Sharp,* 321–22.

92. "Mr. James Reid, Chief in Command in the New Colony of Sierra Leone, to Granville Sharp, Esq.," in Hoare, *Memoirs of Granville Sharp,* 322–23.

93. Hoare, *Memoirs of Granville Sharp,* 336.

94. "To the Worthy Inhabitants of the Province of Freedom, in the Mountains of Sierra Leone," in Hoare, *Memoirs of Granville Sharp,* 329.

95. As Jack P. Greene notes of Barbados's reputation throughout England and its other colonies: "Conventional English moral standards were also reputedly little regarded in Barbados. Drunkenness was so common that it seemed to be the very 'custom of the country.' Lewdness, fornication, adultery, and incest were common, and fist fighting appeared to be the primary vehicle for settling disputes" (Greene, "Changing Identity in the British West Indies in the Early Modern Era: Barbados as a Case Study," in *Imperatives, Behaviors, and Identities: Essays in Early American Cultural History,* 13–67 [Charlottesville: University of Virginia Press, 1992], 25–26).

96. Quoted in Norton, "The Fate of Some Black Loyalists," 420.

97. Wadström, *An Essay on Colonization,* vol. 2, 221.

98. "Elliot to Mr. Granville Sharp," in Hoare, *Memoirs of Granville Sharp,* 320.

99. *Heads of the Speeches, Delivered on the 18th and 19th April, 1791, in a Committee of the House of Commons, on a Motion Made by Mr. Wilberforce, for the Abolition of the Slave-Trade, with Detector's Letters* (Liverpool, 1791), 100, Slavery and Anti-Slavery, http://find.galegroup.com.libdata.lib.ua.edu/sas/infomark.do?&source=gale&prodId=SAS&userGroupName=tusc49521&tabID=T001&docPage=article&callisto ContentSet=ECSS&searchType=AdvancedSearchForm&docId=CW3304 229913&type=multipage&contentSet=ECCO&version=1.0&relevancePageBatch =CW104229913&docLevel=FASCIMILE.

100. For more on early English attitudes toward Black Africans, see my *Black Africans in the British Imagination: English Narratives of the Early Atlantic World* (Baton Rouge: Louisiana State University Press, 2016). See also Alden T. and Virginia Mason Vaughan, "Before Othello: Elizabethan Representation of Sub-Saharan Africans," *William and Mary Quarterly,* 3rd ser. 54.1 (January 1997): 19–44; P. E. H. Hair, "Attitudes to Africans in English Primary Sources on Guinea up to 1650,"

History in Africa 26 (1999): 43–68; Emily C. Bartel, "Imperialist Beginnings: Hakluyt's Navigations and the Place and Displacement of Africa," *Speaking of the Moor: From Alcazar to Othello* (Philadelphia: University of Pennsylvania, 2009); and Mary Wilson Floyd, *English Ethnicity and Race in Early Modern Drama* (Cambridge: Cambridge University Press, 2003).

101. Wadström, *An Essay on Colonization,* vol. 2, 202.

102. "The Old Settlers at Sierra Leone, to Granville Sharp, Esq.," in Hoare, *Memoirs of Granville Sharp,* 332.

103. Ibid.

104. Ibid.

105. Ibid., 331.

106. Ibid.

107. Konstantin Dierks, *In My Power: Letter Writing and Communications in Early America* (Philadelphia: University of Pennsylvania Press, 2009), 5.

108. Sharp's letter to his niece appears in the appendix to Wadström, *An Essay on Colonization,* 223.

109. Hoare, *Memoirs of Granville Sharp,* 339.

110. Wadström, *An Essay on Colonization,* vol. 2, 73.

111. Ibid.

112. Hoare, *Memoirs of Granville Sharp,* 313.

113. Ibid., 317.

114. "Appendix No. XI," in Hoare, *Memoirs of Granville Sharp,* xviii, xxix.

115. "G.S., in Reply, to the Worthy Inhabitants of Granville Town, in the Province of Freedom, Sierra Leone," in Hoare, *Memoirs of Granville Sharp,* 346.

116. Hoare, *Memoirs of Granville Sharp,* 353.

117. Sierra Leone Company, *Substance of the Report,* 6.

118. Anna Maria Falconbridge, *Two Voyages to Sierra Leone, During the Years 1791–2–3, in a Series of Letters* [. . .], 2nd ed. (London, 1794), 62, http://find.galegroup.com .libdata.lib.ua.edu/sas/infomark.do?&source=gale&prodId=SAS&userGroup Name=tusc49521&tabID=T001&docPage=article&callistoContentSet=GKEL &searchType=AdvancedSearchForm&docId=U3603669241&type=multipage &contentSet=ECCO&version=1.0&relevancePageBatch=U103669239&doc Level=FASCIMILE.

119. Equiano, *The Interesting Narrative,* 188.

120. Cugoano, *Thoughts and Sentiments,* 140.

121. Ibid., 140–41.

122. Sharp, *Free English Territory in Africa at Sierra Leone—Called the Province of Freedom* (London, 1790), 10, African History and Culture, 1540–1921, https://info web-newsbank-com.libdata.lib.ua.edu/iw-search/we/Evans/?p_product=EAIX &p_theme=eai&p_nbid=Y5FW60IVMTY2NTMyMjEyOC42MDgyNTA6MT0x NDoxMzAuMTYwLjIoLjExNw&p_action=doc&p_queryname=1&p_docref=v2 :13D59FCC0F7F54B8@EAIX-147E02B708BA8710@9064-15450E4EC313CBC8@3.

123. Fyfe, *A History of Sierra Leone,* 27.

FIVE

"SEND ME OVER ONE WORTHY"

Reimagining Respectability in Sierra Leone

1. For more information about this failed immigration plan, see George E. Brooks Jr., "The Providence African Society's Sierra Leone Emigration Scheme, 1794–1795: Prologue to the African Colonization Movement," *International Journal of African Historical Studies* 7.2 (1974): 183–202. See also Manisha Sinha, *The Slave's Cause: A History of Abolition* (New Haven, CT: Yale University Press, 2016).

2. Many African Americans in the latter eighteenth century were drawn to Methodism because of its liberation rhetoric. For a concise discussion of the denomination's allure, see Dennis C. Dickerson, "Liberation, Wesleyan Theology and Early African Methodism, 1766–1840," *Wesley and Methodist Studies* 3 (2011): 109–20; and Dee E. Andrews, "The African Methodists," chap. 5 in *The Methodists and Revolutionary America, 1760–1800: The Shaping of an Evangelical Culture* (Princeton, NJ: Princeton University Press, 2000). For a general discussion about the religious activity and cultural perceptions of Black Nova Scotians, see Ellen Gibson Wilson, *The Loyal Blacks* (New York: Capricorn, 1976); and James W. St. G. Walker, *The Black Loyalists: The Search for a Promised Land in Nova Scotia and Sierra Leone, 1783–1870* (Toronto: University of Toronto Press, 1992). See also Joanna Brooks, "John Marrant and the Lazarus Theology of the Early Black Atlantic," in *American Lazarus: Religion and the Rise of African-American and Native Literatures,* 87–114 (Oxford: Oxford University Press, 2003).

3. Their reputation for piety also contrasts those white Loyalists who settled neighboring Shelburne in Nova Scotia (see Bonnie Huskins, "'Shelburnian Manners': Gentility and the Loyalists of Shelburne, Nova Scotia," *Early American Studies* 13.1 [Winter 2015]: 151–88).

4. Suzanne Schwarz, "'Our Mad Methodists': Abolitionism, Methodism and Missions in Sierra Leone in the Late Eighteenth Century," *Wesley and Methodist Studies* 3 (2011): 122.

5. For additional biographical information about King, see *Dictionary of Canadian Biography,* ed. James W. St G. Walker, 5 (University of Toronto/Université Laval, 2003), s.v. "King, Boston," www.biographi.ca/en/bio/king_boston_5E.html. See also King, "Memoirs of the Life of Boston King" (1798), in *Unchained Voices: An Anthology of Black Authors in the English-Speaking World of the Eighteenth Century,* ed. Vincent Carretta, 351–68 (Lexington: University of Kentucky Press, 1996).

6. Compare, for example, the opening paragraph of King's narrative with those of Equiano and Briton Hammon, as well as the preface of Wheatley's published volume of poetry.

7. See King, "Memoirs of the Life of Boston King (1798), in *Unchained Voices: An Anthology of Black Authors in the English-Speaking World of the Eighteenth Century,* ed. Vincent Carretta (Lexington: University of Kentucky Press, 1996), 351. Subsequent citations of King's narrative appear parenthetically in the chapter text.

8. See Ryan Hanley, *Beyond Slavery and Abolition: Black British Writing, 1770–1830* (Cambridge: Cambridge University Press, 2018).

9. See David George, "An Account of the Life of Mr. David George from Sierra Leone in Africa, Given by Himself," in *Unchained Voices,* ed. Carretta, 333–50; and John Marrant, "A Narrative of the Lord's Wonderful Dealings with John Marrant," in *Unchained Voices,* ed. Carretta, 110–33.

10. Hanley, *Beyond Slavery and Abolition,* 137.

11. Ibid., 131–32.

12. Wilderness landscapes appear often in early American spiritual narratives, beginning with Puritan accounts of captivity by Natives in the seventeenth century. Other Black autobiographers, like John Marrant, wrote of receiving enlightenment or transformation in the woods.

13. As Joanna Brooks and John Saillant point out, King's missionary work in West Africa reflects a mode of Black Atlantic intellectual thought that "imagined Africa as a place to be redeemed through emigration, colonization, and proselytization by once-enslaved Christian blacks" (Brooks and Saillant, *"Face Zion Forward": First Writers of the Black Atlantic, 1785–1798* [Boston: Northeastern University Press, 2002], 18–19).

14. *Substance of the Report of the Court of Directors to the Sierra Leone Company to the General Court Held at London on Wednesday the 19th of October, 1791* (London: James Phillips, et. al., 1792), 17–19.

15. Ibid.

16. Ibid.

17. Prince Hoare, *Memoirs of Granville Sharp, Esq. Composed from His Own Manuscripts, and Other Authentic Documents in the Possession of His Family and of the African Institution* [London, 1820], 367.

18. See Konstantin Dierks, "Letter Writing, Stationery Supplies, and Consumer Modernity in the Eighteenth-Century Atlantic World," *Early American Literature* 41.3 (2006): 473–94.

19. Bannet defines "letteracy" as the "collection of different skills, values, and kinds of knowledge beyond mere literacy that were involved in achieving competency in the writing, reading, and interpreting of letters." It also entails "associated cultural information, such as common conceptions of letter-writing, awareness of current epistolary practices, basic knowledge about where letter-writing was taught and about how it was taught or to be learned, even how to 'read' and use a letter manual" (xvii). It is apparent that King Naimbanna II understands the cultural work and political value of letter writing (see Bannet, *Empire of Letters: Letter Manuals and Transatlantic Correspondence, 1680–1820* [Cambridge: Cambridge University Press, 2005]).

20. *Substance of the Report,* 13.

21. Srinivas Aravamudan, *Tropicopolitans: Colonialism and Agency, 1688–1804* (Durham, NC: Duke University Press, 1999), 4.

22. For more on transculturation, see Mary Louise Pratt, *Imperial Eyes: Travel Writing and Transculturation* (New York: Routledge, 1992).

23. For more on the importance of letter writing and its political work specifically in Sierra Leone, see *"Our Children Free and Happy": Letters from Black Settlers in Africa in the 1790s,* ed. Christopher Fyfe (Edinburgh: Edinburgh University Press, 1991). Here, Fyfe has compiled a representative mix of letters and petitions that colonists wrote to voice their pleasures and (mostly) displeasures with the Sierra Leone Company's management of the colony. Although Fyfe does not include Perth's letter, he does include letters written by two other women, illustrating that letter writing was not solely a male occupation in the colony.

24. For more about women's roles in the economic life of colonial Freetown, see Suzanne Schwarz, "Adaptation in the Aftermath of Slavery: Women, Trade and Property in Sierra Leone, 1790–1812," in *African Women in the Atlantic World: Property, Vulnerability and Mobility, 1660–1880,* ed. Mariana P. Candido and Adam Jones (Woodbridge, Suffolk, UK: James Currey, 2019), 19–37; and E. Frances White, *Sierra Leone's Settler Women Traders: Women on the Afro-European Frontier* (Ann Arbor: University of Michigan Press, 1987).

25. Though she did not visit Scotland, Perth did travel to England for two years. When Macaulay left the colony in 1799, he took with him some twenty-five indigenous children and Perth. In London, she worked as a caretaker for the children while also seeking medical treatment for a sick daughter.

26. Mary Perth, "Letter," in *Surprising Accounts of the Revival of Religion in the United States of America, in Different Parts of the World, and among Different Denominations of Christians with a Number of Interesting Occurrences of Divine Providence* (Philadelphia: William W. Woodward, 1802), 202–3.

27. Woodward, *Surprising Accounts of the Revival of Religion,* 3.

28. Ibid., 201.

29. Boston King maintained an epistolary relationship with Clarkson after Clarkson left Sierra Leone in 1792. He often wrote to the former governor with updates about the condition of the colonists. They also exchanged goods by mail (see his letters in *"Our Children Free and Happy,"* 54–56).

30. Rose Morral, in *"Our Children Free and Happy,"* 27–28.

31. Susana Smith, in *"Our Children Free and Happy,"* 24.

32. Cassandra Pybus, "'One Militant Saint': The Much Traveled Life of Mary Perth," *Journal of Colonialism and Colonial History* 9.3 (Winter 2008): 12, https://doi.org/10.1353/cch.0.0035.

33. That last group, emerging through the fervor and patronage of Selina Hastings, the Countess of Huntingdon, links back to John Marrant's evangelical work in Nova Scotia. Marrant might have migrated to Sierra Leone if he had not died before the mass exodus occurred in 1792.

34. Zachary Macaulay, *Life and Letters of Zachary Macaulay,* ed. Viscountess Margaret Jean Revelyan Knutsford (London: Edward Arnold, 1900), 54.

35. See Christopher Fyfe, *A History of Sierra Leone* (Oxford: Oxford University Press, 1962), chap. 3, 59–87.

36. Sierra Leone Petitioners, "Letter," in *Life and Letters of Zachary Macaulay,* ed. Knutsford, 146.

37. Clark, "Singular Piety in a Female African: Letter from the Rev. Mr. Clark, Chaplain to the Sierra Leone Establishment, to His Father in Scotland," *Evangelical Magazine* 4 (1796): 460–61. Subsequent citations from this source appear parenthetically in the chapter text.

38. For a discussion of Perth's conversion process, see Pybus, "One Militant Saint."

39. I discuss in more detail the collaborative nature of Black African mediation in early Atlantic narratives in a previous book, *Black Africans in the British Imagination: English Narratives of the Early Atlantic World* (Baton Rouge: Louisiana State University Press, 2016). See also Rafia Zafar's essay "Capturing the Captivity: African Americans among the Puritans," *MELUS* 17.2 (Summer 1991–Summer 1992): 19–35.

40. By 1799, Macaulay had restored Perth to her original good standing, illustrating the capriciousness of respectability. For more on the rift between Macaulay and Perth, see Pybus, "One Militant Saint."

INDEX

Printed in the USA
CPSIA information can be obtained
at www.ICGtesting.com
LVHW091538160923
758130LV00001B/1

9 780807 179796